The Shame of Death, Grief, and Trauma

The Shame of Death, Grief, and Trauma

Edited by Jeffrey Kauffman

Routledge
Taylor & Francis Group
New York   London

Routledge
Taylor & Francis Group
270 Madison Avenue
New York, NY 10016

Routledge
Taylor & Francis Group
27 Church Road
Hove, East Sussex BN3 2FA

© 2010 by Taylor and Francis Group, LLC
Routledge is an imprint of Taylor & Francis Group, an Informa business

Printed in the United States of America on acid-free paper
10 9 8 7 6 5 4 3 2 1

International Standard Book Number: 978-0-415-99748-5 (Hardback)

Library of Congress Cataloging-in-Publication Data

The shame of death, grief, and trauma / [edited by] Jeffrey Kauffman.
    p. cm.
    Includes bibliographical references and index.
    ISBN 978-0-415-99748-5 (alk. paper)
    1. Shame. 2. Bereavement. 3. Death. I. Kauffman, Jeffrey. II. Title.

BF575.S45S54 2010
155.9'37--dc22   2009032758

Visit the Taylor & Francis Web site at
http://www.taylorandfrancis.com

and the Routledge Web site at
http://www.routledgementalhealth.com

Contents

Introduction: Speaking of Shame

Silence surrounds the shame of death, grief, and trauma. The presence of shame as a significant factor in grief has been basically and widely unrecognized. This book is a step in the direction of bringing the shame of death, grief, and trauma out in the open—at least, out into the open enough that shame is taken into account in our self-understanding, our clinical understanding, and our theories.

We cannot, however, actually pull back the curtain and expose shame for what it is. It is not possible to bring this subject completely out into the open because there is something inherently hidden in the nature of shame. The very etymology of the word *shame* leads to the word *hidden*. Often it is taboo to speak of shame. And, beyond taboos against recognizing shame, shame and taboo have very close ties. The power of taboos to prohibit *is*, indeed, shame. And, while shame's power to conceal itself is abiding, it is, nonetheless, our intent here to speak of shame.

The reader may ask, "Why this fuss about *speaking of shame*?" The answer is, in part, that it is an expression of respect for the power of shame. And, so far as shame does disclose itself, does it not do so only in response to a healthy respect for shame? Also, I should say, that in bringing the shame of death, grief, and trauma out into the open and reflecting on it, as the reader is invited to do with this book, there is a tendency to forget what is unspoken and unspeakable, and, in so doing lose awareness of the meaning of shame.

Shame is a powerful word, and talking about it is often fraught with the risk and anxiety that shame will be induced. Speaking of shame can also be redemptive and empowering, such as a person bearing witness to shame endured, in which private shame has public meaning and special sanction. Theories of shame, occurring in a more or less shame-neutral zone, are generally talked about without inducing shame, though shame injunctions may limit how deeply shame as a force in grief is understood.

And, although in a context such as this we do talk about shame in a shame-neutral space—in the wild, shame is a very great and powerful force to be reckoned with.

The aim of this book is to make a case that shame is a common and pervasive feature of the human response to death and other loss, and, in this context, to give an account of some of the many meanings of shame and some of the many ways in which shame works. But the book does not aim for a unified theory of shame, for shame does not boil down to a single meaning. An odd, interesting, and significant aspect of shame is its multiplicity. The multitude of meanings hints at the hidden nature of shame, which does not disclose what it actually is.

In any case, recognizing the significance of shame in grief and trauma opens new meanings and possibilities for understanding death, grief, and trauma. From the shame-hazed shadow land of grief and traumatized consciousness to the many particular ways shame operates in grief and trauma, shame takes many forms, serves many functions, and has many causes.

In this book of observations, reflections, theories, and practices related to the shame of death, grief, and trauma, *freedom from shame* is the constant concern. The therapeutic aim of the book is the liberation from the oppression, disruptions, devaluations, inhibitions, and other woundings of shame.

Although *The Shame of Death, Grief, and Trauma* is a book on the psychology of shame, several authors (Darcy Harris, Susan Roos, and I) found related issues of social justice, social criticism, and morality to be integral to understanding aspects of the relation of shame and grief. This book is, in the first place, a book for clinicians about the experience and meaning of shame in grief and trauma, but concerns about stigma, disenfranchisement, exclusion, and other shame-based moral questions are also a part of the concern brought to bear here.

In an introductory essay, "On the Primacy of Shame," I make a case for the primacy of shame in the phenomenology of grief and put forward a wide range of ways in which shame is a factor in grief and especially in traumatic grief. The text includes a discussion of the *shame of shame* (Lewis, 1971) as a key complicating factor in grief and a discussion of mourning as an occurrence of conscience.

The following chapter is written in the first-person and placed early in the book by way of nodding to the primacy of first-person narratives. Although the intention of this book is to stimulate *conceptual thinking* about grief and grief therapy, I wish, at the outset, to affirm a certain primacy of the individual over the general (Kierkegaard, 1992; and in the thanatology literature see Neimeyer, 2001, and Attig, 1996). The individual as an affective self-positing self is the point of reference for clinical thinking, and the very isolating individuality of shame is a part of our reflection on the shame of death, grief, and trauma. In Chapter 2, shame meanings are implicit in the language and narratives of the story. Shelley Costa describes the alienation of disenfranchised grief, giving a candid and finely nuanced portrait of her experience of disenfranchised grief and the transformation of shame through strengthened autonomy and renewed self-confidence. Her narrative, "Side by Side," seizes the reader with its vocabulary of silence and with her valor and wit in honoring and loving her son.

In Chapter 3, Victor Schermer provides a psychoanalytic perspective, examining developmental experiences that impact bereavement and loss reactions. He identifies shame as a disruptive experience of infancy that influences later mourning. In his chapter, "Between Shame, Death, and Mourning: The Predispositional Role of Early Attachments and the Sense of Self," he examines the influence of the earliest shame "disruptions upon subsequent attitudes to death, dying, and grief."

Charles Figley, David Albright, and Kathleen Reagan Figley, in Chapter 4, "Combat, Combat Stress Injuries, and Shame," make an important contribution to the psychological study of shame among combatants. They develop a concept of combat stress injury (CSI) and examine the complex ways that shame occurs as an aspect of CSI. They point out that shame-related CSI is embedded in symptomatic expressions (such as depression, anger, and substance abuse) and indicate specific psychological circumstances in combat stress, which give rise to shame, showing how deeply shame may be embedded in the stress injury experience.

In Darcy Harris's "Healing the Narcissistic Injury of Death in the Context of Western Society" (Chapter 5), Becker's terror theory provides a conceptual framework for an account of shame being inherent in awareness of mortality and an account of death anxiety as a form of shame anxiety. She examines diverse meanings of death as "the ultimate narcissistic wound" and sheds light on "the avoidance and denial of death in Western society as a means of masking the narcissistic wound of mortality." Harris examines these diverse shame factors in the context of a sociocultural critique of the narcissism in Western culture.

Alex Tyree, in "Shame: A Hospice Worker's Reflections" (Chapter 6), reflects on his experience as a hospice bereavement worker. With sensitive, perceptive insight, he takes note of the shame vulnerabilities of grieving persons he has *companioned*, and with an awareness of himself around every corner, he tells stories of grief shame. Tyree observes common ways in which shame is woven through grief and the everyday life experiences that bear upon the meaning of the loss. He blends a reflection on the meaning of shame with stories of the grieving person's shame. He also reflects on the role of shame in the history of the hospice movement.

"Shame and Death in Cultural Context" (Chapter 7), by Paul Rosenblatt, gives us a cross-cultural survey of a range of ways in which shame operates and ways in which shame and death relate. He carefully weighs questions of universality and diversity, and the significance of each as he sorts through similarities and differences from culture to culture. As well as highlighting diversities from culture to culture, Rosenblatt points out the "diverse ways, even within a culture, for defining shame," the "great diversity in the meanings it is given," and the fact that "the ways that people become shamed or are made aware of their shame vary and change from time to time." He also considers the limitations inherent for any observer, based upon his own cultural context.

In "Mask of Shame, Mask of Death: Some Speculations on the Shame of Death" (Chapter 8), Hilary Clark explores the close relationship between shame and death by an examination of masks. "Masks are objects of deep anxiety and fascination—ritualistic objects across many cultures and over human history—that both manifest death and disguise it," she writes. From the infamous shamed and hooded Abu Ghraib figure to the hoods of the Klu Klux Klan, from masked superheroes to death masks and the hooded Grim Reaper, she examines the subtle interplay of shame and death. Clark develops Wursmer's argument that masks may function to shame death and that the shame-related nature of a mask is "simultaneously a representation of defense and of the failure of defense."

Maureen Underwood and Laura Winters, in Chapter 9, "Using the Representation of Grief and Shame in Contemporary Literature and Film to Train Mental Health Professionals," describe a program they have developed to train bereavement professionals to facilitate psychoeducational support groups for traumatic grief. The trainings incorporate poetry, novels, and film to harness the power of symbolic metaphor for getting in touch with affective grief experience, notably "helplessness, loss of control, and attributions of personal unworthiness and failure in which shame is rooted."

In "The Long Road to Relevance: Disability, Chronic Sorrow, and Shame" (Chapter 10), Susan Roos writes on shame implicit in the social meaning and chronic sorrow of disability. Advocating with a passion for social justice for the disabled, she writes a social-political history of disability, a study of shame-based policies and practices, in which shaming valuations are expressed in "marginalization, rejection, and abhorrence of those who fall too far from acceptable standards." She looks at diverse ways persons and families live with the chronic sorrow and shame of disability. She writes, "Situations of debilitating chronic disease and disability are open invitations for shame." Roos ties her chapter together with first-person narrative and brings our attention back to the first-person reflective self.

Jeffrey Kauffman

REFERENCES

Attig, T. (1996). *How we grieve: Relearning the world.* New York: Oxford University Press.

Kierkegaard, S. (1992). *Concluding unscientific postscript to philosophical fragments* (H. V. Hong & E. H. Hong, Trans.). Princeton, NJ: Princeton University Press.

Lewis, H. B. (1971). *Shame and guilt in neurosis.* New York: International Universities Press.

Neimeyer, R. A. (2001). *Meaning reconstruction and the experience of loss.* Washington, DC: American Psychological Association.

About the Editor

Jeffrey Kauffman, MA, MSS, FT, is a psychotherapist in private practice in suburban Philadelphia. He is the author of *Guidebook for Helping Persons with Mental Retardation Mourn* and the editor of *Awareness of Mortality* and *Loss of the Assumptive World*.

About the Contributors

David L. Albright is completing a PhD in social work and an MS in measurement and statistics at Florida State University. He previously served in the U.S. Army Infantry.

Hilary Clark, PhD, is a professor of English at the University of Saskatchewan. She teaches courses in critical theory (particularly psychoanalysis), life writing, modernism, and contemporary poetry. Her present research focuses on issues of interpretation, symbolization, and ethics in child psychoanalysis. SUNY Press recently published her edited volume *Depression and Narrative: Telling the Dark* (2008).

Shelley Costa is a freelance writer, scholar, and mother currently living near Philadelphia. She is mother to Matthew, born in June 2003; Chloe, born in October 2004; and a daughter born in 2007. The death of her first child shortly before his birth has deepened and defined her experience of loss, life, and motherhood.

Charles R. Figley, PhD, is a founding editor of *Traumatology*; Fulbright fellow and professor, Florida State University; and Florida State University Traumatology Institute director.

Kathleen Regan Figley, PhD, is the president and founder of the Figley Institute.

Darcy Harris, PhD, FT, is the thanatology coordinator at King's University College in London, Ontario, Canada. She maintains a small, private counseling practice with a specialization in the areas of loss and bereavement. She is also an author and lecturer with a focus on issues related to loss, change, and transition.

Susan Roos, PhD, LCSW, BCD, FT, PhD, is a psychotherapist in private practice in Arlington, Texas. She serves as adjunct faculty at the Union

Institute and University, Cincinnati, and the University of Texas at Arlington, School of Social Work, Professional Development Program. She is a consultant to Trauma Support Services of North Texas, an organization providing therapy at no cost to persons who are traditionally underserved. As cochair of the Arts Committee, she serves on the Executive Committee of the Dallas Society for Psychoanalytic Psychology and was president of the society in 2006–2007. She is associate editor of *Gestalt Review*, ad hoc reviewer for *Death Studies*, and contributes regularly to professional journals and books on issues concerning disability, end-of-life, and grief and loss. She is the author of *Chronic Sorrow: A Living Loss* (Routledge, 2002). She has presented on chronic sorrow at numerous professional conferences in the United States and Canada.

Paul C. Rosenblatt, PhD, is Morse-Alumni Distinguished Teaching Professor of Family Social Science at the University of Minnesota. He has published extensively on many topics at the intersection of grief, culture, and families. His most recent books are *African American Grief* (with Beverly R. Wallace), *Two in a Bed: The Social System of Couple Bed Sharing*, and *Shared Obliviousness in Family Systems*.

Victor L. Schermer, MA, LPC, CAC, CGP, FAGPA, is a psychologist in private practice and clinic settings in Philadelphia. He is executive director of the Study Group for Contemporary Psychoanalytic Process, founding director of the Institute for the Study of Human Conflict, and a Fellow of the American Group Psychotherapy Association. He is coeditor of *Leadership in a Changing World: Dynamic Perspectives on Groups and Their Leaders*, *Group Psychotherapy for Psychological Trauma*, *Group Psychotherapy of the Psychoses*, and *Ring of Fire*. He is coauthor of *Object Relations, the Self, and the Group*, and author of *Spirit and Psyche*. He is a regular contributor to professional journals and a frequent presenter at conferences and workshops internationally.

Alex Tyree, MS, has been a hospice chaplain and bereavement counselor for Delaware Hospice Inc. where he has visited bereaved individuals and families in their homes, as well as facilitating groups, for the past 19 years. Working within his local community, he has been involved with end-of-life related agencies in Delaware and Pennsylvania such as the Delaware End of Life Coalition, Wellness Community–Delaware, and Pennsylvania Hospice Network, as well as having taught masters-level courses related to loss and grief at Neumann University in Aston, Pennsylvania.

Maureen M. Underwood, MSW, is a licensed clinical social worker and a certified group psychotherapist with over 30 years of practice experience in grief, trauma, and crisis intervention. She has numerous publications in these areas that include a structured curriculum for children and families recovering from traumatic loss and an evidence-based program for youth suicide prevention.

Laura Winters, PhD, is a professor of English at the College of Saint Elizabeth in Morristown, New Jersey, and an adjunct associate professor in the Caspersen School of Graduate Studies at Drew University in Madison, New Jersey. She is the author of *Willa Cather: Landscape and Exile*, as well as essays on 20th and 21st century literature and film.

SECTION 1

Introductory Essay

CHAPTER 1

On the Primacy of Shame

Jeffrey Kauffman

THE PARTICULARITY OF SHAME AS A PSYCHOLOGICAL REACTION TO DEATH

My aim in this chapter is to make a case that shame is a pervasive feature of the human response to death and other loss, to indicate the significance of shame in grief and trauma, and to expand our understanding of shame. In both our common and scientific views of grief, shame is barely recognized; there is broad sociocultural support in the belief that shame is not central to grief. The argument in this chapter, however, is that shame is both a general and a particular feature of grief. Shame is present in the grieving *self's experience of itself*, and it is a particular feature of grief, co-occurring with other features of the grief experience, as in shame associated with any particular thought, feeling, or meaning.

Death and the bond broken by death can be experienced as devaluing the self. One may feel naked in face of death. Abandonment and broken attachment shame *disconnects* a person from the social world and from oneself. It weakens a person's sense of familiarity in the world and with their own self. Shame prompts disconnection; and disconnection is, itself, experienced as shameful. The disconnective nature of grief is shameful. Any aspect of the self's reflexive reality may disconnect, including disconnection of self from the social world and from itself, a fragmentation of consciousness, loss of a sense of place in time, emotional dislocation, disruption of a sense of identity, or loss of a sense of being or belonging. Disconnection *exposes* the self. Exposure disconnects.

Death may objectify the appearance of the self to its own self, as in *mortification*. The very preoccupation with death and with oneself in mourning is felt to be shameful. The sacred terror of death shames, and believing death to be a moral judgment is being under a burden of shame. The *stigma* of death is shaming. To experience oneself in one's grief to be a *victim* of death is to be ashamed.

Persons are delivered to shame by the inward violence touched off in grief. Grief can arouse anger and rage, about which one may feel ashamed. A person may feel ashamed of the fear of death; and quite remarkably, a person is likely to feel shame about their shame (Lewis, 1971) of death. All of reflexive life may be experienced with shame; and this is especially true of the hypercathected inner world of grieving.

Perceived weakness and failure in grief are shameful. Experienced *deprivation* of any kind can be shameful. Grief, struggling against powerlessness/helplessness in face of death, is, in being vanquished by death, shamed. Grief anxiety that one's world is out of control induces shame and shame heightens loss of control anxiety.

A mourner may experience guilt-shame: a belief that oneself is to blame (shame) prompts belief that one's actions are to blame (guilt). It has often been observed that guilt is the feeling that "I have *done* something wrong," and shame is the feeling that "I *am* something wrong." In grief, so far as my being is at stake, self-blame is shame. The incitement of shame can overthrow a sense of the right to exist, and install inward deadness or other shame dissociative states. To be disenfranchised in grief, to be in a social environment in which grief must be hidden, to be a social outcast in one's grief, is to experience one's grief, and thereby oneself, to be shameful. Shame is, whatever else it may be about, always shame about oneself. The self-reproach and regrets of the dying, whether death is imminent or not, are much more shame than guilt. And in mourning, the will of the deceased, as it is experienced in mourning, is enforced by shame. Guilt, widely recognized to occur in grief, could serve being reevaluated for how much it is actually or primarily shame. Wherever conscience comes into play in grief, which is, I think, far more often than usually accounted, there is guilt, but more potently, there is shame, such as in angry judgments against oneself that accompany, and sometimes drive, object-focused grief experience. The guilt in Freud's melancholia is not guilt, but, in its devaluing self-reproaches, in its very self-preoccupation and self-deprecation, it is shame. And, in the puzzling and fundamental sense in which loss turns a person against himself, the identity-anxiety that is aroused is shame.

There are many ways in which grief arouses shame anxiety, such as shame for being alive while the other is dead, for the inward disorder of grief, for being frightened, being vulnerable to death, being outcast, helpless, and abandoned; shame for the whole inner world of grief and diverse circumstances of grief. Because traumatic grief, in particular, is soaked in shame, any specific grief anxiety is, in traumatic grief, more likely to be shameful.

The initial shock of death's omnipotence knocks the self unconscious. The disconnected self in grief implodes with overwhelming, unfathomable death. Presented to the omnipotence of death, the self covers its eyes and turns in horror—while it *internalizes a shame* of death. Death, lodged at the core of grief, is a shame phenomenon, a shame before death's omnipotence. Grief therapy responds to the needs of the griever, including *the need for shelter in the omnipotence/shame spectrum of grief.* Shame before the omnipotence of death insinuates itself into other feelings about oneself in grief.

The dead body, in the sheer physicality of death, may inspire shame, and its symbolic introject, a subjective representation of the dead body, may be shrouded in awe and shame. Rituals and some practices with the dead body are carefully constructed and carried out to deal with the shame power of the body, particularly the shame of the dead body as a sacred/profane being. Fear of the dead body may arouse shame. Fear of the death that the dead body stands for may be shameful. The uncanniness of a dead body that resembles a living body, which was recently alive and now is not, may result in a feeling of shame for the viewer. There is shame also in the awe and dread and mystery of the dead body. The shared mortality that the dead body signifies may inspire shame.

The experience of grief cannot be understood without taking an account of the shame that is so covert, yet so diverse and powerful a grief force. Each and every way that loss may be typologized has characteristic shame features: shame of a violent death, a suicide, a homicide, a comrade in arms dying, accidental death, a specific illness; the death of a person toward whom one feels responsibility. Every bond, when broken, has shame vulnerabilities; every type of loss and every individual loss has its own unique shame propensities. Death and loss are prone, in various undertows of subjectivity, to be experienced as saying something (shameful) about oneself: shame of one's own mortality, shame at having lost a loved one, shame over not having loved well enough or been loved well enough, shame about one's grief and its vulnerabilities, shame at the self-absorption of grief, shame of being overpowered by grief, and, most remarkably, shame of shame. Shame, co-occurring with specific grief features, is a key risk factor for mourning complications.

The diverse, many-faced nature of shame and the diverse particularity of shame in grief suggest that perhaps shame is less a specific feature of grief than a generalized feature that shows up in the particularities of grief. Perhaps shame is more like a medium of grief, a self-woundedness that bleeds through the particularities of shame in grief.

SEPARATION ANXIETY

Broken attachments not only break a bond with the deceased but tear at the bond of the self with its own self. Exposed by no longer being bonded to an attachment object, the self experiences itself to be abandoned *unto death*, thrown out from under the protective cover of attachment, exposed to an abyss. Exposed by abandonment, overwhelmed in the shame of being disposed of, negated in the sense of not having a right to exist, the shame of separation anxiety diminishes the self, and raises the risk of a pervasive shame-prone grief disposition—which prevents mourning, as well as intimacy with self or others. The most persistent and painful wound of separation anxiety, a pain on which grief "gets stuck," is a shame anxiety that accompanies and sometimes saturates grief. The self is, in separation anxiety, thrown into shame anxiety. That is, separation anxiety is an exposure of the self, a type of shame anxiety. The self-psychology of separation anxiety is in the shame meaning of separation.

Separation anxiety in traumatic grief may propel one into nihilistic panic, with one's sense of being and one's very meaningfulness disintegrating, the self in full shame retreat, covering its tracks as best it can. The collapsing self of traumatic grief is in a state of shame. Traces of separation anxiety shame are also present in "normal" grief. So, shame is not something that is present or absent in grief, so much as being more or less present. The attachment bond is regulated by shame, and disturbances in the bond are disturbances of shame.

SIGNS OF THE DEVELOPMENTAL BEGINNINGS OF SHAME: EXPOSURE ANXIETY IN THE FACE OF A STRANGER

Developmentally, shame may be seen in *stranger-anxiety*, emerging from within the space of the toddler's bond with mother. The expression of stranger-anxiety by retreating, hiding, and covering the face is in response to experiencing an intrusion upon the private space of the maternal bond. Stranger-anxiety is an expressive language gesture. But, it is not simply expressive. It is a communicative act of showing. In stranger-anxiety, shame is enacted by gestures of hiding and covering. In a stranger-anxiety enactment, hiding itself does not simply occur, but hiding is performed, and signals distress over intrusion into privacy. In the hiding gesture the toddler appears to be trying to protect from and negotiate the intrusive gaze of the stranger through performing an act of hiding. Stranger-anxiety is a shame performance for the purpose of warding off exposure. Stranger-anxiety is a sign of developing self-consciousness and an enactment of an early anxiety about securing the boundaries of otherness and self. Stranger-anxiety displays a developmentally early anxiety about the violation of privacy and intimacy.

It is also worth noting that this gesture, signaling a need for safe cover, is sometimes taken by adults as a cue for teasing—as if it registers as shame, but the shame is shameful, and defensively projected back onto the toddler. The intruder's shaming of the baby by his own shame is an unconscious exhibition of shame, a social shame performance. Shame, in this case, leads to covert aggression by the witness of the stranger-anxiety exhibition of shame. The projective shame deployments of teasing give back to the toddler just what the body language of hiding is seeking to protect against. Stranger-anxiety threatens the internal space of "the privacy of the self with itself and mother" where the capacity to mourn is also developing. With the developmental emergence of shame-organized self-consciousness, a baby becomes, in the experience of others and, most probably, itself, a person with the presence and self-awareness of personhood. The capacity to mourn develops along with this.

TRAUMATIC SHAME TEMPORALITY

In traumatic wounding, in terms of memory and expectation, the anxiety that occurs is driven by an implicit certainty that *what has already happened is going to happen* (Winnicott, 1974). The horizon of posttraumatic temporality is that what has already happened but not been experienced (Blanchot, 1994) is anticipated. Posttraumatic consciousness lives into the memory of the trauma as an anxious anticipation, which operates as the *repetition of traumatic shame*.

The temporality of what has already happened, but not yet been "realized," happening again is expressed in the concepts of recurrence, return, and repetition. Freud, for example, proposes the repetition compulsion as a return of death (Freud, 1961). From the first, at the birth of internal time consciousness (Husserl, 1964) death is repressed, and temporality is its return. As time passes, the primary repression of death keeps up the pressure and the boundary of primary repression is breached again and again. The temporality that begins with the repression of death, the temporality of the repetition compulsion, living toward death that has already happened, is the temporality in which anxiety occurs. Primary repression is a concept about what is denied consciousness at the beginning and persists as underlying anxiety, such as annihilation anxiety. Primary repression is a *returning* to consciousness of a primal anxiety buried at the origin of consciousness. Anxiety in the face of death is a surge of indwelling death anxiety returning, triggered by the face of death.

The concept of primary repression hypothesizes a trauma at the origin of consciousness, which establishes a temporality of the return of the repressed as the temporality of selfhood. The traumatic temporality of the return of the repressed and protentional temporality, the openness and intentionality of consciousness toward the future, coexist (in such a way that death is the beginning and the end of consciousness).

The temporality of reflexive consciousness toward death is a repetition compulsion, and anxiety is the vehicle of repetition. Traumatic anxiety works in the same way as primary repression, repeating and reliving dissociated trauma. Shame is the *concealment power* and *enforcer* of repression and dissociation. The shame of the repressed and dissociated returning compels their repetition. The psychoanalytic therapeutics of bringing traumatic repetition to a rest includes, then, a negotiation of the *shame defenses* of the repressed and dissociated. Shame-driven repetition of traumatic grief is brought to a rest by recognizing and reckoning with the split off shame.

TRAUMATIC SHAME DISSOCIATION

Traumatic grief shame occurs in fragmentations or dissociations, defilements and humiliations, helplessness, and other overwhelming grief anxieties. Traumatic shame damages the "protective cover of beliefs," which maintains the integrity of identity and valuations. Traumatic grief destabilizes or disintegrates basic beliefs, which give the self cover— belief that I am, that I am valuable, that order is sufficiently constant and predictable, and that I am safe. Loss of the protective cover of beliefs is a symptom of traumatic shame (Kauffman, 2002).

Disconnections of the self with itself in grief, dissociated fragments of self, and grief are shame phenomena that are particularly noteworthy in traumatic stress anxiety. Traumatic stress anxiety in grief is characterized, in part, by its disconnective, disintegrative force. Fragmentation of self is often not so much like a smashed vessel as it is, rather, a *self-relational* disconnect, a deep shame state. Disconnections of the self with itself in grief and trauma are shame-dissociative phenomena.

SHAME, MOURNING, AND CONSCIENCE

Psychological theory of grief and mourning historically begins with an argument to distinguish between normal and not normal, to make clear and distinct the difference between mourning and melancholia. In 1917, during World War I, Freud wrote a paper about the difference between normal mourning and not-normal mourning. This distinction has been an underlying concern throughout the history of grief and mourning theory. In "Mourning and Melancholia," Freud (1959) separates self-reproachful self-preoccupation in grief and calls it *pathological*. This distinction establishes the psychology of mourning as a normative science and defines a norm, which Freud decribes as a process of reality testing. This natural process is interfered with by self-preoccupations, which he calls guilt, which causes the loss to be repeated and not, as in the normative process of mourning, mitigated. Guilty self-preoccupations complicate grief.

Now, Morrison and Lansky, in *The Widening Scope of Shame* (1997) are correct in pointing out that Freud misunderstood the phenomenon he was observing in melancholia. He is not describing guilt but shame when he describes the psychodynamics of self-reproaching intentionalities in reaction to death. Self-reproach in grief is a shameful act of *turning against oneself*, shaming oneself. Such a shame infection of mourning is a common characteristic of complicated and traumatic grief. Self-preoccupied reproach in grief is deviant from the norm and from the normal momentum of mourning, but is part of the normal course of grief experience.

In "Mourning and Melancholia," Freud describes mourning as an ego function, and this is how it is generally understood. The reality testing process he describes is certainly an ego function, but the mourning process also involves the self's relationship with itself, including shame-regulated positions and judgments about oneself. Disturbances of self-preoccupation in grief are self and superego activities.

THE OPPOSITE MEANINGS OF SHAME

A problem with understanding the opposite meanings of shame, such as in the pair *shame as exposure* and *shame as cover,* is that shame as cover has little currency in speech. Shame as exposure—humiliation, embarrassment, devaluation, and objectification—is recognized, but the shame variants humility, modesty, discretion, honor, redemption, pride, and so forth are not recognized to be shame phenomena. The sense of the word shame, for example, as cover, humility, modesty, discretion, and so forth is not familiar. We do not usually regard these as shame phenomena. But, if we are able to recognize shame and pride to exist in relation to each other, as two parts of the same dynamic, we can begin to consider the psychodynamics that operate between the opposites *cover* and *exposure*, *pride* and *shame*, and so forth, as variations of each other.

The psychodynamics between pride and its opposite (shame) is a shame dynamic. The self-regard of pride and its opposite is a shame phenomenon. The power that authorizes and energizes the reflexive reality of pride and its opposite is the power of a *cover–exposure dynamic*. What is said here of pride may be said of many shame variants, such as dignity and shame, honor and shame, validation and shame, autonomy and shame, and so forth.

Banishment or exposure, as well as redemption, liberation, meaning and identity, on the other hand, are also shame variants. The mysterious internality of death in human experience is inscribed by shame. The nature of the sacred/profane is psychologically a shame phenomenon.

Self-regard, self-consciousness, and self-attention are examples of shame dynamic fields. Mourning operates in a self-relational, shame dynamic field. By a shame dynamic field I mean a force field defined by shame and its opposites, as two sides of the same force. With shame and pride, opposites of self-regard, for example, shame is the name of one of the pair of opposites, but it is also the force that regulates the field (Kauffman, 2010). Shame enforces normative law. Signal shame (Fenichel, 1945; Gilbert & Andrews, 1998; Kauffman 2001, 2002; Levin, 1967, 1971; Morrison & Lansky, 1997; Tompkins, 1963) is a shame signal that does not cross the threshold of consciousness, which enforces normative order.

Shame regulates by its power to create a very painful emotion, and it is this emotion that is usually called to mind by the word shame. This operates as an enforcer of self-valuation and social order. It regulates through constituting experiences of valuational privation, such as dishonor, disgrace, devaluation, dehumanization, stigmatization, failure, subjugation, annihilation, defilement, exclusion, objectification, and so forth. The protective cover of belonging, affirmative self-valuation, and enclosures of identity are breached in the overwhelming anxiety of acute, complicated, and traumatic grief.

SELF-CONSCIOUSNESS

Self-consciousness is a word with two meanings. In one sense it is the reflexivity of consciousness, and in the other it is a painful sense of exposure. It is not a coincidence that self-consciousness has these two meanings. The two are norm and deviance, two sides of the meaning of shame as regulator. The pain of exposure and the reflexive construction of, for example, identity, exhibit two sides of shame, suggesting that self-consciousness is itself a shame phenomenon. Darwin (1965) observes that shame is the *emotion of self-consciousness*. He sees the origin of self-consciousness in the awareness of self, which occurs in and through the eyes of the other. The boundary between self and other, like the boundary of the self's relationship with itself, is regulated by shame.

The shame of self-consciousness is the shame of one's own death. The act of recognizing oneself through the eyes of the other is generated from *death at the seat of self-consciousness*. This is, also, the genealogy of the superego in Freud (1960), that is, moral self-awareness is constituted from internalizing the death power of the other (father) and from death that is always already there in the unconscious. The enforcement power of Freud's superego agency, he says, overlooking the great power of shame, is guilt.

The shame of death is the crux of the self-relational organization of consciousness and conscience. And when death impacts on life, the impact occurs not only in the ego, but in the shame-organized conscience. In mourning, the relationship of self with itself and with the deceased occurs in shame-organized internality. The genealogy of self-consciousness from the shame of death originates in the hidden meaning of death in the unconscious and leads, through mourning, to the formation of human conscience, identity, and transcendence.

ON DEATH'S SACRED AND PROFANE NATURE

The presence of death calls for special discretion. Death's sacred nature may be transgressed or violated, shaming a person who is grieving. Rules of discretion provide a protective cover for mourning, and indiscretion induces shame. The discretion called for in the presence of the bereaved involves the performance of social manners that protect the bereaved from exposure. A sacred bond with the deceased—and with oneself—is violated by social indiscretion. Discretion shelters mourning from the shame of nonrecognition. In traditional cultures social behavior in relation to mourning is prescribed and ritualized to assure sacred cover of the disturbance that death arouses. The practice of social isolation of the bereaved quarantines death as unclean. And, being thus an outcast in grief, alone with the profanity of death, mourners are oppressed by the shame of their grief.

Discretion, beyond being a mere social gesture, is, psychologically, an act of holding within oneself the shame woundedness of the other. In being discreet toward mourners, the social environment bears within itself the sacred wound of death. Discretion in the presence of the bereaved, in refraining from wounding, holds within the sacred grief shame of the other. Exposure of the mourner to indiscretions, disenfranchisements

(Doka, 2001), or other ruptures of the sacred privacy of grief in which the griever is shame vulnerable, violates, objectifies, and *profanes the mourner.*

Profaning the bereaved by indiscretion and disenfranchisement is an act of shame-induction and moral pollution. The profaned mourner experiences contamination, alienation, shame-panic, inner deadness, and such. Death sanctifies life and curses it, and transforms human animal nature into a sacred–profane nature. The psychology of shame motivates and enforces the sacred–profane dimensions. During a crisis of being in psychological proximity to death, the sacred and the profane tend, in the charged and volatile *sacred–profane climate,* to dedifferenti-ate. The cover–exposure dynamics of sacred and profane—as in clean–dirty or in morally valued–defiled—is a shame dynamic operating in the moral proximity of death.

Awe, as defined in the *Oxford English Dictionary* (OED, www. oed.com), is "an immediate and active fear." Awe is a subjective state of being in a reflexive relationship with the all-powerful otherness of death, filled with immediate and active fear—and shame. The *OED* further says that awe is "dread mingled with veneration or respectful fear … in the presence of supreme authority, moral greatness or sublim-ity, or mysterious sacredness." Each of these (shame-dynamic) acts (i.e., dread, veneration, and respect) and each of these (shame-based) entities (i.e., the presence of supreme authority, moral greatness or sublimity, and mysterious sacredness) are experienced from the position of *shame-receptivity* to the power of death. Sacred shame-receptivity before the awful power of death is a fear that embraces the fearful, and receives it. The sacred meaning of death discloses itself, not to knowing, but to awe. The gravity of the soul is its shame.

When Gorer (1987) wrote that death had become pornographic, he was saying that death was no longer under the traditional cover of rituals and other traditional meaning-giving acts, and that people are by virtue of this sociocultural change exposed to death as a profanity, an exploita-tion, defiling and meaning-rupturing. Weakening the sacred cover of tra-ditional meanings and practices exposes the individual to the profanity of death. Death is not a matter of fact in consciousness; it is a profanity in search of a sacred cover.

THE POSTTRADITIONAL STIGMATA
OF DEATH AND GRIEF

Increasingly, so it appears over the past 200 years, as the power of tradi-tion to define death has weakened, the mourner increasingly has become a social outcast, unsheltered, unredeemed, and stigmatized by death. Since the decline of the authority of traditional norms and practices, the regulative power of shame to provide cover for mourning has become more unstable. The historic challenge of postmodernity has been to find an adaptive response to this sociocultural disorder, or to find a metanarrative about the dilemma.

The mourners in Aries' (1974) "age of thy death" mourn not their own deaths, as had been the case from the 12th to the 18th centuries, according to Aries, but the death of the beloved other—*thy death*. In the age of thy death, mourning, as a pathway of resolving broken attachment anxiety, has become more problematic, such as in the late 20th century observations of Gorer or in Walter's (1994) observation that mourning has become *privatized*, cut off in grief from the social enclosure and, in one's privacy, alone and deprived of an implicit sense of belonging and being. The late 20th century observation that grief is becoming more traumatic (e.g., Rando, 1993; cf. Bracken, 2002; Caruth, 1996; Davoine & Gaudillière, 2004; Farrell, 1998; Marder, 2001) is a recognition of a historically progressive difficulty with mourning. In an age of grief as broken attachment anxiety, mourning has progressively developed complications, which Freud (1959) had first diagnosed as a type of self-preoccupation.

The age of thy death is an age of alienation and abandonment. Death has been expelled from the self and the social world, only to reappear as a foreign, otherworldly invader. To keep this danger under control, new death meanings and practices are replaced by newer ones at an accelerating pace, for new meanings are full of promise, but not long lived. Death, unbound from traditional norms, prompts a restorative urge to redefine mourning, to conserve what is already lost. An increasingly rapid rate of change is a sign of an instability of the socioculturally "grounded validity" and vitality of death's meaning. Aries writes that in the age of thy death, which began in the 18th century and continues today, death is hidden and shameful.

ECHOES IN THE SILENCE: THE MORAL CONTEXT OF DEATH

When Darwin asked "What is the emotional expression which distinguishes man from other animals," he concluded that it was the blush, which he says is an expression of shame, the emotion of self-consciousness. He begins his account by describing the nature of blushing as "a sense of shame gorged with blood" (Darwin, 1965, p. 309). That is, blushing is shame expressed in a particular physiological way.

For shame to expresses itself as a blush is an act of self-betrayal, disclosing what it wills to conceal. Self-betrayal is a key aspect of shame's pithy nature. Blushing, the blood-pumped flush of self-consciousness, an "involuntary" bodily expression, betrays a secret. Darwin, commenting further on the self-betrayal nature of blushing, describes a mechanism by which the very effort to hide leads to disclosure. Darwin (1965) says of the blush that "the wish to restrain it, by leading to self-attention, actually increases the tendency" (p. 320). The urge to restrain and prevent exposure by hiding results in an increased lack of restraint and is, indeed, the vehicle of self-exposure. Blushing, an exhibition of shame, is an enactment of self-betrayal. It is also possible that blushing expresses a wish for relief from hiding or that self-betrayal is a sort of shame tic, which Darwin's mechanistic psychology of the blush may suggest.

Darwin gives another example of the expressive language of shame: "An ashamed person can hardly endure to meet the gaze of those present, so that he almost invariably casts down his eyes or looks askant" (p.321). The shame gesture of averting the gaze of another is, like the blush, a social gesture that demonstrates what shame is. In both instances, the concealment nature of shame betrays itself by exhibiting itself. Both ethological observations selected by Darwin to exhibit the phenomenon of shame are gestures of yielding power to the other through a demonstration of submission to the power of the other. Both the blush and the averted gaze express *being exposed and subordinated to the power of the other.* The emotion of self-consciousness, shame, which distinguishes human emotional life from the emotional life of other animals, is the ordering power of identity and social order. A naturalist psychology of moral relationships, of which mourning is an instance, is based on the power of shame as regulator.

Self-consciousness originates in the power of the other, through whom the self posits itself, signifying death. The self, through shame, posits itself. Darwin calls this self *personal appearance.* In talking about personal appearance, Darwin thinks like a psychologist of self-consciousness. Personal appearance does not mean a body image, but means, rather, the appearance of oneself to oneself through the eyes and power of the other. Darwin (1965) writes, "many reasons may be assigned for believing that originally self-attention, directed to personal appearance, in relation to the opinion of others, was the exciting cause [of self-consciousness]; the same effect being subsequently produced, through the force of association, by self-attention in relation to moral conduct" (p. 325). Personal appearance, the object of self-attention, excited by experiencing oneself as an object of "the opinion of others," is a shame phenomenon that originates moral consciousness and identity.

EXPOSURE AND EMPATHY IN GRIEF THERAPY

Clinical space, as space for the disclosure of the grieving self, is a space in which the therapist's awareness of and clinical attunement to shame protects and guides the clinical interface, allowing the griever to disclose herself. Shame inhibits disclosure, to others and to oneself, so that grief shame may be numb, mute, and unrecognized. Therapeutic processing of grief involves being present with one's own grief or being receptive to oneself through disclosure in grief therapy. The interface of the mourner and the therapist is established and maintained as a safe place in which the mourner may, through a psychotherapeutic structure and practice that provides security against the risk of exposure, experience herself in grief.

The interpersonal space of grief therapy is established as an exposure risk safe zone. Anxieties and painful grief meanings are held by the therapist's empathic, implicit grasp of exposure anxiety and vulnerability. The term *holding* (Winnicott, 1965), a description and metaphor of maternal care, has often been used to indicate a basic sense in which the therapist is present with and for the client. Holding, in the therapeutic situation, is regarded by self psychology (Kohut, 1971) as a mirror that accurately reflects. The space in which the client experiences herself with the therapist is a space secured by a mirroring that does not shame. Mirroring and holding, here, are metaphors for "giving interpersonal cover" from shame vulner- abilities, which flow beneath the surface of speech and therapeutic interaction.

Grief deploys narcissistic defenses, in particular, shame defenses against self-devaluation and against the diverse shame negations of the self in grief. Narcissistic defenses are, however, self-defeating in that they block mourning and give neither security nor restora- tion. Grief shame defenses seal off regions of the grieving self from the exposure risk of clinical space. Therapeutic space, which is safe from narcissistic shame defenses of the grief therapist, permits self- disclosure.

TITCHENER'S MUSCLE

The various visual images which I have referred to as possible vehicles of logical meaning, oftentimes share their task with kinaesthesis. Not only do I see gravity and modesty and pride and courtesy and stateli- ness, but I feel or act them in the mind's muscles. This is, I suppose, a simple case of empathy if we may coin that term as a rendering of

Einfühlung; there is nothing curious or idiosyncratic about it; but it is
a fact that must be mentioned. And further: just as the visual image
may mean of itself, without kinaesthetic accompaniment, so may the
kinaesthetic image occur and mean of itself, without assistance from
vision. (Titchener, 1909, pp. 21–22)

Titchener is here concerned with the thought processes of visual imagery
and kinaesthesis. Logical meaning disclosed by empathy, he argues, is
based on visual and kinesthetic imagery. Visual and kinesthetic imagery
are thought processes but not, in a narrow sense, cognitions. Empathy,
as a thought process, involves the imagistic thinking of the mind's eye
and imaginative enactments, which are performed independent of reason and may act independently of each other. Titchener's empathy is an
apperception of a specific range of objects, exemplified by "gravity and
modesty and pride and courtesy and stateliness." These are not objects in
the physical world, but are themselves thought processes, and in particular are thought processes in which self-relational and social valuations
are at stake.

With regard to gravity, we will immediately see that it does not
appear to fit with the others in the series. Modesty, pride, courtesy, and
stateliness are, however, valuational positions of the self in relation to
itself and in social relations, which matter to us because of the psychological and social gravity in the experience of these valuations. The gravity of such valuations is in the significance of self-valuation in ordering
the reflexive self. The inward gravity of modesty and pride, for example,
is the weight, influence, and authority of these valuations in regulating
shame dimensions of the self. Gravity is an analogy to shame as the
psychological force of self-relational valuations, such as in the gravity of
pride and modesty. Courtesy and stateliness are social manners deployed
to manage interpersonal shame variables. Courtesy and stateliness are
sets of social rules authorized and enforced by shame, which display
behaviors for the purpose of providing shame covers; what is grave with
courtesy and stateliness is the shame injury they each protects against.
So, gravity does not seem to be a member of this series as much as it is
the name of the series. There is, however, an old sense of the word gravity as "a title of honor or respect" (i.e., empathy; *OED*, www.oed.com),
which might also be the name of this series. Empathy is empathy for *the
gravity of the other,* as in honor and respect.

Courtesy is expressed in this example from the *OED* of an early use
of the word gravity, in which it means honoring the social standing of
the other, as in "I offer it to you with all singular affection, and bend-
ing submission to your grauitie (gravity)" (i.e., gravity; *OED*, www.oed.
com). Courtesy is a gift of recognizing the gravity of the other.

Shame constituted in the difference between "grauitie" and submission defines a *region of esteem*. The gravity–esteem series consists of instances of the shame-ordered regulation of self-worth and social status. The object of empathy, which Titchener helps us to see, is this shame-valuational, hierarchically ordered region of human experience. Empathy is a type of thinking whose object is the shame-based self-valuations of another, the valuational gravity of the human existence of another. Empathy is a thought process that bonds the human world (giving cover); exposure anxiety is the power of disconnection.

Titchener's account of empathy as a thought process suggests that *seeing*, and its distance from the object, may have no privilege over *feeling* and *enacting*, which together apprehend the object, each operating with a different degree of perceptual and psychological proximity to their object. Seeing, feeling, and enacting-in-thought operate together in empathy.

To return to the gravity series, modesty and pride are shame variants, that is, they each exist as psychodynamic shame opposites: modesty–shame, pride–shame. Shame operates in modesty and pride as a regulative self-ordering authority and as psychodynamic opposite. Modesty and pride exist relative to shame, that is, are shame variants, normative opposites of shame; the exemplary case in this essay being the opposition of exposure and cover.

On an experiential level, the meaningfulness of modesty and pride, their valuational significance in the self's experience of itself, is rooted in shame-variant dynamics, which organize identity. The shame-variant organization of identity is described by Erikson as a developmental processing of shame–autonomy (Erikson, 1980; also see Lynd, 1958). Autonomy is a shame-variant norm, an integrative cover of developmentally early exposure anxiety. And, when, in traumatic loss, dissociative shame panic flight from self is set in motion, and autonomy is shattered.

Pride and modesty, also, may be paired to mean being with excess (pride) or without excess (modesty) in self-judgment. Valuational excesses, such as overvaluation (including idealization) and devaluation are shame operations. The realm of valuational excesses is taken by Kohut (1971) to be the central concern of self psychology, as in his descriptions of transference and pathologies of self-valuational distortions.

The term *empathy* did not come into the English language through everyday speech and common usage but was coined by the academics Titchener (1909) and Lee (1912). Lee uses the term empathy to describe the psychology of aesthetic perception. He calls empathy a "sympathetic

aesthetic feeling." Titchener's empathy, as we have seen, is an appercep-
tive muscle of the other's valuational experience.

BEING NORMAL

A common question that mourners ask is "What is normal?" The question of normalcy has emerged as the power of traditional mourning
norms has weakened in the culture, leaving persons in need of an affirming seal of normalcy. Anxiety about grief not being normal is a part of
the contemporary grief scene and, in some circumstances, finds its way
into coremost grief anxieties. Experiencing and believing one's grief to
be "not normal" stigmatizes and isolates the mourner. Without good
enough sociocultural mourning rules, mourners are prone to experience
their grief as not normal. The power that authorizes traditional mourning norms, however, is today invoked by a psychological concept of normalcy, though the uncertainty that gives rise to the question "What is
normal?" is not quelled.

   Normalcy is a term of differentiation and functions as a protective
cover differentiated from (the shame of) exclusion from the enclosure of
normalcy. *Normal* is a term of differentiation by which abnormal is also
constructed. The idea of normalcy sorts and casts out the shame of death
and grief as not normal. What is excluded in this way, however, persists
in a trajectory of return, reappearing as anxiety.

   The cover of normalcy may come to function as a hiding place from
a shame of identity and uniqueness, hiding out under the cover of normalcy. To the extent that normalcy functions as a hideout, the identity
and uniqueness of being human is compromised. So it is with grief. In
grief that is masked by normalcy, a person is, in being normal, not himself. In such a circumstance, no deviance from psychological health may
be evident. There is a socioculturally syntonic factor in the escape from
grief to normalcy, as society supports the false self-mirroring of such a
grief fugitive. In the unsure sociocultural landscape of a time in history
when the authority of traditional sociocultural norms is on the wane, the
mourner who asks what is normal may be seeking refuge by identification with prescriptive normal grief.

   Now, normalcy itself stakes a valuational claim in its very differentiation from not normal. However, it is possible to make a judgment
about the value of normalcy. And, so far as we are able to suspend judgment about the value of normalcy, then we are free to consider other
possibilities, but to take that first step subverts the a priori value claim of
normalcy. Suppose there were reason to value some deviant grief greater
than or incommensurate with normal grief. Suppose, for example, that

the basic norm of psychosocial adaptation is not of greater life-affirming value than some grief recognized to be deviant. Or, perhaps the grief of those afflicted with a chronic sorrow (Roos, Chapter 10, this volume) has deeper redemptive power than normalcy.

Normalcy comes up as an existential question for grievers only in a sociocultural circumstance in which normative authority has lost vigor. In this situation, novel ways of grieving become critical for sociocultural adaptation and may contribute to changing mourning norms.

Perhaps, the American jeremiad (Bercovitch, 1978; Breitwiesser, 2007), which protects the shame of a nation, nurturing its spirit, has lost its potency in affirming the meaning of life through the self-criticism that inheres in mourning. Even as thanatology in America opens up the public sphere to dialogue, educational agendas, authoritative norms, new grief practices, media attention, psychotherapy, and grief supportive institutions; even as scholarly work in philosophy and the humanities finds itself thinking in relation to death, as depth psychology finds its depth in death (or, in the shame of death); and as the psychological study of grief and mourning flourishes, the American jeremiad grows more ineffectual and supplanted by the shame of self-destructive narcissistic/fear-of-death *defensive trends;* the republic is forgetful of its suffering.

NARCISSISTIC DEATH ANXIETY IS A HUNGRY GHOST IN THE CHAMBERS OF GRIEF: EXPOSURE AND GRIEF PSYCHOPATHOLOGY

Self-preoccupation in grief, turning attention to oneself in self-blaming shame devaluations, commonly called self-pity and, by Freud, called melancholia, is a loss-of-self anxiety reaction to the loss of a valued object. The psychopathology of grief, as identified in folk anxieties about the dangers of grief and in psychoanalytic conceptualizations of mourning, is a self-preoccupation driven by helplessness anxiety, self-blaming shame anxiety, and by an elusive generalized shame anxiety. Loss-of-self anxiety in grief becomes exacerbated when the effort to recover oneself becomes spellbound by helplessness and shame. In traumatic grief, likewise, powerful underlying traumatic shame, which fragments and pollutes the self, is the disintegrative undertow. Shame wounding of the grieving self is a key danger that societal mourning norms aim to protect against. Such norms operate to secure safe passage through the shame-dangerous passageways of grief.

The quicksand of shame's self-preoccupation, the pithiness of the self's inward collapse in melancholia, are disturbances of the very reflexive structure of shame, namely, that shame is prone to be itself shameful. Lewis (1971), who appears to have been the first to notice this, spoke of this as the *shame of shame*. Self-pity or melancholia is not simply a disposition of shame in reaction to death and other loss; it is the shame of shame or, more precisely, a *shame of* the shame of the grieving self. The shame of shame describes a disintegration of the self's cohesion or integrity, a narcissistic pit of self-absorption trying to hold itself together, a self-disconnect.

A very common part of the grief reaction is to experience shame at being abandoned and helpless; shame at the shock of death and at one's own mortality; shame inspired by the all-powerful, ultimate, invisible meaning of death; shame at the whole strange and wounded inner world of grief; shame at being stigmatized or polluted by death; and so forth. Inherent in the experience of death or of grief is a risk of being preoccupied in self-absorbed (shame) anxiety. The disintegrative psychodynamics of this shame anxiety is the guarded and reckless flight of the shame of the shame of death and of grief.

REFERENCES

Aries, P. (1974). *Western attitudes toward death: From the middle ages to the present* (P. Ranum, Trans.). Baltimore: Johns Hopkins University.

Bercovitch, S. (1978). *The American jeremiad.* Madison: The University of Wisconsin Press.

Blanchot, M. (1994). *The instant of my death* (E. Rottenberg, Trans.). Stanford, CA: Stanford University Press.

Bracken, P. (2002). *Trauma: Culture meaning and philosophy.* London: Whurr.

Breitwiesser, M. (2007). *National melancholy: Mourning an opportunity in classic American literature.* Stanford, CA: Stanford University Press.

Caruth, C (1996). *Unclaimed experience: Trauma narrative and history.* Baltimore: John's Hopkins University Press.

Darwin, C. (1965). *The expression of emotions in man and animals.* Chicago: The University of Chicago Press.

Davoine, F., & Gaudillière, J. (2004). *History beyond trauma* (S. Fairfield, Trans.). New York: Other Press.

Doka, K. (Ed). (2001). *Disenfranchised grief: New directions, challenges and strategies for practice.* Champaign, IL: Research Press.

Erikson, E. (1980). *Identity and the life cycle.* New York: W.W. Norton and Company.

Farrell, K. (1998). *Post-traumatic culture: Injury and interpretation in the nineties*. Baltimore: Johns Hopkins University Press.

Fenichel, O. (1945). *The psychoanalytic theory of neurosis*. New York: W.W. Norton.

Freud, S. (1959). Mourning and melancholia. In J. Rivere (Trans.), *Collected Papers* (Vol. 4, pp. 152–170). New York: Basic Books. (Original work published 1917)

Freud, S. (1960). *The ego and the id*. (J. Riviere, Trans.) New York: Norton.

Freud, S. (1961). *Beyond the pleasure principle* (J. Strachy, Ed. & Trans.). New York: W.W. Norton.

Gilbert, P., & Andrews, B. (1998) *Shame: Interpersonal behavior, psychopathology, and culture*. New York: Oxford University Press.

Gorer, G. (1987). *Death grief and mourning in contemporary Britain*. Salem, NH: Ayer Company Publishers. (Original work published 1965)

Husserl, E. (1964). *The phenomenology of internal time-consciousness*. (M. Heidegger, Ed. & S. Churchill, Trans.) Bloomington: Indiana University of Press.

Kauffman, J. (2001). The psychology of disenfranchised grief. In K. Doka (Ed.), *Disenfranchised grief: New directions, challenges, and strategies for practice* (pp. 61–77). Champaign, IL: Research Press.

Kauffman, J. (2002). Safety and the assumptive world. In J. Kauffman (Ed.), *Loss of the assumptive world* (pp. 205–211). New York: Routledge.

Kauffman, J. (2010). Making sence of being human. In J. Ciprut(Ed.), *On meaning*, Cambridge, MA: MIT Press.

Kohut, H. (1971). *The analysis of the self*. New York: International Universities Press.

Lee, V., & Anstruther-Thompson, C. (1912). *Beauty & ugliness: And other studies in psychological aesthetics*. London: John Lane.

Levin, S. (1967). Some metapsychological considerations on the differentiation between shame and guilt. *International Journal of Psychoanalysis, 48*, 267–276.

Levin, S. (1971). The psychoanalysis of shame. *International Journal of Psychoanalysis, 52*, 355–362.

Lewis, H. B. (1971). *Shame and guilt in neurosis*. New York: International Universities Press.

Lynd, H. M. (1958). *On shame and the search for identity*. New York: Science Editions.

Marder, E. (2001). *Dead time*. Stanford, CA: Stanford University Press.

Morrison, A. P., & Lansky, M. R. (1997). The legacy of Freud's writing. In A. P. Morrison & M. R. Lansky (Eds.), *The widening scope of shame* (pp. 3–40). Hillside, NJ: The Analytic Press.

Oxford English Dictionary (*OED*). Retrieved December 1, 2009, from http://www.oed.com.

Rando, T. (1993). The increasing prevalence of complicated mourning: The onslaught is just beginning. *Omega: Journal of Death and Dying, 26*, 43–59.

Titchener, E. B. (1909). *Lectures on the experimental psychology of thought-processes*. New York: Macmillan.

Tompkins, S. S. (1963). *Affect, Imagery, Consciousness: Vol. 2. The negative affects*. New York: Springer.

Walter, T. (1994). *The revival of death*. London: Routledge.

Winnicott, D.W. (1965). *Maturational processes and the facilitating environment: Studies in the theory of emotional development*. New York: International Universities Press.

Winnicott, D.W. (1974). Fear of breakdown. *International Review of Psychoanalysis, 103*(1), 103–107.

A Personal Narrative

CHAPTER 2

Side by Side

Shelley Costa

*To the bravery of those
who, by word or gesture,
have tipped their hats
to one they could not know,
dissolving in friendship
the shame of the unrecognized.*

When a child dies, society grieves. Those entirely unknown to the family ache when they hear of the loss of one who has caused admiration and laughter, one who taps into one's own memories, unburdening a cherished phase in life. The death of a child is a tragic jolt, perennially moving.

But the younger a baby is, the less a community speaks of the child. With a few, treasured exceptions, people defer to speaking about the parents. This is their anchor. The baby comes to represent not a lost person, a lost present, or even one's own lost innocence (infancy preceding conscious memory), but an unfulfilled future, a path not taken. Collective lifetimes steeped in social custom effectively blunt the magic of infants not yet socialized. Guided by the highest of motives, a sympathetic community erases the lost life in order to focus on the bereaved and to wish them the best in *moving on.*

People force on the bereaved what they can comprehend. To a parent negotiating condolences, the baby is lost all over again.

My own struggle against such alienation has been anchored in the body. First, the body of my child. My son died at full term, before birth, of an umbilical cord accident. I had the privilege of constantly feeling his many strong movements as well as the remarkable privilege of honoring his existence by giving birth to him. Neither I, nor anyone else, had the privilege of seeing or holding him alive: thriving, squirming, sleeping, breathing. But we *did* have the privilege of seeing and holding him as the newborn that he was.

The awe of looking on one's firstborn child is an incomparable experience. There are many who have assumed that the birth of my eldest daughter finally brought me this feeling. When each of my beautiful daughters was born healthy, I felt joy, amazement, and relief. But it was not the world-shifting, irrational pride of the firstborn. This happens only once.

A handful of relatives and friends came to the hospital. I felt accepted and loved in their choice to come to us in this life-changing and unusual situation, in the naturalness with which they enfolded our swaddled child. In the months that followed, I felt the most comfortable in their presence. With them, I felt whole and honest even when not speaking directly about our loss. In the presence of others I felt overwhelmed by a sin of omission. Normal, everyday discourse washed over me as thoroughly dishonest, yet mentioning my son was awkward and inappropriate, a burden on the listener. In some cases I acknowledged my child and lived with the social breach; in others, I refrained. Internally destroyed by either choice, I kept public interaction to a minimum.

Six weeks later we moved hundreds of miles from our child's birthplace. Now every interaction was an introductory one. Person after person unwittingly met a husk, a mirage. There was no way to explain, to run, or to warn *them* to run. Unmoored, I was thankful to have part-time work that forced me out of bed. But being in the presence of others, drained my energy. Minor jolts or unexpected events reduced me to tears. I became accustomed to frequent physical feelings of alarm completely out of context, as if an invisible practical joker had a habit of taunting me with a completely inaudible "Boo!" When I opened the door to a crowded meeting, the sudden increase in noise felt like a slap in the face. I learned to keep my eyes lowered.

These were the first public arenas of my grief. But what was at stake in public judgment had impressed itself upon me before my son was born. In that moment, I was consumed in tears on my kitchen floor, my ear pressed to the phone. My spouse stood near me, looking on with suffering and concern. My doula—a professional birth assistant whose support and experience brought me essential focus—was asking me if we were planning to bring our camera to the hospital.

For me, the idea of taking photographs was, in that moment, as abstract and unreal as everything else that one imagines to follow a first birth. I recognized with dread that taking pictures under the circumstances would be fairly incomprehensible, perhaps even shocking, to the world at large. At the same time, I suspected that I would want visual memories of our child, especially to share with future siblings. In the midst of tears, confusion, and fear, I felt impossibly torn between wanting to make the right decision for myself and my family and wanting to avoid seeming horrid, shocking, morbidly sentimental ... wrong.

My spouse also felt the weight of imagined public condemnation. When he heard me answer that the decision to bring our camera had not crossed our minds, he reacted abruptly: "NO! No pictures." I transmitted his wishes through sniffles. My doula spoke very clearly, very firmly. "If you pack the camera, you do not have to ever take it out of your bag. But if you change your minds, and you don't have the camera, you may regret it for the rest of your lives." The logic was mercifully irrefutable. We packed the camera.

Later that evening, two friends came to bring us supper, to listen, weep, give support. I shared my worries, rehearsing fears about what I had eaten or how I had moved. I withheld just one emotion: a sense of overwhelming embarrassment for imposing on others a nine-month-pregnant form, a silhouette that misleadingly represented joy. An apology for my appearance rose silently to my tongue and froze. As it did, I realized that I was sparing myself the vehement, almost angry denial that I knew would (and should) come if I uttered it. I felt wrong and foolish as well as embarrassed. I was ashamed of being ashamed.

By the end of that evening, my confusion and grief had mustered on two battlegrounds: the body of my child and my own pregnant body. Neither, it seemed, was worthy of being seen in the full light of day.

Day did arrive, and with it the natural birth of my son. It was a cherished experience that allowed my spouse and I to find joy in the midst of our profound loss. I learned that my body was powerful and that it could deliver beauty as well as tragedy. Moved by fatherhood, my spouse changed his mind about photographs once he saw his child. Our small digital camera allowed us to take intimate, delicate portraits of our newborn in natural light. We remain deeply thankful for them—and for the gift of our first child.

From the start I longed for him to be recognized for having lived as much as for having died. And from the start it felt like walking amid spring-loaded traps. I designed a handful of birth remembrance announcements and agonized over who might appreciate the child they represented versus who might simply see them as evidence to feel sorry for me. Not wanting to presume or to exclude, I sent them to people in both categories. Printed on some cards was a small black-and-white photo; some cards had no photo. On them all was printed a poem by T. S. Elliot about the silence of love within a family.

At birth, my son weighed seven and a half pounds. He was nineteen inches long. His announcement cards declared these traits as they would have done for any other newborn.

Withdrawal brings safety; but as solace, it is incomplete. Overall, my need to have my son perceived as an individual was met with support, with tenderness, and at times (most rewardingly) with genuine gratitude. Sometimes, either in speaking to someone I knew well, or in truthfully answering the frequent "Is this your first?" during my next pregnancy or during my elder daughter's subsequent babyhood, I did feel jostled by the awkwardness, as well as the bare loneliness of feeling misunderstood. For each such instance there had been many more expressions of support. But negative moments touched sore spots. More than once I privately wondered, in tears, why I bothered. But the compulsion was so deep as to eliminate choice. For me, silence punished my son by revoking the natural and unconditional acceptance he would have received had he not died. *It was not his fault.*

We held two events: a birth memorial and a first birthday reflection. Through them I shared my own poetry, music, and artwork. I designed a memorial Web site. Each creative process was healing and transformative. The two memorial events and the Web site have allowed my son a small place within a community. But in seeking to be understood there is always some level of risk. Who is looking? What are they thinking?

At no point did anyone overtly scold or wag a finger. Quite the contrary. In the first weeks and months I received kind, wise, and well-timed words to counter instinctive maternal self-blame. Many, many relatives and friends made their support very clear. I also benefited from books, Web sites, and support groups on pregnancy and infant loss that were not available to previous generations. Most crucially, I had the good fortune of giving birth with midwives who viewed my and my spouse's emotional health as equal to my and our child's physical health, and a hospital staff well trained in compassionate postnatal care for mothers who have experienced loss. All of this was an antidote to feelings of shame.

These resources could not entirely prevent maternal self-blame. In the first phase of grieving I endured self-directed emotions similar in intensity, and in irrationality, to the embarrassment I had felt the evening before the birth. But the wealth of available support and information helped me to marshal reason over and over again against these feelings. I needed forgiveness, but recognized very early on that that was an internal battle. I saw that anyone who knew *me* very well automatically forgave me; that anyone who thoroughly understood the science of pregnancy automatically forgave me; and that anyone in between who had an undisrupted illusion of control—naive young couples, for example, who thought physical fitness automatically led to healthy children, a lovely fiction like an unpopped balloon—could not be entrusted with the power to judge, even if they believed themselves to hold this power.

Because of all this, if I had been asked, say, a year or so after my son's birth whether I had experienced *shame* during my grieving process, I would have said no. But were I to be asked whether I had experienced *judgment*, I would have said yes. This judgment had a constant, hovering presence, and was the source of the bulk of my suffering. In such perceived, disembodied judgment, the experiences of grief and shame come together.

Rather than being about the cause of my child's death, the judgment that affected me had to do with the value of his life.

Those who sat at the bench did not intentionally bang the gavel. My accusers wounded me unknowingly. What they had in common were remarks, gestures, or responses that in some way confirmed my fear—or knowledge—that there was little room in the world for my child. At the same time, these *same* individuals also exhibited sadness, kindness, and support.

The confusing display of fidelity on the one hand and abandonment on the other caught me off-balance more than once. But the betrayal was not personal. These individuals took refuge in social convention. They blindly condoned what was universally permissible (sympathy for a survivor) and distanced themselves from what was not (regard for a dead baby). They were acting as social drones. If I didn't want their sting, it was easy to see which choice I should make.

The choice was a false one; the alternative, meaningless. What is sympathy if it is not openhearted listening? What is it to grieve if one cannot speak of the dead?

Very, very early in my loss, before anyone had a chance to trip over their tongues, I sought to anchor a receding reality. I thought of onions, potatoes, and flour—they come in five-pound bags, two-pound bags. If I ever felt like I was losing it, I told myself, I could just go to the supermarket and hold a couple of these bags. Seven pounds, eight and a half ounces.

I soon began, relatively often, to imagine *hitting people* with these bags as a way of getting across my son's personhood. Not specific individuals, just people on the street. Innocent people. I was not comfortable with the violent imagery, but there it was. *Whoom.* A five-pound bag of flour to the face. (I usually spared my victims the remaining two-and-a-half pounds of potatoes or onions.) *That's* what the world is missing.

Even in those fantasies, I felt for the flour-covered people as they blinked through the white powder of their innocence and confusion.

My son occupies a quiet place in our immediate family. I have always felt supported in this from many quarters, and I continue to be. Conflicting opinions no longer matter. Over the course of healing, a confidence in my own views has replaced a fear of being wrong in the eyes of those with whom I disagree.

I now realize that in navigating my grieving, I have played a role—the most crucial role—in giving credence to an ill-informed and shapeless public judgment. I am through. Instead of fearfully imagining myself as seen from a critical height, I invite others to share in my perspective.

The pairs of eyes that matter most to me now are not those of censure. They are the ones that have always been at my side.

Psychological Reflections on Shame and Grief

CHAPTER 3

Between Shame, Death, and Mourning

The Predispositional Role of Early Attachments and the Sense of Self

Victor L. Schermer

When a child is born, although she cries, she has no well-formulated idea of the end that awaits her, although if we are to believe Wordsworth, she may have "intimations of immortality." Hence, too, eternity's opposite, mortality, may be presaged during infancy, especially during painful disruptions in the continuity of the child's relationship to her caregiver. Bowlby (1958, 1968, 1973) alluded to such an early form of death aware-ness when he pointed to the role of primary attachments and the threat to the child's security when absence or loss occurs.

Among the disruptive experiences of infancy is shame. As Tomkins (1963, 1964, 1991) observed, shame is an emotion expressed in infancy in the face-to-face interaction with the mother. In addition, there are other brief and extended disruptions of the mother–infant relationship. The influence of such early disruptions upon subsequent attitudes to death, dying, and grief, however, is difficult to discern and has received relatively little attention by researchers and clinicians. Nevertheless, it is important to consider how such formative experiences may impact bereavement and loss as they occur later in the life cycle. In what follows, I will utilize a self-psychological and relational psychoanalytic perspec-tive to develop some potential theoretical linkages between the earliest disruptions of attachment and shame-based attitudes toward loss and grief that emerge in the course of development. I will then discuss the clinical implications of these linkages as they manifest in the counseling and psychotherapy of adults.

THEORY

Preliminary Reflections on Shame and Death

The emphasis of this volume, courageously initiated and convened by Jeffrey Kauffman, is on the relationship between shame and death. One wonders why it took until now for social scientists to focus on this connection, and it is worth taking a moment to ponder why that is so.

While much has been written about the connection between guilt and mourning (Becker, 1973; Freud, 1917; Perera, 1986), the relationship of guilt's close cousin, shame, to death, dying, and grief has not been addressed to such an extent partly because shame, although it plays a powerful role in life, literature, and the arts, has only recently become of ongoing interest to the social sciences and helping professions. Only with the relatively recent work of Bradshaw (1988), Kaufman (1989), Lewis (1987), Nathanson (1987), and others has shame been given a central role in the understanding of the personality.

Guilt, on the other hand, is an emotion closely related to social, religious, and juridical requirements of conduct, and therefore has been discussed in multiple contexts for millennia (Curren, 1989). In addition, guilt has taken precedence over shame because it is easier to verbalize and more amenable to cognitive processing than shame. In Western culture shame is primarily experienced as an aversive physical and kinesthetic sensation and in many instances is privatized and privileged. Further, shame, while clearly a social emotion that regulates interpersonal behavior, is very much related in our society to the acute consciousness of the individuated self that arose during relatively recent historical periods. Shame both informs and is informed by the sense of self as it evolves throughout the life cycle. The acute self-awareness that fuels shame only gradually became a focus of increased attention in the eras of romanticism and modernity, peaking, of course, with the introspective rigors of Freud and psychoanalysis. Moreover, within that latter discipline, it is no accident that shame could only be grasped within an emerging *self psychology* (Kohut, 1977) in which self-esteem and narcissism occupy a central place.

Despite the scholarly neglect of the shame–death nexus, it is a common observation that death often evokes shame both in those who know that their death is imminent and in those close to them. Shame is manifest in the awkwardness attendant on discussions of death, in the avoidance of contact with the dying, in such ritualistic elements as shrouds and coffins, and in superstitious avoidance of the mention of the dead. These ways of minimizing contact with the dying are designed to keep such inevitabilities from "view." Similarly, shame is the specific emotion that early on leads to avoidance of eye (= "I") contact (Tomkins, 1963), and later to brief or prolonged "exile." In such expressions of shame, an element of dissociation is also involved, as if contact with the dead or dying puts the one so shamed at risk for death himself. But that only betrays a still greater sense of shame, as if to die itself is a reason to be further excluded or banished, as if death is not enough. Thus, one of the implicit attributes of death is that it is a shameful act, sometimes making it the quintessential instance of blaming the victim.

Why should one be ashamed of death, which in itself is a fact of life having no actual implications regarding ones worthiness, social status, or personal acceptability? (After all, everyone dies, and death is the "great equalizer.") The reason is that death, like other "facts of life," takes on meanings embodied in ritualistic acts, narratives, and myths. One of those connotations embodied in culture-based stories and enactments is *exclusion*, a teleological meaning attached to death's finality. It is not merely that the life ends. Rather, phenomenologically in its reification, death creates a barrier or wall that makes the dead mute and inaccessible. Such a notion of death as exclusion is potentiated by the Darwinian imperative of the quick removal of the deceased's body, both for sanitary reasons and so as not to attract prey. These biological necessities surely led through evolution to a predisposition to regard death as shameful and repulsive: the dead begone! In addition, and especially pertinent to the subject matter of this chapter, the fact that the dead no longer exist in "real time" can easily be interpreted by the child as similar to isolation as a punishment or, more consequentially, of parental neglect and deprivation. Thus, in a sense, the dice are loaded regarding the perception of death and dying as shameful conditions of exclusion rather than normative aspects of the life cycle.

On the other hand, death and shame are not inevitably bound to one another. Indeed, one observes a spectrum of attitudes toward death and dying, not only across cultures, but within a given culture. Thus, there are the extremes of, on the one hand, Elisabeth Kübler-Ross's (1969) pioneering encounters with the dying, and on the other, the fictional death-denying "Big Daddy" of Tennessee Williams's (1955) *Cat on a Hot Tin Roof*, who insists we should "go without knowin' it." Much of this variation can be accounted for in terms of orientations toward death internalized from others—parents, peers, popular culture, religion, and so on—but it may also reflect the earliest relational experiences that come about well before "death" can be known and verbalized as such. I will now consider this possibility.

The Impact of Early Attachments on the Death–Shame Nexus

Since emotions and attitudes emerge early in the process of development, the wide variations in orientations toward death and dying suggest that the dynamics of attachment to the caregiver and the emerging
sense of self may play a role in the extent to which death later connotes
and evokes shame and other affects. Although it is true that these patterns develop throughout life, it is likely that the ground for them is
seeded in the earliest relational experiences of the infant with caregivers as the infant develops a sense of selfhood conditioned by these
interactions.

Just as the connection between shame and death has been neglected,
so too has the impact of the earliest preverbal relational experiences.
With the notable exception of Melanie Klein, who regarded Freud's
(1920) "death instinct" as an innate predisposition conditioning the
balance of libido and aggression and impacting on the earliest object
relations (Klein, 1977, p. 250), most psychologists and psychoanalysts
do not attribute death awareness to the infant. It stands to reason,
however, that the infant's "procedural memories" and templates of
anxiety, insecurity, absence, and aloneness would subsequently attach
themselves to what the infant later encounters about death and dying
when these concepts can be symbolically and imagistically elaborated.
Furthermore, the affect of shame would enter the equation both in the
earliest interactions and later on, as cognitive structuring, social learning, symbolization, the sense of self, and intersubjectivity emerge more
fully. Thus, a rationale for a fourfold linkage of attachment, shame, the
sense of self, and death/mourning could be constructed in terms of the
developmental process. However, before developing this idea further, a
particular gap in such theorizing has emerged in the literature and must
be pointed out.

On the Relationship Between Attachment Theory
and Bereavement Studies

It is curious that in the recent acceleration of studies of attachment
(Cassidy & Shaver, 1999), grief and loss are only peripherally discussed.
The partial "disconnect" between the two disciplines exists despite the
fact that Bowlby (1958, 1968, 1973, 1980), who provided the impetus
for many of these investigations, related primary attachments and grief,
holding that mourning is a normative, innate response to disruptions in
the security afforded by the presence of the caregiver. Thus, in Bowlby's
once controversial and now widely held view, *bereavement and stages*

of grief emerge in the earliest attachments and are universal. As the Talmudic saying goes, "As soon as a man is born, he begins to die" or at least to experience abandonment and loss.

In the past two decades, Bowlby's perspective, earlier the target of criticism by more traditional psychoanalysts, most notably Melanie Klein and Anna Freud (Edgcumbe, 2000, pp. 68–76), has led to a wave of empirical and theoretical studies of the attachment situations of children and their impact on later development, especially with regard to the so-called attachment disorders, that is, psychiatric disturbances resulting from disrupted bonding. Such studies include, above and beyond attachment behaviors as such, considerations of affect regulation and mentalization (Fonagy, Gergely, Jurist, & Target, 2002), and neural plasticity (Nelson, 2002).

As a consequence of their pragmatic and empirical emphases, and despite Bowlby's associate Parkes's (1996, 2006) influential contributions on attachment theory and grief, many recent studies that have emerged from Bowlby's work have removed themselves from the understanding of the mourning process, which Bowlby considered inseparable from the nature of attachment. For example, in Fonagy's (2001) comprehensive analysis of attachment theory and psychoanalysis, less than two pages are devoted to grief and mourning. Further, in empirical studies of attachment behavior, the relational variations and distortions that result from difficulties of bonding are not regarded so much as forms of grief as they are considered cognitive-behavioral "attachment disorders," that is, clusters of self-regulative patterns of the child in relation to the caregiver. Whether "secure," "insecure/avoidant," or "insecure/disorganized," these patterns are investigated primarily in the context of recurrent mother–child interactions and disruptions rather than with respect to the death or extended absence of the maternal object. Thus, grief is only peripherally considered in relation to these disorders. The emphasis is rather on the adaptations the child must make to the caregiver's brief absences, problematic attitudes, miscommunications, and abandoning behaviors.

Although such studies are of great interest in terms of their implications for mental health, they obscure Bowlby's seminal observation that grief results from disrupted attachments, and conversely, that damaged attachments are a form of grief, points earlier articulated by Freud in his seminal paper, "Mourning and Melancholia" (1917) and elaborated in a different way by Bowlby. Freud suggested that the lost loved one is taken into the ego, sometimes leading to disturbances in mood and tendencies toward irrational guilt and self-punishment. Bowlby focused on the way in which attachment affords security, so that loss implies a trauma to the self for which normal mourning is ultimately reparative. Both held that the dynamics of attachment, the self, and mourning are interrelated, an idea that has suffered a degree of neglect by both developmentalists and bereavement specialists with respect to the neonatal and infantile phases of development in particular. One purpose in what follows is to rekindle that dialogue by suggesting some of the mechanisms that link the earliest attachments to death awareness and mourning, and by providing some case examples. In making that reconnection, shame plays an essential role.

It is important to note that the gap separating attachment research from the study of subsequent loss and mourning is partly the result of the difficulty inherent in making inferences about the connection between the two. The earliest nonverbal attachments persist as predispositions that one hypothesizes are related to later symbolic representations, for example, of death and dying. But the actual relationships between the two are difficult to identify and articulate. There must be a process whereby the earliest experiences are "absorbed" into the later understanding and explanation of death and loss. Jung (1933) understood it as a function of the "numinous," the child's intuitive grasp of the spiritual realm. For Jung, the primary relationship to the mother is an archetype, a universal symbol that manifests in the child's dreams, stories, and struggles that emerge in the process of individuation. For Freud (1919), the primary relationships later become manifest in "the return of the repressed," with its consequent regression, whereby the conflicts of the Oedipal phase evoke longings for an earlier state of affairs.

More recently, self psychology and relational psychoanalysis have led to a somewhat different account, holding that the primary relationships are ongoing and evolving. Rather than being repressed, they continue to develop. Thus, regarding death and mourning, the child acquires ideas and feelings about them in day-to-day explorations of the world within the interpersonal context of striving to establish a secure, esteem-enhancing sense of self vis-à-vis significant others. The child, for example, finds a dead bird in the garden, or has a dream containing a threatening image, or reads a story about death as a punishment for evil deeds, or plays a video game in which she gleefully wipes out bad personages. These become related in diverse ways to experiences of deprivation, frustration, and loss that challenge the child's security and sense of self. Mortality takes on a powerful meaning. As the child strives to sustain and restore security and esteem, her individuating sense of self retains the legacy of the earliest infantile experiences with the caregiver/mother. The primary attachments thus "color" the understanding of death and loss as they become assimilated into her picture of the world and the ongoing narrative of her life.

This latter account is the basis of the linkages I shall now draw between early disruptions of attachment and subsequent attitudes toward death and grief.

A Working Set of Hypotheses

To delineate the relationship between grief, attachment, and the self from a contemporary perspective, it is important to note that, as many recent studies of infant development have shown, attachment is not simply what Bowlby viewed as the instinctive mechanism wherein the child maintains protective proximity to the mother. Modern infant research has shown that relationships serve a multitude of crucial functions for the infant. Not just safety and security, but cognitive and motor development (Cornish et al., 2005), affect regulation (Schore, 1994), self-awareness and self-cohesion (Tolpin & Kohut, 1980), intersubjectivity (Benjamin, 1999), identity (Erikson, 1959), and emotional growth (Symington & Symington, 1996, pp. 85–91) all depend on sustained interactions with significant others. Not only the infant's physical safety but his or her being and becoming, existence and essence, and constancy and change depend on ongoing interchanges with others.

This hierarchical primacy of relationships was first articulated by the psychoanalyst Fairbairn (1952, p. 33), who stated that for the infant "pleasure is the signpost to the object," meaning that the infant does not so much seek the mother for pleasure or reward (milk, nourishment), but that the pleasurable feeling helps identify the presence of the mother. Thus, for Fairbairn, a relationship is the primary "drive" that conditions all the other drives. In his time (1930s–1940s), this idea was new and controversial. Since then, countless research studies and psychoanalytic reconstructions have supported it, suggesting that infants seek and initiate relationships (Cohn & Tronick, 1988), and that disruptions are a major factor in mental and developmental disorders (Berlin, Ziv, Amaya-Jackson, & Greenberg, 1999). Paradoxically, the individuated self and mind are established through relationships (Foulkes, 1948, pp. 10–11). The brain itself is social (Cozolino, 2006), and brain cells called "mirror neurons" (Iacoboni, 2008) respond equally to self-initiation of behavior and the same behavior enacted by another person. Self and relationship are two sides of the same coin.

How do these findings about the importance of primary relatedness inform our understanding of mourning and attitudes toward death? If death were merely a physical ending to a biological process, it would have minimal psychosocial "meaning" and arouse no strong emotions. Rather, the death of the self is what makes physical cessation meaningful and powerful. And since the self is defined through relationships, we can hypothesize that *the "anlage" or precursor of what the person later knows as "death" is a disruption of interconnectedness, belonging, and relatedness* experienced as early as birth and perhaps, judging from perinatal research (Janus, 1997), even before. This hypothesis is further confirmed by the observation (Ainsworth & Andry, 1962; Spitz, 1945; Spitz & Cobliner, 1965) that with prolonged deprivation or absence of the caregiver, infants begin to literally "shut down," that is, their vital functions begin to diminish, leading to apathy and depression. The infant's contact with caregivers plays such a vital role that it makes life possible for them. Conversely, a lack of connectedness may be psychophysiologically equated to dying, or at the very least a loss of vital energy.

From such considerations, one can suppose that interruptions of the "flow" of the mother–infant interaction establish parameters in the self that are later equated symbolically with death and dying. Such derailments may include the emotional or physical unavailability of the mother, failures of attunement and empathy, and hostility or overintrusiveness. All have potentially damaging or traumatic consequences for further development. In the latter instances, such "gaps" would later be internalized not only as insecurity, as suggested in attachment studies but also symbolically represented as a profound fear of death and preoccupation or identification with it. Subjectively, death is often experienced as a severe and disruptive hole, gap, or absence within the continuity of the self that implies exile and impermanence. As one patient said, with respect to early and severe disruptions in her relationship to her mother, "Sometimes I feel as if I don't *exist*." Such discontinuities emerge as early as the birth process itself and in the interactions of the infant with caregivers, and we can surmise that one way discontinuities become permanentized is through the subsequently evolving consciousness of death and dying.

How, then, does shame enter this picture of such disruptions in attachment, bonding, and relationships?

Shame as a "Disconnect" or "Exclusion" Presaging Death

From the aforementioned perspective, shame becomes related to death as a "disconnect" between mother and infant. Tomkins (1964), in his pioneering work on emotions communicated in mother–infant interactions, theorized that the basic emotions of infancy, namely, anger, fear, disgust, sadness, shame, surprise, and happiness, manifest as preverbal facial communications as much as they are gut (internal physiological) reactions. In particular, when "ashamed," the infant looks down and to the side to avoid meeting the eyes of the other. The eyebrows arch outward in a nonaggressive expression and the mouth droops in sorrow. Usually the head is tilted forward or bowed. Thus, in shame, the infant cuts himself off from visual contact. Importantly for the present context, there is also in shame an element of what will later become the emotion of grief. Shame implies that something has been lost, whether a part of the self or the link to the significant other.

Among the several derailments such as absence, deprivation, and empathic failures, shame has several special characteristics that give it a singular importance. First, shame occurs actively within the "here-and-now" interaction. That is, as Tomkins's observations show, it is a relational emotion. Second, shame includes a proactive self-deprivation: the infant averts her gaze. Third, shame simultaneously protects the infant and paradoxically makes the infant more vulnerable. Avoidance of eye contact serves as a primitive defense against mother's "disapproval," but it also creates a vulnerability of isolation from her. Thus, shame is a mechanism of the self that has the specific connotation of being disapproved, rejected, and cut off. As an active process, it is an "admission of failure" in the eyes of the (m)other.

Subsequently in the life cycle, shame becomes related to mourning insofar as death and dying are perceived as isolation from human interaction and an exile from human contact. Shame makes "to die" an active rather than passive verb, and death a source of disapproval and rejection. It repeats the early derailments between mother and infant in a permanentized form tinged with a recognition of a "basic fault" (Balint, 1979) in the self. Shame absorbs the other "gaps" of the infant's experiences, such as emptiness, absences, and frustrations, giving them a "loading" of social rejection and the loss of status and identity.

When an attachment is traumatically disrupted through death or other difficult circumstances, the self is diminished in several ways. First, through identification, a part of the self is felt to die, suffer, or be damaged. Second, the rupture of the bond leaves the self fragmented and helpless, establishing or rekindling disorganized and anxious attachment styles. Third, the "assumptive world" (Janoff-Bulman, 1992) or what Winnicott (1965a) called the "holding environment" is challenged, leading to a break in the flow of ordinary experience and mutual trust. Thus, where shame and trauma predominate, the grieving self cannot repair sufficiently to undergo healthy transformation and form new attachments. For many patients, the healing of this rupture and blockage in development is a major objective of counseling and psychotherapy, and particularly where the presenting problem is bereavement.

The role of the counselor in such instances includes not only support of the mourning process, but also the facilitation of the growth of the self in such a way that it can endure not only the loss of the loved one but also the resultant damage to the self. Thus, counseling and psycho-therapy are where one can most clearly discern and address the relation-ship between death or mourning and the earliest attachments, especially as the latter are relived within the therapeutic relationship.

CLINICAL PRACTICE AND ILLUSTRATIVE EXAMPLES

On Attachment, Self, and Shame in Counseling and in Psychotherapy*

Connections between disruptions of infantile relational experience with death and mourning remain theoretical abstractions until we can utilize them and find evidence for them in the process of addressing grief and loss, especially, but not exclusively, with adults who are in mourning or facing their own death. With adults in psychoanalysis, it is possible to "reconstruct" the infantile relationship with the mother and other caregivers, and, through dreams and free associations, trace thoughts about death and dying back to this earliest relationship. In the cases of psychoanalytic therapy described next, I was able to achieve such reconstructions and "tracings" to a greater or lesser extent, utilizing the patients' transference and my own countertransference feelings as a guide. However, most grief counseling with those with terminal ill-nesses are relatively time limited and the empathic counselor must focus on what is highly significant in the present moment of the mourning process.

Thus, for example, with Jonah,† a male patient dying of AIDS, with whom I made home and hospice visits, it would have been counterpro-ductive in the few months prior to his death to help him understand how his primary maternal relationship affected his feelings about AIDS, medical care, and dying. However, in lieu of such reconstruction, I chose to step in to fulfill a need. I was able to put myself in the place of a "good enough mother" to provide a "holding environment" (Winnicott, 1965a), which enabled Jonah to sort out his conflicting emotions and to die with dignity and grace. As his disease worsened (this was before the advent of antiviral medications that stave off the disease), Jonah experienced and

---

* The terms counseling and psychotherapy overlap considerably. In the present context, counseling refers to time-limited interventions that emphasize grief and loss, whereas psychotherapy consists of open-ended treatment with a broader scope of aims and goals.
† In all case examples discussed in this chapter, patient names and other identifying infor-mation have been modified to protect confidentiality.

expressed gaps and disruptions in bonding sometimes caused by severe pain, and sometimes by the empathic failures and benign neglect of physicians who could do only so much to assist him.

One gap that was especially painful to him was the "exile" implied by the interruption of the relationship with his estranged father, who was "turned off" by his son's homosexuality. I helped Jonah contact his father and engage in conversations with him that repaired the damaged bond. As Jonah felt renewed affection with his father, he felt less ashamed of his sexual orientation and medical condition, and his sense of self became more cohesive, enabling him to accept hospice care with grace and dignity. As he was dying, I sat with him at his bedside and he told me that although he did not want to die, he could accept its inevitability and that "there must be something better on the other side." During the several months of counseling, he moved from a person terrified by his condition and the prospect of death to one who courageously dealt with pain, made peace with those around him, and died with a sense of completion. The "holding" provided by counseling, and by his father, his gay partner, and the hospice staff alleviated his shame and mitigated the gaps and disruptions in the continuity of his self, allowing him to die with dignity.

My experience in briefer, time-limited therapy both with dying patients and those in mourning suggests that the theoretical perspective developed earlier is best utilized with a basic model of maternal care forming a background for the process. Most elements of the model are "standard" for many bereavement counseling approaches (Worden, 1991). The emphasis that is specific to primary attachment dynamics involves ongoing attunement and interventions to address disruptions, hurts, shame, losses, and gaps in the flow of "holding" as the client experiences them. The model has the following components.

First, the counselor/therapist, as she accumulates relevant information, strives for an empathic bond with the client. This is usually known as "rapport" and involves good communication, suitable boundaries with optimal closeness/distance tailored to each client, and a sense of the emotional wounds and shame-based patterns. (These are the gaps and disconnects referred to earlier.) In addition, the counselor helps the client formulate the "unfinished business" that must be dealt with to achieve acceptance and closure.

Second, and most relevant to the specific aspect of "maternal care," the counselor attunes to disruptions, gaps, and empathic failures in the counselor–client relationship and in the more general caregiving the client is receiving (medical treatments, family responsiveness, memorial services, and so on). The counselor then aims to facilitate a "holding environment" in which the client feels safe and develops a faith* that between his or her own inner resources and caregiver responsiveness, acceptance, resolution, and completion is possible.

Third, the counselor facilitates a "working through" of the loss, mourning process, or dying that the client brings for healing. This involves an exploration of memories relevant to the loss. The counselor attends to shame-based responses through empathic acceptance and by a dialogue that helps the client mitigate the feeling of anxious apartness and exile. She also helps the client to access inner and outer resources that may fill the various gaps, emptiness, and perceived abandonments that are experienced within the grieving process.

Finally, the counselor helps the client identify "unfinished business" that can be sufficiently addressed to give closure and completion to the grieving or dying. As the client, insofar as practically feasible, completes the unfinished business (for example, by having a family meeting), the counselor sustains the holding environment. Included here is the unfinished business of counseling itself, making for an authentic and compassionate closure between counselor and client.

It should be said that the patient cannot and should not be sheltered from the inherent existential aloneness that is a necessary and important part of authentic grief. The counselor's goal is to help the client discover that he or she need not fragment nor endlessly suffer from this aloneness, which, under good circumstances, can become a source of personal growth.

I will first illustrate this fourfold process with an example of a client who came to me shortly after the death of his father. Then I will provide a more extensive case study of a woman who, in a 3-year psychoanalytic psychotherapy, worked through several losses and blows to her self-esteem, where the earliest infantile "disconnect" formed a central part of her autobiographical narrative. Finally, I will discuss a case in which shame and a defective sense of self were implicated in a patient's death wish toward herself. In each instance, I will make inferences about how the primary attachment to the mother/caregiver played a significant role.

Mourning the Father's Death in a Shame-Based Client

Luke came to me in a state of disorganization shortly after the death of his father, who had divorced his mother a long time before but

---

* Eigen (1985) hypothesized that faith develops in the primary relationship to the mother as a result of her optimal timing of her nurturing responses. The infant gradually acquires "faith" in the eventual meeting of the need during periods of the mother's absence. Such a belief later generalizes to spiritual/religious life.

maintained frequent contact with the patient. When his father died from a carcinoma that resulted in progressive weakening, weight loss, and debilitation, Luke felt not only loss, but also helpless, hopeless, and disappointed. In a self-curative attempt to restore his esteem and ability to cope, he used amphetamines, threw himself into his work, and began a relationship with an attractive woman who mirrored his need to be handsome and the center of attention. When none of these coping mechanisms alleviated his depressed mood and psychosomatic symptoms, he sought treatment. He viewed therapy initially as a magical solution, hoping that a "good doctor" could "fix me up and make me feel better." He quickly overidealized me as such a caregiver.

In taking a history, I found that Luke's self-esteem had been dealt two major blows. The first was in infancy and early childhood. His depressed mother displaced her hurt and angry feelings toward her absent husband onto the boy, and therefore both neglected him and viewed him as an extension of herself, so that she led him to feel worthwhile only insofar as he fulfilled her dependency needs and gained her approval. Thus, he never developed genuine self-sufficiency and individuality. To compensate, he overidealized his father, who in fact had often failed him by his absence from the home. When his father became ill and debilitated, Luke felt ashamed to see his father, whom he previously thought of as invincible. When last he saw his father weakened and taken to the hospital to die, he was devastated and began to use drugs to cope. Both his early experiences with his mother and his father's more recent illness led him to feel deeply ashamed of himself, and to compensate for the shame, he developed a grandiose façade exaggerating his importance to others and believing that he could magically control them with his ability to entertain them and manipulate their feelings. His relationship with his attractive girlfriend reinforced his feelings of being special and "in control." When his father finally died, however, Luke felt helpless and impotent. Wandering around the city late at night, he hallucinated his deceased father coming around street corners or standing beside him, only to vanish as quickly as he came. Denying the reality of his father's death, his mourning process could not proceed.

My sense was that Luke would not be able to properly mourn until he achieved some restoration of his self-esteem and individuality. Therefore, pertinent to the model, I decided to provide him with a holding and mirroring environment, listening intently and reflecting empathically on his shifting emotions. As a result of this nonintrusive process he developed mirroring, idealizing, and twinship transferences in which he strove to impress me with his importance, idealized me as a faultless "doctor," and noticed "how much alike" we were (Kohut, 1971).

After some time, I decided to break into this blissful symbiosis (Mahler, Pine, & Bergman, 1975), or else, I thought, Luke would never go through a mourning process. I began gently to point out some of the kinks in his armor, as well as to note his expressions of shame, grief, and loss. Clarifying the roots of his shame in his mother's attitudes and his dismay upon seeing his father's strength diminished by illness facilitated a normal mourning process, in which he grieved not only the death of his father, but the loss of self-esteem as he perceived his idols, namely, his father, his girlfriend, and me, lose their luster and become all-too-human in his eyes. As he resolved his grief, he gave up his use of amphetamines, consolidated his career, and reached a more balanced perspective on both himself and me.

This case illustrates the implicit disruptions or gaps in the maternal attachment (as well as to his absent father) that needed to be healed in order for a relatively mature acceptance of death and genuine grief to occur. In Luke's case, the disruptions consisted in his mother's harsh, critical shaming and rejections, further reinforced by his father's absence and death. For Luke, this led to a narcissistic behavior disorder (Kohut, 1977, p. 193) with episodes of partial fragmentation of the self compensated by grandiose control of others and acting out with drugs. The therapeutic mirroring process allowed for sufficient strengthening of his self to allow mourning to occur and be resolved.

A Shame–Grief Nexus, the "Story" of Which Began Prenatally

Although Luke gave me an understanding of how disruptions in both childhood and adulthood could impact the mourning process, some of the details remained obscure. His treatment was relatively brief and somewhat urgent, so that I needed to focus on his immediate needs, and his narrative was disjointed. By contrast, circumstances allowed me to "study" another grieving patient in greater depth and detail, both because she was an excellent reporter of her history and current emotions, and because she sought "understanding" as much as she desired "cure."

Lisa came to treatment as a young adult when she felt as if everything was falling apart inside her and around her. A relationship had ended in an angry manner. She began to abuse alcohol, amphetamines, and marijuana. Family relations had deteriorated. Her work as a financial consultant was in jeopardy because of her hostile relationship with her boss. She told me how she felt alternately superior and inferior to the latter as they "locked horns." Her identity and sense of self were fragmented and disorganized. For instance, she forgot appointment times, had difficulty completing work tasks, and engaged in compensatory maneuvers such as brief sexual liaisons, drug abuse, verbal expressions of rage, and social isolation as means to temporarily restore her sense of self.

Lisa, however, possessed a strong "life force" and will to thrive, and also was a good "historian," providing rich information about her family life, which was built on intensely ambivalent bonds. We learned early in treatment that some of her current troubles could be attributed to the death of her father during her adolescence. The loss was complicated by her being his caregiver, and by her confusion about his doting but errant husbanding and fathering, since he was a grandiose, manipulative womanizer.

However, Lisa quickly disclosed that her deeper insecurity was rooted in her love–hate relationship with her mother, the stage for which was set before she was born. Her mother became pregnant with Lisa in her forties, 15 years after her firstborn daughter, when she no longer wished to bear a child. During pregnancy, Lisa's mother decompensated, was briefly hospitalized, and placed on antipsychotic medication. It is possible she had a death wish toward the fetus within her (Sonne, 1996), but when Lisa arrived, her mother partly recovered, and while anxiety-ridden and possibly suffering from postpartum depression, she nevertheless devoted herself, although erratically, to childrearing. One could infer that as a result of her mother's confusion and ambivalence, Lisa formed an "anxious-disorganized" attachment that mirrored her mother's own conflicts and that she repeated in her relationship to her older sister, women in general, and with me in the transference. At one point in treatment, she read Nancy Friday's My Mother, Myself (1997), noting how well the book articulated her own ambivalent and intense bond and identification with her mother. Lisa had also internalized her mother's ambivalence, alternating between hopefulness and self-destructive death wishes manifest in suicidal ideation, drug abuse, and unsafe sex. She also had displaced her feelings toward her mother onto her much older sister and, more recently, her boss. However, in the positive transference, she experienced me as the unconditionally accepting, holding, and containing mother she never had. Within this transference and therapeutic alliance, Lisa was able to "create" and "use" me as a therapeutic "object" in unique and constructive ways.

As Lisa found that she could safely express and partially resolve her feelings of rage, sadness, hope, and disappointment, she resumed dating and abstained from drugs. I had become a "good enough mother" for her to whom she could safely express her emotions and thereby reconstitute her daily life. However, I noticed that my attitude toward her was in fact too benign, and that I failed to clarify and interpret her aggression. I corrected my course and began to address her anger and point out that her negative cognitive distortions toward her sister and her boss were rooted in her ambivalence toward her mother. Although she acted out her refusal to at first accept these interpretations by coming late to sessions, she was eventually able to see their validity. Concomitantly, her relations not only with her sister and her boss but also with the men she was dating improved.

At around this time, she began a prolonged (1 year) process of unremitting mourning, not only for the loss of her father, but, more profoundly, for the damage to the bond with her mother. I first recognized this phase in my countertransference. Lisa was wearing a brooch on which my gaze became fixated. I soon realized that the item had brought to my mind a similar piece of jewelry that my beloved grandmother had worn. When I mentioned the brooch to Lisa, she said that it was a family heirloom that her mother had given her. Not only did the piece represent for Lisa a "linking object" (Volkan, 1982) to her mother and intergenerational family, it also served during sessions as a "transitional object" (Winnicott, 1971) between Lisa and myself. Through the jewelry, Lisa had become for me a representation of my "good grandmother," further establishing a mutual healing relationship through which we both grieved, she openly, and me internally. Lisa, in a sense, was helping me in a way that she was unable to rescue her mother, providing a moving example of "the patient as therapist to his therapist" (Searles, 1975).

As Lisa described her relationship with her mother in greater detail, it became apparent that what she was mourning were periodic gaps in their primary bond. That is, her mother would episodically decompensate into a depressive psychosis, becoming relatively incommunicado, and then reconstitute for periods of time during which she became passionately devoted to Lisa. Her devotion was almost heroic, as if to make reparation for her emotional absences. In addition, her mother may have suffered from bipolar disorder and during her hypomanic phases would become almost a "supermother."

However, during this extended mourning, Lisa curled up in her chair in a womblike position and wept, stuffing her used Kleenex under the chair cushion, which I only realized and cleaned out after she terminated treatment, a matter to which I will return shortly. She wept for almost everything and everyone she knew. At one juncture, she expressed grief for me, as she recognized my loneliness and the difficulty of my work. But what suggested that she was mourning the gaps in her relationship to her mother were her frequent phone calls to me during this time, expressing anxiety and a need for reassurance. Yet at no time did she decompensate or require hospitalization; it was as if the phone calls simply served the purpose of restoring contact with me in order to sustain a sense of my ongoing presence and "object constancy" (Lax, Bach, & Burland, 1986). Toward the end of this period, Lisa gained further insights about the distorted aspects of her relationships with her mother, father, and sister, forming realistic and consistent pictures of them and restoring her "family image" (Sonne, 1991) to its rightful place in her psyche.

Only toward the end of her treatment was the element of shame expressly considered. Lisa spoke of the teasing and taunting that her older sister, who served as part-time surrogate parent during mother's depressive episodes, inflicted on her during her childhood. She also felt ashamed of some of her father's extramarital affairs, and about her own failures in her work and her difficulty establishing a lasting love relationship. Her shame, ultimately, was related to her feeling that she was an "unwanted" child and a "second-rate" sibling to her sister.

As Lisa verbalized and resolved her feelings of shame, a healthy narcissism and sense of self began to emerge. This was first expressed in an interest in music. She found herself singing songs from Broadway musicals and the American Songbook on a daily basis, and soon took private singing lessons. She brought a new cheerfulness to sessions, dressed seductively, and her anger toward me modulated into lighthearted jokes. She began a new relationship with a man who really cared about her and whom she eventually married. She commenced, with optimism and excitement, a new career.

After further working through of her practical daily life issues, I initiated the termination of her treatment, which she perceived affirmatively as a chance to "go it on her own," while tearfully expressing a sense of loss. At her final session, she summarized her entire therapy in a single gesture. She brought me a gift of a trash can for my office, stating that my patients could put their Kleenex into it. Then she explained that, during her period of mourning, she had stuffed her tissues into the seat cushion as she curled up into a womblike position. It must have been by a slight of hand, because I never noticed it. After she left, I looked under the cushion, found a wad of tissues there and tossed them into the trash can she had just given me.

In Lisa's case, the disruption of the maternal bond began in the womb. Antipsychotic medications can cross the placental barrier (Lieberman & Murray, 2001, p. 70), but above and beyond this possible biological disruption, Lisa's earliest relationship with her mother was disrupted by her mother's depressive episodes. The maternal rejection was also encoded as a "family story" in the factual knowledge that Lisa had about the circumstances of her birth. By assuming a womblike position in the cushioned chair, she perhaps expressed both her feelings of abandonment as well as a wish for rebirth. During her protracted period of mourning, it was as if I could witness the gradual repair of the disorganization in her psyche that stemmed from her periodic "exile" from her mother's good care. The trash can perhaps symbolized both her mother's womb and also my role as a "container" into which she could place her grief, her anger, her shame, and her "dead inner objects."

"I Feel As If I Don't Exist": Damage to the Sense of Self Leading to Shame and Self-Destructive Behavior

Rita was a product of a disturbed home environment in which she, her brother, and her sister all developed clinical depression and personality disorders with borderline features. Although Rita's relationships with both parents and her brother were problematic throughout her childhood and adolescence, I will focus here on her early relationship to her mother and how it led to her shame-based sense of self and a profound death wish that was directed from her "false self" to her "true self" (Winnicott, 1965b).

Rita's mother, she recalled, was self-consciously concerned for her children. However, she acted in a very detached manner toward them, and her parenting was mechanical, based as it was on religious and moral scruples rather than empathic attunement. Thus, as far back as Rita could remember, her mother communicated a shaming and absolute sense of "right" and "wrong," approval and disapproval regarding even basic activities like playing, eating, eliminating. She rarely responded to her children with her own emotions of pleasure and delight, or, for that matter, upset, anger, or genuine concern. As a result of the mother's detachment and judgmental stance, both children felt ashamed and response-starved. They competed aggressively for mother's attention in order to obtain enough of her short supply of emotional engagement. Mother appeared to have very little capacity to relate authentically and responsively to her children.

Rita came for treatment during a time of ongoing professional development with persistent feelings of inadequacy and failure that were invariably contradicted by the positive feedback she received from her colleagues. In addition, she was just beginning to engage in sexual and romantic relationships that held great meaning for her and in which she allowed herself to feel dependent and needy after an adolescence and young adulthood of relative social isolation. She expressed the hope that, through therapy, she could overcome her defeatism about her career, and, even more importantly, achieve a successful romance which included genuine intimacy and mutual honesty. She felt that the latter would rectify the emptiness and disconnect she experienced with her mother and nuclear family.

The depth of Rita's shame and fragmentation was not immediately apparent. She possessed what we both later came to see as a "false self" façade that gave a misleading impression of a woman on the go with strong inner resources. The first indication of her fragility was the way she coped with rejection by a man whose love interest she was desperately trying to attract. She experienced him initially as "the answer to all my prayers" for someone she could relate to on a deep level of intimacy. When he lost interest in her, she became despondent, went on a drinking binge, displayed shameful behaviors to her friends (such as verbal tirades, which she later regretted), and acted inappropriately seductive at parties and other gatherings. She felt suicidal and expressed a wish to die. Within a few days, she forcefully began to patch herself up, stop drinking, and get on with her life. This pattern recurred as a "repetition compulsion" several times thereafter with potential partners who after a while invariably frustrated her advances, possibly on account of her neediness.

Each time this pattern repeated itself, Rita felt angry and humiliated, describing herself as a "total failure" and hopeless about ever succeeding at love. Her sense of failure was extreme and connected to a feeling of nonexistence in which she felt as if she literally died as a result of her inability to connect to the lover. Her feeling of not existing became the central focus in her treatment, since she felt wretched about its persistence. Not existing meant for her a combination of rejection and depersonalization, as well as a self-fulfilling prophesy about the outcome of her death wishes toward herself. Rita's "self-cure" was to go to her family members, especially her mother and sister, and attempt to repair their relationships with her, efforts to which they did not respond. She did, however, maintain a secure connection to me as her therapist, which she used to restore some hope that she could recover her lost selfhood.

Rita had a profound wish to repair the "hole" in her psyche. She repeatedly emphasized to me how nothing would satisfy her other than to face it and find a way to fill it with an authentic relationship to me and others. Her suicidal self-destructive wish was inseparably intertwined with her self-healing desire. She brushed aside my attempts to give her perspectives and understanding that would at least partially compensate for the emptiness and nonexistence that haunted her. Her drinking binges had more risky consequences, but she was unreceptive to alcoholism treatment as such. She expressed suicidal ideation more frequently, to the point where her friends feared for her life. At the same time, she paradoxically became more successful in her career and her attachment to me became stronger. She always "contracted for safety" and dug in more intently on her self-defined therapeutic task of "existing" by becoming whole. Curiously, the more desperate she became, the more she was able to function in her work and the more related to me she became. This was a contradiction I have rarely if ever encountered in another patient. It was as if she felt that "to die" made her stronger and more "real."

Rita's therapy continued with only moderate success. In time, she was able to avoid drinking episodes, tolerate rejection, communicate her feelings more appropriately, and moderate her suicidal wishes. However, the emptiness in her psyche and the feeling of nonexistence persisted despite long-term therapy and antidepressant medication. She has since sought various approaches to treatment from other providers. The damage to her sense of self appeared highly resistive to change, but, on account of Rita's persistence, a deeper level of healing in the future cannot be ruled out.

Rita's earliest relationship to her mother was severely disrupted by her mother's lack of empathic attunedness and shame-based approach to childrearing. In Rita's case, this must have only led her to pursue the attachment to her mother even more urgently, rather than withdraw from it. As she grew up in such an environment, she apparently acquired the shame-based notion that "if I die and cease to exist, I will be loved." Thus, to love and be close to others could only be expressed in suicidal and self-destructive wishes and a feeling of depersonalization. Rita illustrates one kind of connection between the primary attachment, the sense of self, shame, and the symbolic understanding of one's own death that develops later in the life cycle. Specifically, the infantile "derailments" were ongoing and sufficiently depriving to lead to a fundamental damage to her sense of self in which survival and death were falsely equated. One could speculate that Rita's mother may have had a necrophilic preoccupation with death that she communicated unconsciously to her daughter. However, this dynamic did not emerge during the patient's treatment with me. What was clear was that her death wishes resulted from a severely damaged self that was ruled by shame and a level of rejection that led her to feel that she literally did not exist.

SUMMARY AND CONCLUSIONS

The relationship between shame and death/mourning has been obscured by the long scholarly lacuna in exploring the affect of shame. Similarly, the relationship between the earliest attachments and subsequent attitudes toward death and grief has been limited as the result of a partial neglect of mourning in the study of attachment disorders despite the fact that Bowlby had pointed out their fundamental relationship. In this chapter, I have tried to build a rationale for restoring these important linkages, using clinical examples to illustrate how early disruptions of attachment play a role in grief, attitudes toward death, counseling, and psychotherapy. In so doing, I have suggested that shame plays a significant, though not exclusive, role in the damage to the sense of self and the denial of loss that complicates and pathologizes the mourning process.

Although early infant–caregiver interactions, mourning, and the affect of shame have each independently been the subject of extensive research efforts, the relationship between them has not. In my discussions of Jonah, Luke, Lisa, and Rita, I have presented clinical material that supports such a connection and has a certain face validity. A logical next step would be further clinical and empirical research to test and define these hypotheses more sharply and to give them a stronger empirical foundation. For example, a study of children's early perceptions of death and dying correlated with attachment patterns, and the sense of self and identity could shed light on this important subject. One well-known study that bears some relation to the matter was A. Freud and Burlingame's (1943) report of their work with children separated from their parents during the London Blitz, suggesting that disrupted attachments had more adverse effects than exposure to the bombings themselves. What have not been conducted, to my knowledge, are longitudinal studies of evolving connections among early relational dynamics, predominant affects, and means of coping with grief and loss. Such investigations, while difficult to implement, would provide important information for understanding how the earliest relationships and their context impact on mourning throughout life. Such studies could include counseling interactions as such, and it would be especially interesting and important to consider case studies of children in which the mother–child relationship is observed in vivo along with the child's emerging understanding of death and dying.

Meanwhile, my intention has been simply to stimulate the reader's thought about the ways in which early relational experiences and the emerging sense of self inform subsequent attitudes and complexes regarding bereavement, death, and dying. To that purpose, a trialogue between bereavement specialists, psychoanalysts, and developmental psychologists would be most helpful as well.

ACKNOWLEDGMENTS

I thank Walter N. Stone, MD, for his helpful critique of a preliminary draft of this chapter.

REFERENCES

Ainsworth, M., & Andry, R.G. (Eds.). (1962). *Deprivation of maternal care*. Geneva: World Health Organization.
Balint, M. (1979). *The basic fault*. New York: Brunner-Mazel.

Becker, E. (1973). *The denial of death*. New York: The Free Press.

Benjamin, J. (1999). Recognition and destruction: An outline of inter-subjectivity. In S. A. Mitchell & L. Aron (Eds.), *Relational psychoanalysis: The emergence of a tradition* (pp. 181–210). Hillsdale, NJ: Analytic Press.

Berlin, L. J., Ziv, Y., Amaya-Jackson, L., & Greenberg, M. T. (Eds.). (1999). *Enhancing early attachments: Theory, research, intervention, and policy* (Duke Series in Child Development and Public Policy). New York: Guilford.

Bowlby, J. (1958). The nature of the child's tie to his mother. *International Journal of Psychoanalysis, 39*, 1–23.

Bowlby, J. (1968). *Attachment and loss: Vol. 1. Attachment*. New York: Basic Books.

Bowlby, J. (1973). *Attachment and loss: Vol. 2. Separation, anxiety, and anger*. London: Penguin Books.

Bowlby, J. (1980). *Attachment and loss: Vol. 3. Loss: Sadness and depression*. New York: Basic Books.

Bradshaw, J. (1988). *Healing the shame that binds you*. Deerfield Beach, FL: Health Communications.

Cassidy, J., & Shaver, P. R. (Eds.). (1999). *Handbook of attachment: Theory, research, and clinical applications*. New York: Guilford.

Cohn, J. E., & Tronick, E. Z. (1988). Mother-infant face-to-face interaction: Influence is bidirectional and unrelated to periodic cycles in either partner's behavior. *Developmental Psychology, 24*(3), 386–392.

Cornish, A. M., Mcmahon, C. A., Ungerer, J. A., Barnett, B., Kowalenko, N., & Tennant, C. (2005). Postnatal depression and infant cognitive and motor development in the second postnatal year: The impact of depression chronicity and infant gender. *Infant Behavior and Development, 28*(4), 407–417.

Cozolino, L. (2006). *The neuroscience of human relationships: Attachment and the developing social brain*. New York: Norton.

Curren, R. (1989). The contribution of Nicomachean ethics iii.5 to Aristotle's theory of responsibility. *History of Philosophy Quarterly, 6*, 261–277.

Edgcumbe, R. (2000). *Anna Freud: A view of development, disturbance and therapeutic techniques*. London: Routledge.

Eigen, M. (1985). Toward Bion's starting point: Between catastrophe and faith. *International Journal of Psycho-Analysis, 66*, 321–330.

Erikson, E. H. (1959). *Identity and the life cycle* (Psychological Issues Monograph: 1). New York: International Universities Press.

Fairbairn, R. W. D. (1952). *Psychoanalytic studies of the personality*. London: Routledge and Kegan Paul.

Fonagy, P. (2001). *Attachment theory and psychoanalysis*. New York: Other Press.

Fonagy, P., Gergely, G., Jurist, E. L., & Target, M. (2002). *Affect regulation, mentalization, and the development of the self*. New York: Other Press.

Foulkes, S. H. (1948). *Introduction to group analytic psychotherapy*. London: William Heinemann Medical Books.

Freud, A., & Burlingame, D. T. (1943). *War and children*. London: Medical War Books.

Freud, S. (1917). Mourning and melancholia. In *The standard edition of the complete psychological works of Sigmund Freud* (Vol. 14, pp. 237–260). London: Hogarth.

Freud, S. (1919). The uncanny. In *The standard edition of the complete psychological works of Sigmund Freud* (Vol. 17, pp. 226–256). London: Hogarth.

Freud, S. (1920). Beyond the pleasure principle. In *The standard edition of the complete psychological works of Sigmund Freud* (Vol. 18, pp. 3–64). London: Hogarth.

Friday, N. (1997). *My mother, my self: The daughter's search for identity*. New York: Bantam.

Iacoboni, M. (2008). *Mirroring people: The new science of how we connect with others*. New York: Farrar, Strauss, and Giroux.

Janoff-Bulman, R. (1992). *Shattered assumptions: Towards a new psychology of trauma*. New York: Free Press.

Janus, L. (1997). *The enduring effects of prenatal experience: Echoes from the womb* (T. Dowling, Trans.). New York: Jason Aronson.

Jung, C. (1933). *Modern man in search of a soul*. New York: Harcourt Brace.

Kaufman, G. (1989). *The psychology of shame: Theory and treatment of shame based syndromes*. New York: Springer.

Klein, M. (1977). *Love, guilt, and reparation and other works: 1921–1945*. New York: Delta.

Kohut, H. (1971). *Analysis of the self*. New York: International Universities Press.

Kohut, H. (1977). *Restoration of the self*. New York: International Universities Press.

Kübler-Ross, E. (1969). *On death and dying*. New York: Macmillan.

Lax, R. F., Bach, S., & Burland, A. (1986). *Self and object constancy: Clinical and theoretical perspectives*. New York: Guilford.

Lewis, H. B. (1987). *The role of shame in symptom formation*. New York: Lawrence Erlbaum.

Lieberman, J. A., & Murray, R. (2001). *Comprehensive care of schizophrenia: A textbook of clinical management*. London: Informa Health Care.

Mahler, M., Pine, F., & Bergman, A. (1975). *The psychological birth of the human infant*. New York: Basic Books.

Nathanson, D. (Ed.). (1987). *The many faces of shame*. New York: Guilford.

Nelson, C. A. (2002). Neural plasticity and human development. *Current Directions in Psychological Science, 8*(2), 42–45.

Parkes, C. M. (1996). *Bereavement: Studies of grief in adult life* (3rd ed.). London: Routledge.

Parkes, C. M. (2006). *Love and loss: The roots of grief and its complications*. London: Routledge.

Perera, S. (1986). *The scapegoat complex: Toward a mythology of shadow and guilt*. Toronto: Inner City Books.

Schore, A. (1994). *Affect regulation and the origin of the self: The neurobiology of emotional development*. Mahwah, NJ: Lawrence Erlbaum.

Searles, H. (1975). The patient as therapist to his analyst. In P. L. Giovacchini (Ed.), *Tactics and techniques in psychoanalytic therapy* (Vol. 2, pp. 95–151). New York: Jason Aronson.

Sonne, J. C. (1991). Triadic transferences of pathological family images. *Contemporary Family Therapy, 13*(3), 219–229.

Sonne, J. C. (1996). Interpreting the dread of being aborted in therapy. *International Journal of Prenatal and Perinatal Psychology and Medicine, 8*(3), 317–339.

Spitz, R. A. (1945). Hospitalism: An enquiry into the genesis of psychiatric conditions in early childhood. *Psychoanalytic Study of the Child, 1*, 53–74.

Spitz, R. A., & Cobliner, W. G. (1965). *The first year of life: A psychoanalytic study of normal and deviant development of object relations*. New York: International Universities Press.

Symington, J., & Symington, N. (1996). *The clinical thinking of Wilfred Bion*. London: Routledge.

Tolpin, M., & Kohut, H. (1980). The disorders of the self: The psychopathology of the first years of life. In S. I. Greenspan & G. H. Pollock (Eds.), *The course of life* (pp. 425–442). Bethesda: NIMH.

Tomkins, S. (1963). *Affect, imagery, consciousness: Vol. 2. The Negative Affects*. New York: Springer.

Tomkins, S. (1964). *Affect, imagery, consciousness: Vol. 1*. New York: Springer.

Tomkins, S. (1991). *Affect, imagery, consciousness: Vol. 3. The negative affects: Anger and fear*. New York: Springer.

Volkan, V. (1982). *Linking objects and linking phenomena*. New York: International Universities Press.

Williams, T. (1955). *Cat on a hot tin roof*. New York: New Directions.

Winnicott, D. W. (1965a). Theory of the parent-infant relationship. In *The maturational processes and the facilitating environment: Studies in the theory of emotional development* (pp. 37–55). New York: International Universities Press.

Winnicott, D. W. (1965b). Ego distortion in terms of true and false self. In *The maturational processes and the facilitating environment: Studies in the theory of emotional development* (pp. 140–152). New York: International Universities Press.

Winnicott, D. W. (1971). Transitional objects and transitional phenomena. In *Playing and reality* (pp. 1–25). New York: Basic Books.

Worden, J. W. (1991). *Grief counseling and grief therapy* (2nd ed.) New York: Springer.

CHAPTER 4

Combat, Combat Stress Injuries, and Shame

*Charles R. Figley, David L. Albright,
and Kathleen Regan Figley*

Sgt. Rock Reno was in the second month of his first deployment to Iraq as a Marine squad leader on patrol in Ramadi, a city 68 miles west of Baghdad. On the day Sgt. Reno sustained a combat stress injury he was responsible for clearing a building, something he was well trained to do. Unfortunately, a child was accidentally killed during the exercise. The death traumatized the Marine. Reno found himself living with a considerable sense of shame over his role in the incident, a shame that roiled through his sleep and dreams.

A chapter about shame in the context of combat might suggest a causal relationship; that shame is a result of one's actions in combat. We suggest a far more complex relationship, building on a model of combat stress injury outlined in recent years by Nash, Hall, and Figley (Figley, Hall, & Nash, 2009; Nash, 2007; Nash & Figley, 2007). After defining the critical concepts and describing a theory of combat stress injuries, we address the implications of shame for war fighters.

DEFINITIONS

Combat and combatants. Most would define combat as a fight or fighting in war. Modern war combat is complex and includes collective actions of fighting forces that involve tactics carried out by highly trained military personnel or combatants, sometimes at a distance from the field of battle. War combatants are those who serve one or more roles in battle and by doing so are at risk of dying and being injured. They also risk killing or injuring others, including enemy combatants, civilians, and friendly forces.

Combat stress and combat stress reactions. Combat stress is the perceived demand to perform under combat conditions. Combat stress reactions are both the wanted and unwanted consequences of those actions. More specifically, combat stress is the mental, emotional, or physical distress, tension, and strain resulting from participating in war.

Combat stress injuries (CSIs). CSIs are combat reactions causing measurable mental, neurological, or emotional harm to combatants. These may be a consequence of the physical conditions; physical injury; death or harm to self or others; horror, fear, and loathing; or psychic injury (moral dilemma) that can include shame and humiliation. Paradoxically, unwanted combat stress injuries are caused by exposure to the same physical and mental combat stress reactions that bring about the wanted actions that win battles and wars.

Stigma. Stigma is defined as a perception of being marked by a sign of disgrace, discredit, or shame, which sets a person apart from others. This sign is often related to social context, rather than to anything as concrete as a defect of appearance. For example, the stigma of mental illness remains a powerful negative attribute in most social contexts, with slang terms for mental illness being part of a common societal vocabulary of ridicule.

Sociological interest in psychiatric stigma was given added vigor with the publication of Erving Goffman's *Stigma: Notes on the Management of Spoiled Identity* (1963). He identified the process of assigning values to attributes possessed by individuals who differ from the norm of society and the effect that attribution has on the individual to whom it is assigned.

Goffman discussed two types of stigma: *Discredited stigma* cannot be concealed. These external characteristics are evident and easily discoverable by others, such as facial scars, loss of a limb, or blindness. These represent visible injuries and disabilities. *Discreditable stigma* can be concealed from others. These are internal characteristics that may not be readily or immediately apparent, but which may be discovered and judged by others, such as mental illness, combat stress injury, or postconcussion syndrome. These represent invisible injuries and disabilities.

Goffman's notion of stigma is composed of a twofold process: First, the individual possessing potentially stigmatizing characteristics internalizes the values assigned to the trait by society. This is significant because combat veterans are assigned particular traits by both the society at large and by the particular culture of their military unit. Second, the individual may develop fear and anxiety about being treated differently from others like themselves. Combat veterans may, for example, perceive being viewed as inferior, cowardly, or weak as worse than being killed. It is not surprising, therefore, that this type of shame may lead to addiction, suicide, and other reactive behaviors.

In the last two decades, psychiatry has taken up the serious study of stigma as a barrier to professional mental health services. In 1989, the theme of the American Psychiatric Association's (APA) annual meeting was "Overcoming Stigma." Indeed, overcoming the stigma related to mental disorders was the centerpiece of Dr. Paul Jay Fink's term as president of the APA (Fink & Tasman, 1992). Nearly a decade later, the Royal College of Psychiatrists (2008) for the United Kingdom and Ireland initiated a 5-year "Changing Minds" antistigma campaign focusing on mental disorders. Its aim was to increase understanding, challenge preconceptions, and increase acceptance of six of the most common mental disorders.

It is not surprising, then, that stigma as a barrier to combat stress injury treatment has been recognized as an issue from the beginning of the current U.S. wars in Afghanistan and Iraq. In 2004, Charles W. Hoge et al. published a groundbreaking report in the *New England Journal of Medicine* titled "Combat Duty in Iraq and Afghanistan and Mental Health Problems." They found that after duty in Iraq, combatants had a significantly higher rate of meeting strict screening criteria for major depression, generalized anxiety, or posttraumatic stress disorder (PTSD; 15.6% to 17.1%) than after duty in Afghanistan (11.2%) or before deployment to Iraq (9.3%). As expected, the largest difference was in the rate of PTSD. Alarmingly, only 35% to 45% of soldiers and Marines who met the strict screening criteria for a mental disorder indicated an interest in receiving help and only 23% to 40% reported receiving professional help in the past year. Compared to combatants who did not meet screening criteria for a mental disorder, those who did were about twice as likely to report concerns about being stigmatized and about other barriers to receiving mental health care.

More recently, Anna Stowe Alrutz (2006) completed a survey of the spouses of active duty Army soldiers. She found that spouses who receive most of their useful information from nonmilitary sources report higher levels of perceived stigma associated with combat stress than do spouses who receive their useful information from the military.

In the current U.S. military, the stigma associated with combat-related mental disorders is real. This is especially important since it appears that the stigma of the shame of being labeled with a mental disorder may be a major stumbling block to accessing mental health services. The next section discusses how shame emerges within the context of the stigma experiences that ensue from any mental health consequences from military services, especially combat.

Shame. Although there is no commonly agreed upon definition of shame (Gilbert & Procter, 2006), for the purpose of this chapter it is defined as the fear of knowledge about one's own failings, often accompanied by the fear that these failings will be discovered or known by others of significance. Thus shame is the consequence of stigma (Gilbert, 2003).

This is consistent with Gilbert (1997, 1998) who suggested there are two types of shame: *Internal shame* is associated with the fear of violating one's own moral, ethical, or religious codes of conduct and thought. *External shame* is associated with the fear of violating other's standards of conduct.

Applied to combat veterans, internal shame is the fear of violating one's own codes of conduct in the execution of their duties or upon reflection of past behaviors. We will suggest that maintaining this internal shame carries considerable costs. These costs and their causes will be the focus of much of the content to follow.

COMBAT AS A CONTEXT FOR SHAME

"War is hell" stated William Tecumseh Sherman in his address to the 1879 graduating class of the Michigan Military Academy.

> I confess, without shame, that I am sick and tired of fighting—its glory is all moonshine; even success the most brilliant is over dead and mangled bodies, with the anguish and lamentations of distant families, appealing to me for sons, husbands, and fathers ... it is only those who have never heard a shot, never heard the shriek and groans of the wounded and lacerated ... that cry aloud for more blood, more vengeance, more desolation. (Sherman, 1865)

War, like shame, is psychological and stress is the primary metric (Figley & Nash, 2007). The combat environment offers boredom, friendship, loss, moral ambiguity, and events of intensity that are hard to contextualize. Combat exposure includes, but is not limited to, the fear of being killed; the exhilaration of strategy and risk; the rollercoaster dips of boredom, routine, and social politic, and peaks of search and destroy missions; killing and avoiding being killed or wounded; and achieving your mission. Recent developments in the theory and research of combat and its psychosocial and biobehavioral consequences have resulted in a cascade of wisdom about modern combat and its immediate and long-term effects on the warfighter.

A THEORY OF COMBAT STRESS INJURY RESILIENCE

The psychological reaction to combat stress has remained relatively unchanged throughout the history of warfare. However, the dominant perspective on how those reactions are viewed by the military and civilian communities has changed. Therefore, the role and source of shame for these warriors must be understood to effectively help them and their families.

Combat stress injury (CSI) is an adaptive response that may be symptomatic of something more serious (Figley & Nash, 2007). The term is being proposed to subsume prior nomenclature and shift away from a pathological focus toward one that encourages resilience. The changes in terms and emphasis are important to note because they have guided the psychological and medical treatment of troops who have experienced emotional distress after exposure to combat. New nomenclature can provide new awareness, acceptance, and potentially more effective preventive and acute treatment modalities.

Nash (2007) advocates the concept of CSIs as a way to understand the development of not only combat-related posttraumatic stress disorder, clinical depression, anxiety, and substance abuse, but also a wide variety of reactions that are normal for warfighters. He suggests that the nomenclature for wartime trauma shifts to differentiate between normal adaptive responses to stress and reactions that may be symptomatic of something more serious.

Nash identifies three mechanisms of CSIs and resiliencies, suggesting that CSIs can be divided into three types:

1. Fatigue stress injury, caused by the wear and tear of accumulated stress
2. Grief stress injury, caused by the loss of someone or something that is highly valued
3. Traumatic stress injury, caused by the impact of terror, horror, or helplessness

He suggests that they are not mutually exclusive. Each requires acute care as soon as possible.

Recently, a fourth injury set was added (R. Westphal, personal communication, 2009), moral injury, which is caused by a sense of contradiction between what one values and the awareness of one's actions.

One of the strengths of the CSI model is its emphasis on a four-pronged view of the development of combat stress injuries that helps account for the emergence of a host of wanted and unwanted consequences (Figure 4.1). Shame is one these consequences.

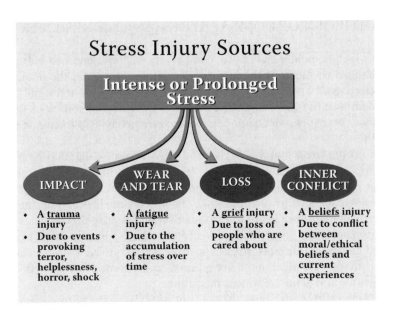

FIGURE 4.1   Combat stress injuries.

The model is process-oriented instead of oriented toward patho-logical outcomes. It emphasizes a shift within the paradigm for helping military combatants move from pathology to normalization that implies a move away from the medical model toward a psychosocial adapta-tion model. The model suggests an awareness of the complex interplay between adaptation and resilience that may lead to emergent opportuni-ties for prevention and management of combat and operational stress disorders. The CSI model has four possible mechanisms or causes:

1. Impact—Due to traumatic life-threatening situations provoking terror, horror, or helplessness.
2. Wear and tear—Due to fatigue and accumulation of prolonged stress, including from nonoperational sources, without sufficient sleep, rest, and restoration.
3. Loss—Grief due to the loss of close comrades, leaders, or other cared-for individuals.
4. Inner conflict—An injury to an individual's belief system due to conflict between moral/ethical beliefs and current experi-ences, such as taking action outside of the rules of engagement or where there is harm to an innocent life or in not preventing harm to a buddy. Shame is a by-product of this injury.

CSI AND SHAME

Shame emerges in combatants, if at all, at a point when the combatant recognizes there is a conflict between what is experienced and the expectations from self and others. If expectations and experience diverge widely, there is inner conflict. This is called cognitive dissonance. The extent to which cognitive dissonance is stressful determines the degree of inner conflict stress injuries.

CSIs caused by shame-related inner conflict are similar to other kinds of CSIs in terms of provocative memories as well as subsequent physiological, behavioral, and emotional symptoms. These symptoms include:

- Losing control of one's body, emotions, or thinking
- Being frequently unable to fall or stay asleep
- Waking up from recurrent, vivid nightmares
- Feeling persistent, intense guilt or shame
- Feeling unusually remorseful
- Experiencing attacks of panic or blind rage
- Losing memory or the ability to think rationally
- Being unable to enjoy usually pleasurable activities
- Losing grounding in previously held moral values
- Displaying a significant and persistent change in behavior or appearance

Most combatants recover on their own or through informal networks that enable the combatant to reset psychologically after combat events (see Castro & McGurk, 2007a, 2007b, 2007c; MHAT IV, 2006). Having a unit that is open and supportive is vital. When combatants feel supported and accepted they are more likely to process emotional trauma when it occurs. Such support helps ensure that combatants have resilience to the effects of both emotional and physical fatigue. Unit support is an invaluable asset to prevent combat stress injuries that may be characterized by sleep dysfunction, depression, low energy, hyperarousal, tension/anxiety, irritability, and anger (Figley & Nash, 2007). Moreover, families play a large part in modulating CSI effects and promoting recovery in returning combatants (Alruzt, 2006).

HELPING COMBATANTS WITH SHAME-RELATED CSIS

Rarely is shame the presenting problem for combatants or loved ones who accompany them to counseling. Most often, shame-related CSIs are embedded in such problems as depression, anger, or substance abuse.

However, the assessment and treatment of CSIs by knowledgeable clinicians can uncover and mitigate the burdens of shame rather quickly.

In the following we provide some broad guidelines that we hope are useful. An ongoing research program on war shame would help improve the precision and details of the guidelines we provide. We address two important questions as a way of summarizing what we know about shame-related CSIs.

When Do Combatants Most Often First Discover Shame?

The study of shame in combatants is in its infancy. Both the emergence of the CSI model and public acceptance of the stigma of shame as a barrier to mental health services for combatants represent recent developments. As a result, the answer to the question is based exclusively on anecdotal data and the theoretical formulations noted earlier.

The first feelings of regret regarding their own behaviors or those of others in their fighting unit that reflect badly on themselves represent the dawning of shame in combatants. This regret would then be reinforced by any psychological conflict that is not eliminated by normal methods, such as introspection, prayer, or discussion within informal buddy networks within the unit.

Initial attempts at mitigation involve a rather spontaneous, informal process of self-analysis that includes addressing the five traumatic incident questions (TIQs; Figley, 1995):

1. What happened to me?
2. Why did it happen to me?
3. Why did I act like that at the time?
4. Why have I been bothered by it since then?
5. What if something like this happens again?

If this internal dialogue does not produce a sufficient rationale to solve the conflict, the combatant turns to others to engage in a conversation. This exchange both permits the combatant to hear himself or herself for the first time and to gauge the reactions of others. He or she could engage in a dialogue with a loved one, trusted fellow combatant, friend, superior, or chaplain. However, clinical shame, a form that probably requires treatment, is embedded in the fear of being disliked, marginalized, or a source of humiliation.

A case example of the emergence of shame in a combatant is based on an actual case. Rock (not his real name) was in the second month of his first tour in Iraq as a Marine squad leader on patrol in Ramadi and responsible for clearing a building. He and his five-member squad were following rules of engagement (ROE) and were taking incoming fire from insurgents in the building. As they went from room to room, Rock fired at a movement in a darkened corner of a closet. He discovered that he had shot a child hiding under a blanket.

His immediate reaction was horror and regret that was followed immediately by his responsibility to his squad members who were continuing to clear the building. Only after the building was clear did he report the incident to his platoon leader by radio. Rock and his squad continued to clear the area and hours later completed their mission.

Another squad arrived at the site, removed the child and found that insurgents had killed the family the previous day. No charges were filed against Rock because he had followed the ROE. Rock sensed no negative evaluations from his superiors or squad members. They recognized that Rock had not intended to kill a child, that there was no way of knowing or preventing it from happening.

Yet, Rock had nightmares for several evenings in a row and on the morning after the third night of turmoil he spoke with a chaplain for the purpose of talking about his troubled sleep. Only after probing did he describe the dream content and discuss the incident. For the first time he was able to thoroughly talk about and address the five TIQs.

In contrast to the others with whom he briefly discussed the incident and dismissed it as an unfortunate and regrettable accident with a clear signal that he should cease thinking and talking about it, the chaplain mostly listened and only spoke to ask questions that were various forms of the TIQs. Following is a rough estimate of Rock's story:

[What happened?] I was clearing a three-story building. We had just moved up to the second story (the shooters were on the third). We were moving from room to room in sync so I had little time to waste. I saw a movement in the corner of my eye and shot it the direction with a burst of three rounds. I rush to insure the insurgent was down; found a blanket and a female child of around 5 years old shot twice and had no pulse. I quickly went to the next room to retain the pace of the search in order to kill the shooters. After the building was cleared I called my platoon leader to report the incident. He said he would send a standby squad to "clean up" (handle the corpse, make a report, and turn the child over to next of kin). I was ordered to continue the search of the adjacent buildings for insurgents. I was asked to relate the incident to the squad leader leading the investigation. I briefly talked with others to brief them on what happened. Their reactions were like mine: regretted the kid being killed but angry that no one had bothered to help the child get to a safe place and out of harm's way. War sucks. Nothing more was said. I had bad dreams three nights in a row and talked to the chaplain to get my head straight.

[Why did this happen?] Bad luck. The kid was at the wrong place at the wrong time. I had no choice. Friendly fire happens in a war zone. [Why did I do what I did?] I did what I had to do. It could have been an insurgent hoping that I did not see him then attack us when we were vulnerable. [Why have I been bothered by this?] Despite following ROE, everyone being supportive and in agreement that I was in the right I did not join the Corps and fight in war to kill a kid. [Why wouldn't *anyone* be bothered?] I am bothered because I am a decent, God-fearing, upstanding human being. [What if something like this happens again?] I don't know. I hope it won't but I don't know how I will be completely convinced that it won't happen again no matter what I do. I guess I will be on guard to avoid killing innocent people but I had and will have only seconds to make a determination. I will pray more to give me the guidance in those split second points of time.

What Are the Options for Eliminating the Unwanted Consequences of Shame and Enhancing Those Consequences That Are Valued?

Shame emerges and is maintained when the combatant experiences one or more CSIs. The assessment process is vital because the treatment for shame, perceived stigma, and any one or a combination of CSIs varies greatly. The following list represents four kinds of CSIs combatants may experience:

Fatigue injury—This type of injury is due to the accumulations of stress due to wear and tear over an extended period of time and sufficient rest and acceptance often leads to a quick recovery. When resilience and stamina return, shame is often not a consequence. As with the other injuries, the assumption should always be that the warfighter is resilient and, with sufficient resources, support, and self-care, will spring back and not only be fully recovered, but may attain considerable pride and self-respect for enduring such difficult conditions for so long. In Rock's case, his fellow Marines also sought and found sufficient rest and recuperation from the wear and tear of war during and following their deployment.

Grief injury—Because this type of injury is due to a specific loss, the shame varies with the loss because the sense of responsibility for the loss varies. Sometimes the loss is associated with innocence, feelings of invincibility, or some other intrapsychic resource the warfighter had prior to exposure to adult realities and the hellish nature of war.

A more serious problem with shame is associated with the guilt of culpability, of feeling responsible for the death or injury of another or injury to oneself. The more the shame is hidden from others, the more toxic and more difficult it will be to detect and correct by others. One of the most difficult and toxic combinations of CSIs occurs when all four clusters of symptoms coexist in association with guilt regarding the loss of a fellow warfighter. In Rock's case, although he did not lose any fellow warfighters due to his own perceived actions, the child was killed by the weapon he controlled.

Belief injury—Because this form of injury is associated with a conflict between one's core moral/ethical beliefs and one's experiences in war, it is more personal than any of the other three injuries. Indeed, the warfighter may wrongly believe that he or she is the only one with such a dilemma. In Rock's case, the values he learned as a child from a deeply religious Baptist family, who helped those less fortunate and condemned all forms of killing, including abortion, forced a reevaluation when he was confronted with being part of a killing machine. Gradually, he shed those attitudes about the value of human life, to the situational ethics learned in Marine basic training, to experiencing the exhilaration and competition of battle. His challenge following his first tour was to be able to coexist and thrive in both contexts: the battlefield and everywhere else. The sense of shame diminished with reconciling and modulating the values of his childhood with those of his warfighter role.

Impact: A trauma injury—This type of CSI is due to events provoking terror, helplessness, horror, and shock. It is most associated with PTSD and clinical depression and their recognized consequences, such as violent behavior, substance abuse, social isolation, and others. Shame can often be a critical feature because the diagnosis, the symptoms (e.g., startle responses, flashbacks), and related behaviors can bring about considerable embarrassment, condemnation, the attention of law enforcement, disciplinary actions, and punishment.

As noted earlier, the stigma of being diagnosed with a mental disorder is one of the major reasons warfighters avoid mental health treatment. The fear of being labeled with a mental disorder is appropriate since it may result in loss of status within a military unit, including delays in advancement and the denial of sensitive positions or security clearances. It may also impact civilian employment in areas such as law enforcement and other high risk and high trust professions.

Professional and lay helpers who wish to assist members of the military must recognize the appropriateness of these fears and the very real consequences a warfighter may face following a diagnosis of a mental disorder, otherwise the helper may inadvertently act in ways that increase resistance and denial.

Trauma-related CSIs are especially challenging to assess and treat when they coexist with any of the other three manifestations of CSIs and especially when all coexist together. Traumatic stress injuries, because they are primarily a problem of memory management, cause unexpected surges of fear linked to the traumatic experiences. It is as if the traumatized are constantly vulnerable to the winds of memories that blow in unexpectedly, lasting from seconds to hours, and demanding immediate attention. These types of injuries, in combination with any of the other three, are a frightening cocktail of emotions. In Rock's case he hid these reactions from most people, except his best friends and his family.

Implications for Treatment

Beyond our overview of shame in the context of combat and through the prism of the CSI model, there is little else we can offer other than some fundamental guidelines until a more fully formed protocol emerges based on evidence of effectiveness. We offer seven guidelines for clinicians and hope this chapter stimulates considerable debate, experimentation, and suggestions for improvement:

1. *Adopt an injury model of assessing and helping warfighters.* This is in stark contrast to the prevailing orientation of the medical model that focuses on illness, psychopathology, and despair (Figley & Nash, 2007).
2. *Expect clients to not only recover from their injuries, but to show evidence of growth and pride when shame is discovered and vanquished.* Hope, positive expectations, and forgiveness are fundamental to confronting the climate of stigma around injured warriors. This kind of attitude makes it easier to find evidence of growth and pride.
3. *Draw upon the contextual facts within which their shame emerged and was maintained.* This requires considerable work on the part of the client that includes acquiring information and perspectives from fellow warfighters. Gilbert and Procter (2006) suggest an approach, compassionate mind training, to overcome shame and self-criticism, particularly using a cognitive behavioral therapy-based program. Rational emotive behavior therapy (REBT) may be particularly helpful with its philosophical and therapeutic emphasis on home practice and unconditional

acceptance of self, others, and life, even when very bad things have happened.

4. *Allow the shame to coexist with new and competing feelings and emotions as long as necessary.* Self-forgiveness takes time. As with grief and the loss of a loved one, realization of the loss and adaptation to one's new life is gradual and cannot be forced.

5. *Enlist the help of injured warfighters who have recovered* (or are well on the way to recovery) in a crusade to help other warfighters confront, challenge, and eliminate shame, as well as modeling the skills to do so as part of the program of treatment. It may not work with some warfighters, but we have found that if it does, it enhances the effectiveness of the treatment. Clients and peer-helpers are less likely to relapse and they feel more motivated to be shame-free and remain so for the sake of their fellow warfighters.

6. *Adopt a humble, inquisitive, and patient style as a therapist. Such a stance is more like a student seeking knowledge and answers rather than a professor who is dispensing them.* Warfighter shame is an extremely humbling and embarrassing state—the exact opposite sensation from the "conquering hero" mentality frequently ascribed to the current cohort of warriors by the more sensational media.

7. *Practice self-care.* The therapist needs to have a sound self-care plan and follow it. It can be extraordinarily stressful being a shame therapist to warfighters. It demands extraordinary intellectual rigor, patience, perseverance, tolerance, and humility. The memories of sessions can invade one's sleep and interrupt one's daily routines and dispositions. Thus, it is wise to possess a skills set that enables the therapist to know when and how to modulate the emotional toxicity of delivering good services during and long after the sessions.

CONCLUSION

We have defined shame as a fear reaction based on one's knowledge about one's own failings and the potential consequences of these failings when others discover them. Stigma is the condition of the social context that defines such failings. The stigma of mental illness in the military, we noted, has never been greater and thus the shame of warfighters has never been greater. Rock's internal shame was never shared with anyone until he sought counseling and he felt safe enough to disclose it, to tell the awful truth he has lived with for years. Rock's feelings were reinforced by the external shame, his perception that others would condemn not just his errors in combat, but the emotional and mental consequences that could make him unfit for combat or a return to a productive civilian life.

Although research in this area is at the beginning stages and no data are available to estimate how many combatants experience shame, Rock's case is not unique. We would guess that most have overcome their shame completely; others have managed to compartmentalize their shame and control it in other ways so that it does not disrupt their lives significantly or for long. The few who continue to struggle with warfighter shame deserve efficient and effective help not only because their shame was acquired in the line of duty, serving their country, but because they are also needed in a peace-loving society and in families and communities who would benefit from the wisdom derived from military service in war and especially because their shame is derived from the very moral convictions that maintain civil societies.

Shame is the interface between meeting and not meeting established standards, having a moral compass that helps to determine right from wrong and the courage to do right when doing wrong would be easier. If shame is the fear of violating one's own moral, ethical, or religious codes of conduct and thought, then shame is good in moderation.

Future scholars and practitioners, we hope, will help further guide all of us to emphasize this reality and make the study and practice of moral and ethical reasoning and atonement a centerpiece in enabling our warfighters to live lives filled with joy and the awareness of a grateful nation.

REFERENCES

Alruzt, A. S. (2006). *The role of communication, prior experience and beliefs as factors influencing combat stress recommendations from military spouses.* Unpublished master's thesis, Florida State University, Tallahassee.

Castro, C. A., & McGurk, D. (2007a). The intensity of combat and behavioral health status. *Traumatology, 13*(4), 6–23.

Castro, C. A., & McGurk, D. (2007b). Battlefield ethics. *Traumatology, 13*(4), 24–31.

Castro, C. A., & McGurk, D. (2007c). Suicide prevention down range: A program assessment. *Traumatology, 13*(4), 32–36.

Figley, C. R. (1995). *Compassion fatigue: Secondary traumatic stress disorders in those who treat the traumatized.* New York: Routledge.

Figley, C. R., Hall, N., & Nash, W. (2009, June 6). *Combat stress injuries: Toward a psychoneuroimmunological model for research, treatment, and prevention.* Paper presented at the 16th Annual Psychoneuroimmunology Research Society Meeting, Breckenridge, Colorado.

Figley, C. R., & Nash, W. T. (Eds.). (2007). *Combat stress injury: Theory, research, and management.* New York: Routledge.

Fink, P. J., & Tasman, A. (1992). *Stigma and mental illness.* Arlington, VA: American Psychiatric Press.

Gilbert, P. (1997). The evolution of social attractiveness and its role in shame, humiliation, guilt and therapy. *British Journal of Medical Psychology, 70,* 113–147.

Gilbert, P. (1998). What is shame? Some core issues and controversies. In P. Gilbert & B. Andrews (Eds.), *Shame: Interpersonal behavior, psychopathology and culture* (pp. 3–36). New York: Oxford University Press.

Gilbert, P. (2003). Evolution, social roles, and differences in shame and guilt. *Social Research, 70,* 1205–1230.

Gilbert, P., & Procter, S. (2006). Compassionate mind training for people with high shame and self-criticism: Overview and pilot study of a group therapy approach. *Clinical Psychology and Psychotherapy, 13,* 353–379.

Goffman, E. (1963). *Stigma: Notes on the management of spoiled identity.* New York: Simon & Schuster.

Hoge, C. W., Castro, C. A., Messer, S. C., McGurk, D., Cotting, D. I., and Koffman, R. L. (2004). Combat duty in Iraq and Afghanistan, mental health problems, and barriers to care. *The New England Journal of Medicine, 351,* 13–22.

Nash, W.T. (2007). Combat/operational stress adaptations and injuries. In C. R. Figley & W. T. Nash (Eds.), *Combat stress injury: theory, research, and management.* New York: Routledge.

Nash, W. P., & Figley, C. R. (2007, February). *Combat stress injuries: An update.* Presentation at the 2nd National Symposium on Combat Stress Injuries, Florida State University Traumatology Institute, Tallahassee, Florida.

MHAT IV (Office of the Surgeon Multinational Force-Iraq and the Office of the Surgeon General of the US Army Medical Command). (2006, November 17). *Mental Health Advisory Team (MHAT) IV Operation Iraqi Freedom 05-07 Final Report.*

Royal College of Psychiatrists. (2008). *Changing minds.* Retrieved April 25, 2009, from http://www.rcpsych.ac.uk/campaigns/previouscampaigns/changingminds.aspx

Sherman, W. T. (1865). Letter to General Halleck. In Col. S. M. Bowman & Lt. Col. R. B. Irwin, *Sherman and his campaigns: A military biography* (p. 488). New York: Charles B. Richardson.

Sherman, W. T. (1879). Graduation speech to the 1879 graduating class of the Michigan Military Academy, Orchard Lake, MI.

CHAPTER 5

Healing the Narcissistic Injury of Death in the Context of Western Society

Darcy Harris

INTRODUCTION

This chapter will explore how the Western societal context of shame profoundly affects individuals who are facing death or who have experienced a significant loss through death. I will begin with an exploration of the social and political influences in Western society that define shameful experiences, and how social responses to death and death-related subjects are essentially the same responses that are recruited in dealing with shame. I will then explore how social norms in Western society influence the experiences of individuals facing death and loss, and the therapeutic implications for bereaved individuals.

SOCIAL INFLUENCES IN WESTERN SOCIETY

Current Western society is a predominantly capitalistic, material-oriented society,* which is governed by the high value placed upon productivity, competition, and consumerism. In a capitalistic society, the active seeking of economic growth, expansion, consumption, control

---

* It is understood that a society as a grouping of people who live in a geographic area will be made up of many cultures, and that there is a dynamic interplay between culture and society in regard to norms, values, and social rules.

over outcomes, and the view of unlimited possibilities are highly prized (Reynolds, 2002). A capitalistic, consumer-driven culture values control and rationality in order to foster productivity (Bottomore, 1985). The human body is viewed as a machine and medical care focuses on using technology to fix the part that is broken (Bolaria, 1994). Value of the self is measured through one's work ethic, accumulation of material wealth, ability to control outcomes and exercise personal power, independence, and being identified externally with the "image" of success. Individuals who live in such a society learn to value themselves and others through the lens of social expectations that are shaped by the devaluing of subjective experience in favor of objective outcome measures and productivity, the compartmentalization of experiences and affect through the maintenance of a veneer of stoicism, and faith in the power of technological advances to overcome human maladies and foibles (Wood & Williamson, 2003).

Common sources of shame are manifest in social contexts, and in Western society, shameful situations are those that expose some form of socially defined weakness, such as poverty, dependency on others, accepting charity, loss of control or inability to control outcomes, or having a reputation as someone who is not generally "successful" in some way (Wurmser, 1981). Here, the importance of the interaction between the individual and the society in which that individual exists becomes a key element in how shame is interpreted and experienced.

THE WORM AT THE CORE

Ernest Becker, a cultural anthropologist who explored the issue of mortality in Western society, posited that underneath the awareness of our impending death is the "worm at the core" of our existence, which continues to spin us into an anxious frenzy of activity and accomplishment as a distraction from an inevitable and completely unacceptable outcome that we cannot control (Becker, 1973). Becker presumed that the combination of our animal instinct to survive and our human awareness of the inevitability of death creates the potential for a terror that could make life itself unbearable. In his perspective, we attempt to eliminate our fear of death in our actions as an attempt to deny or overcome our fate by the use of repression, personal preoccupation, social games, and personal deceptions (Becker, 1973, 1975). In further expansion upon Becker's thoughts, Solomon, Greenberg, and Pyszczynski (1991) state that the entire process of growing up involves the assimilation of the cultural values, causes, ideals, and the pursuit of personal significance, which mask over an individual's fears and anxieties about death.

Human beings have the capacity to think symbolically, to project themselves into time, and to imagine things that have not yet happened. They can think in terms of cause and effect and reflect back upon time and existence in the past, present, and future. These thoughts render us acutely aware that we will die. We possess the consciousness that we desire to live, yet the unique awareness that we will die. It is our awareness of our mortality that makes us unique beings in this existence. It is also this same awareness that has the potential to cripple us into paralysis as the very mechanism of psychological shame (the denigration of the self) becomes manifest in existential shame (the annihilation of self) through the realization of one's mortality.

In this context, death anxiety can be seen as a specific form of shame anxiety, or even of Wurmser's (1981) "narcissistic mortification" in a very literal sense. Death denial and avoidance could therefore also be explained in the same way that shame avoidance is often described—the avoidance of a horribly negative experience through denial, repression, or projection in some way. The focus on materialism and productivity, combined with the devaluing of subjective experiences in the dominant Western culture, provide just this type of avoidance and denial in a ready-made, socially sanctioned way.

DEATH AND SHAME

In a society that values productivity, stoicism, and control, death represents the shameful loss of all of these things. Dying people are not productive and they consume the resources of other productive individuals through their need for care. Being terminally ill involves not just the loss of one's life, but also the loss of one's functioning and valued independence. Becker (1973) stated that most individuals are motivated to prove their worth and value through various accomplishments as a means of countering their terror of death and annihilation. However, in studies of death anxiety, most individuals in Western society state that they are not afraid of death so much as they are terrified of the process of dying, which could involve intractable pain, dependency upon others, and loss of functionality (Leming & Dickinson, 2002). This topic is often the source of debate in favor of euthanasia, as the dying process is seen to involve so much indignity that ending one's life by choice is often viewed as a viable alternative to enduring the shameful aspects of the dying process.

Dying people also represent the failure of prized medical technology, as the inability of current medical technology to cure or to prolong life is rendered ineffective by terminal illness. No matter how much one accomplishes in life or how great an individual's contribution to society has been, death is the ultimate insult that returns all beings, no matter what their level of achievement has been, back to the earth through the process of decay. Death is essentially the ultimate narcissistic wound, bringing about not just the annihilation of self, but the annihilation of one's entire existence, resulting in a form of existential shame for human beings, who possess the ability to ponder this dilemma with their high-functioning cognitive abilities. Human beings are basically ashamed of their mortality and frail physical existence and attempt to overcome this reality through diversion and accomplishments, similar to how individuals with narcissistic personality traits attempt to overcome their deep-seated feelings of inferiority and shame by projecting grandiosity and using various strategies that deflect the pain of their deep-seated insecurity and fragility (Martens, 2005).

Terror management theory (TMT) emerged as an expansion upon Becker's hypothesis that the fear of death underscores all of the activities of human beings. TMT assumes that death-related anxiety is the most fundamental source of anxiety, based in the human knowledge that all beings die at some point. According to TMT, people create and engage in cultural or religious affiliations or practices to assuage this anxiety. One's way of life, culture, and religious affiliation provide meaning, structure, order, and, hopefully, a sense of immortality as a defense against death (Solomon, Greenberg, & Pyszczynski, 1991). Terror management involves certain mechanisms that individuals employ to counter the huge anxiety that is felt when there is exposure to concrete or symbolic threats to one's life. These mechanisms may involve increased identification with one's culture as a means of feeling included in something larger than oneself (an example might be the surge of nationalism in the United States after the events of 9/11), or association with a symbolic representation of something that might afford symbolic immortality, such as a religious tradition, or the creation of something that might afford the originator a status of cultural immortality (such as the creation of a famous work of art, establishment of a trust, or influence in a social institution in some way).

SHAME FROM AN INTRAPERSONAL PERSPECTIVE

We now move to an exploration of how shame is experienced internally, from the perspective of the individual. Although the original definition of shame has the meaning of both exposure and cover (Kauffman, 2001; Schneider, 1977; Straus, 1966), this discussion will focus mostly on exposure, as this aspect is what becomes problematic. From a therapist's perspective, shame can be seen as the root of many difficulties in clients who seek help with psychological difficulties (Johnson, 1987; Lowen, 1985; Martens, 2005; Tantam, 1998). It is also the reason why many clients are unable to continue in therapy, as the basic response to shame-based experiences includes the need to hide or to "cover up" the source of shame, or to avoid it completely (Wurmser, 1981), which is anti-thetical to the therapeutic process. Shame is an acutely painful affective state that is typically accompanied by a sense of "shrinking," or "being small," or seeing oneself as worthless and powerless. The depth of the pain that results from shame leads one to desire to escape and hide from the painful affective state, as within shame, the self is seen as denigrated, unworthy, and reprehensible (Tangney & Dearing, 2002). When an individual feels shamed, there is a sense that something is basically flawed at the core of his or her being—in essence, the self is seen as flawed, useless, and despicable. In this description, shame can be identified as a threat to the self (Lewis, 1971; Martens, 2005).

Wurmser (1981) describes "shame anxiety," which is a specific form of anxiety evoked by the "imminent danger of unexpected exposure, humiliation, and rejection" (p. 49). This same author describes the previously mentioned extreme form of shame reaction, labeled as "narcissistic mortification," which occurs when shame anxiety or other types of anxiety reach traumatic proportions, engendering a sense of terror in an individual (p. 51). Martens (2005) describes this type of shame as an "inner torment," which can lead to great personal vulnerability, reactivity, and the potential for self-destructive or other-destructive tendencies. Such a powerful negative experience has great potential for shaping individual behaviors in order to avoid being shamed. Parents, for example, may find that shaming their children is a highly effective (although potentially devastating) means to control children's behavior and choices. Social groups may develop strong adherence to accepted codes of behavior by the threat of shame to individuals who do not adhere to the social norms of that particular group. MacDonald and Leary (2005) have recently presented the *social pain theory*, which gives further credence to the power of conformity to group norms, as they have demonstrated that the threat of rejection or abandonment in a desired relationship or social group can cause pain that is mediated along physiological pathways, which would be an additive factor to the negative affective state of shame experienced in social settings.

Lewis (1971) posits that shame engenders such strong feelings of anger and hostility toward the self that the individual may be overwhelmed and paralyzed by it. Wurmser (1981) elaborates further on the response to shame by suggesting that individuals will go to great lengths to avoid feeling shamed in social contexts. Shame is generally differentiated in

the literature and in clinical practice from the experience of guilt, with
the former being experienced as a flaw in one's character or basic sense
of self, whereas the latter is related to specific behaviors or situations
where one feels remorse and is able to attempt to rectify the situation
in some manner (Lewis, 1971; Martens, 2005). Whereas the experience
of guilt may have the potential for self growth and reconciliation, the
experience of shame in this regard seems to hold no such potential for
such good outcomes. In guilt, one has a sense of remorse for doing something or not doing something; in shame, one has a sense of remorse for
one's being. Guilt may actually be functional for bereaved individuals,
as when one feels guilt, there is a sense that something could be done
that may change an outcome, and even though this way of thinking may
be unrealistic, it may assuage the anxiety felt by experiencing a significant loss that has a profound impact upon the individual but that is also
outside of the individual's control. The relationship between shame and
pathological narcissism is also well documented in the psychoanalytic
literature, as the extreme avoidance of shame may lead to the projection of a false image of success and grandiosity as a defense against the
crippling effects of shame on the fragile self (Lowen, 1985; Martens,
2005). Maintenance of this image (or "false self") takes precedence over
all other functions because the affective experience associated with the
underlying shame and its implications is too painful to bear.

THE IMPACT UPON BEREAVED INDIVIDUALS

The previous discussion has unique implications for bereaved individuals, whose personal experiences of grief are mediated through the social
expectations of their culture. Earlier, we discussed the avoidance and
denial of death in Western society as a means of masking the narcissistic
wound of mortality. However, the ability to deny death or to avoid death
is no longer possible for those who have experienced the loss of a loved
one. Bereaved individuals represent our absolute inability to overcome
death or to control outcomes. Because the bereaved have violated the
social norms for death denial (and the negative effects of grief upon their
ability to be productive members of society), they are governed by specific social rules regarding their grief. Doka (1989) defined the social
rules of grieving as a set of norms that attempt to determine who, when,
where, how, how long, and for whom people should be sanctioned to
grieve. These norms are the "shoulds" and "should nots" that govern
individual responses to loss, and they exist as an attempt to limit the
extent to which grief can impede upon the social need for death denial
and terror management in a death-denying culture. These rules also

preserve the values of productivity and market stability for individuals whose experience would threaten these values.

Violation of any of the socially accepted norms of grief can have a deep impact upon the bereaved individual, as these social rules govern the social support, economic benefits, and exemptions from responsibilities that are extended after the death of a loved one. Social support is one of the most predictive factors in bereavement adjustment, and bereaved individuals will readily adopt these social rules about their grief in order to prevent abandonment of their social support system due to lack of conformity to these unwritten rules (Nichols, 2002). Individuals whose experience falls outside of these rules experience a profound sense of shame over the loss of control, inability to function, and demonstration of "weakness" in their grief responses. This shame can profoundly affect their ability to grieve in a way that is healing because it inhibits the grief response, which, if unhindered, would assist the individual to integrate the loss into his or her life.

Bereaved individuals may not fit neatly into the responses to death that are described by TMT. According to TMT, exposure to death-related themes and the reality of one's mortality fosters a need in many individuals to find security in culturally mediated representations of belonging to a powerful group or association with a powerful being to assuage the "wound" of mortal fragility and the shame associated with this reality (Schimel, Hayes, Williams, & Jahrig, 2002). However, bereaved individuals who attempt to align themselves with the dominant cultural values in Western society find that identification with these social values leads directly to an imperative to shun or to hide their grief because it interferes with the mandate to produce, perform, and function in the material-based culture. Efforts to further identify with religious traditions may be met with similar messages meant to assuage the grief by focusing on aspects of the afterlife, maintain the homeostasis in relationships within a faith community, and to the extent that the religious community identifies with the capitalistic society in which it is functioning, there may be religious overtones to the capitalistic messages regarding stoicism and maintenance of functionality. Some religious communities may subtly imply that open grief is shameful because it either does not acknowledge God's will regarding what has happened, or that open manifestations of grief may be a sign of doubt in one's faith after a loss occurs.

THERAPEUTIC IMPLICATIONS

Janoff-Bulman (1992) discusses how the assumptions that individuals have formed about the world and others can be shattered when traumatic events occur, such as when there is a significant loss. Beliefs about whether the world is still a "good" and safe place, that people are generally trustworthy, that there is meaning in life experiences, and that the individual has value and worth are all challenged by death and grief. The following common questions exemplify how basic assumptions are challenged by death:

- If I, as a human being, acknowledge the potential ending of my existence by death, am I diminished in my value and worth?
- Does life still hold meaning if I or others who are close to me die?
- Is the world still a good and safe place when death is present?
- How do I live when I realize that I have no control over my death or the death of those who are close to me?

These questions are often reworked in the therapeutic context with terminally ill and bereaved individuals. The grieving process is a necessary one, which helps to integrate the shattered assumptive world into a new world view that incorporates death, loss, and change into a schema that can "cover" the shame of death and the alterations in functionality that are brought upon by the processes of dying and of grief.

In therapy with bereaved individuals, the work is often to find ways to cover the shame associated with the grieving process, while at the same time to uncover the implicit norms of Western society that cause shame to these individuals in their grief. Shame basically leaves one feeling unsafe, exposed, and vulnerable. Maslow (1943) identified safety as a foundational component of human needs that must be in place before an individual can begin the process of self-actualization (or in this context, healing from the wound of loss). Safety in this context does not mean simply being safe physically from harm or violation. The deeper aspect of this concept entails safety in one's experience—to be free from judgment, criticism, social constriction, and paralyzing shame.

I use the phrase, "safety outside, safety inside" to describe this basic therapeutic necessity for healing to begin. In the therapeutic context, "safety outside" refers to the external conditions (such as support given by others to the bereaved individual) that allow the person to grieve in a manner that is congruent with that individual's needs, and the possibility of freedom for the bereaved individual to flow back and forth in the grieving process without interference. "Safety inside" refers to the internal conditions within the person that determine how that individual perceives his or her experience and how he or she allows himself or herself to respond to loss. These internal beliefs, mechanisms, and defenses are usually formed as a result of early socialization in the family system and other social structures such as schools, religious communities, and political structures. These internalized schemata may profoundly affect the bereaved individual's ability to allow for the healthy manifestation of grief, especially if grief is construed as a sign of weakness, self-preoccupation, vulnerability, or failure in some way. Kauffman (2002) discusses a related view of safety in the construct of disenfranchisement and enfranchisement of grief. If a bereaved individual self-disenfranchises his or her grief, the experience is most likely being internally interpreted as one that is shameful and the self-disenfranchisement serves the purpose of avoiding shame by "hiding" the shame-inducing grief. The concept of safety is expressed well in the idea of self-enfranchisement, or the acceptance of the value of one's experience and the choice to honor it, rather than to hide it or avoid it.

Some researchers and clinicians have explored the topic of compassion as a means of countering the harmful effects of shame. Compassion is defined as the ability to demonstrate kindness, understanding, and nonjudgmental awareness toward human responses, especially those that involve suffering, inadequacy, or perceived failure of some sort (Bennett-Goleman, 2001; Brach, 2003; Neff, Kirkpatrick, & Rude, 2007; Salzberg, 1997). These same authors state that compassion serves as a buffer against anxiety and leads to enhanced psychological well-being. Berlant (2004) sees compassion as a way of responding to others out of the recognition of shared human experience. She discusses the withholding of compassion as a form of cruelty that can be manifest in individual and social responses. Templeton (2007) discussed the concept of expanding circle morality, part of which involves a spiritual practice of compassion toward mortality salience in order to enhance an individual's ability to integrate death awareness into life experiences. Compassionate responses embrace human experience, including those that may be perceived as failures by set social standards. The therapeutic equivalent of compassion might be the unconditional positive regard as discussed by Rogers (1972), which is described as the foundation of establishing a safe milieu in therapy. By modeling this compassion in the therapeutic alliance for clients, there may be the opportunity for these individuals to internalize a different set of beliefs about their response to death that would allow for the integration of mortality and grief into lived experience, rather than shame and avoidance, which can hinder healthy human functioning.

The narcissism of Western culture is manifest in the grandiose ideas that we can somehow rise above our mortality through technology, creativity, and just plain hard work that denies the limitations of the body (Becker, 1973; Lowen, 1985). This same societal narcissism implies that we can continue to be fully functional and emotionally staid in the face of the shattering of our worlds through death and loss. Bereaved individuals are thrown into a situation where "the emperor has no clothes," and despite the social pressure to minimize or to deny death and grief and act as if nothing of significance has occurred, the experience of death and grief are real, and they can indeed be crippling. The work of therapy in this context is to "uncover" this narcissism by exposing the unrealistic grieving rules and mandates about death and loss so that they can be seen as false expectations and treated as such by grieving individuals.

Western culture extols and glorifies the body when it is manifest as a lean, sleek machine, but loathes this same body, which has limitations and dies. Death and grief are identified with the aspects of the body that Western society despises—and yet, in therapy, the wisdom of the body in setting limits and informing an individual of important needs is enlisted to assist in healing. The predominant social values of productivity, consumerism, stoicism, and functionality are, in this context, in direct conflict with the ability of human beings to reflect upon and embrace mortality, and to experience death and grief as part of the significant, meaningful experience of being human.

CONCLUSION

In a society that is based upon the celebration of achievement and productivity, death represents failure and loss of control. As such, experiences that relate to one's mortality are very difficult to integrate into everyday experiences of the individuals who live within Western social norms. The strong social codes about independence and maintenance of functionality exist to maintain the material-based culture, but these same codes serve the purpose of marginalizing and stigmatizing individuals who are terminally ill or who are bereaved.

Grief is often referred to as a healthy, integrative experience that has been instinctually developed in human beings through evolution as part of our attachment system (Parkes, 1988). As such, it serves a purpose to reestablish feelings of safety and security in our mortal existence. In Western society, the healthy and integrative aspects of grief are often overshadowed by the high emphasis placed upon achievement and productivity, which creates a scenario of death denial and shame in regard to death-related experiences. Death and grief must be normalized as part of the human experience to remove the shame and stigma attached to them, and the underlying social narcissism in Western society that promotes death denial and avoidance needs to be exposed to allow for the full range of human existence to be manifest.

REFERENCES

Becker, E. (1973). *The denial of death*. New York: Free Press.
Becker, E. (1975). *Escape from evil*. New York: Free Press.

Bennett-Goleman, T. (2001). *Emotional alchemy: How the mind can heal the heart*. New York: Three Rivers Press.

Berlant, L. (2004). *Compassion: The culture and politics of an emotion*. New York: Routledge.

Bolaria, S. B. (1994). Sociology, medicine, health, and illness: An overview. In B.S. Bolaria & H. D. Dickinson (Eds.), *Health, illness, and health care in Canada* (2nd ed., pp. 1–18). Toronto, CA: Harcourt Brace.

Bottomore, T. (1985). *Theories of modern capitalism*. London: George Allen & Unwin.

Brach, T. (2003). *Radical acceptance: Embracing your life with the heart of a Buddha*. New York: Bantam.

Doka, K. (1989). *Disenfranchsed grief: Recognizing hidden sorrow*. Lexington, MA: Lexington Books.

Janoff-Bulman, R. (1992). *Shattered assumptions: Towards a new psychology of trauma*. New York: Free Press.

Johnson, S. M. (1987) *Humanizing the narcissistic style*. New York: Norton.

Kauffman, J. (2001). Shame. In G. Howarth & O. Leaman (Eds.), *Encyclopedia of death and dying* (pp. 407–408). London: Routledge.

Kauffman, J. (2002). The psychology of disenfranchised grief: Liberation, shame, and self-disenfranchisement. In K. J. Doka (Ed.), *Disenfranchised grief: New directions, challenges, and strategies for practice*. Champaign, IL: Research Press.

Leming, M. R., & Dickinson, G. E. (2002). *Understanding death, dying, and bereavement* (5th ed.). Toronto: Nelson.

Lewis, H. B. (1971). *Shame and guilt in neurosis*. New York: International Universities Press.

Lowen, A. (1985). *Narcissism: Denial of the true self*. New York: MacMillan.

MacDonald, G., & Leary, M. R. (2005). Why does social exclusion hurt? The relationship between social and physical pain. *Psychological Bulletin, 131*, 202–223.

Martens, W. H. J. (2005). Shame and narcissism: Therapeutic relevance of conflicting dimensions of excessive self esteem, pride, and pathological vulnerable self. *Annals of the American Psychotherapy Association, 8*(2), 10–17.

Maslow, A. (1943). A theory of human motivation. *Psychological Review, 50*, 370–396.

Neff, K. D., Kirkpatrick, K. L., & Rude, S. S. (2007). Self-compassion and adaptive psychological functioning. *Journal of Research in Personality, 41*, 139–154.

Nichols, D. L. (2002). Social support of the bereaved: Some practical suggestions. In J. D. Morgan (ED). *Social Support: A reflection of humanity* (pp. 33–43). Amityville, NY: Baywood.

Parkes, C. M. (1988). *Bereavement: Stories of grief in adult life.* London: Routledge.

Reynolds, J. J. (2002). Disenfranchised grief and the politics of helping: Social policy and its clinical implications. In K. J. Doka (Ed.), *Disenfranchised grief: New directions, challenges, and strategies for practice* (pp. 351–388). Champaign, IL: Research Press.

Rogers, C. (1972). *On becoming a person.* Boston: Houghton Mifflin.

Salzberg, S. (1997). *Lovingkindness: The revolutionary art of happiness.* Boston: Shambala.

Schimel, J., Hayes, J., Williams, T., & Jahrig, J. (2007). Is death really the worm at the core? Converging evidence that worldview threat increases death-thought accessibility. *Journal of Personality and Social Psychology, 92*(5), 789–803.

Schneider, C. (1977). *Shame, exposure, and privacy.* Boston: Beacon.

Solomon, S., Greenberg, J., & Pyszczynski, T. (1991). A terror management theory of social behavior: The functions of self-esteem and cultural worldviews. In M. Zanna (Ed.), *Advances in experimental social psychology* (Vol. 24, pp. 93–159). San Diego, CA: Academic Press.

Straus, E. (1966). Shame as a historiological problem. In E. Straus (Ed.), *Phenomenological psychology* (pp. 217–224). New York: Basic Books.

Tangney, J. P., & Dearing, R. L. (2002). *Shame and guilt.* New York: Guilford Press.

Tantam, D. (1998). The emotional disorders of shame. In P. G. Gilbert & B. Andrews (Eds.), *Shame: Interpersonal behavior, psychopathology, and culture* (pp. 161–175). New York: Oxford.

Templeton, J. L. (2007). Expanding circle morality: Believing that all life matters. *Dissertation Abstracts International, 68*(02), 1342B. (UMI No. 3253419)

Wood, W. R., & Williamson, J. B. (2003). Historical changes in the meaning of death in the Western tradition. In C. D. Bryant (Ed.), *Handbook of death & dying* (Vol. 1, pp. 14–23). Thousand Oaks, CA: Sage.

Wurmser, L. (1981). *The mask of shame.* Baltimore: Johns Hopkins University Press.

CHAPTER 6

Shame
A Hospice Worker's Reflections

Alex Tyree

FOR SHAME

I approached the front door and rang the bell as I have been doing for the past 16 years of making home visits as a hospice bereavement worker. After some minutes a slight woman slowly opened the door with a half smile. She led me down the hall to her living room, and we sat down. Her dog hopped up on the couch beside her and put his head in her lap. Sue sighed before beginning to speak. Her son had disappeared some weeks ago and had been found dead in a shallow body of water. He had drowned, and there was no explanation for this tragic incident. Though this was not a hospice case, this mother had consulted our services from the community.

Sue was hard pressed to explain the pain she was experiencing and found herself struggling with the simplest tasks. Recounting the course of events leading up to the discovery of her son's body, she paused saying, "I knew he was dead when he didn't come home after two nights, but I didn't want to believe it." She was clearly upset with herself for having held onto the hope that there was an alternative ending to this story and castigated herself for her attempts at self-protection, the notion that he was still alive.

As a person whose job it was to communicate with groups, it was now ironic that she found that she was unable to leave the house, at least not without great determination. Going to the store or having lunch with a friend was a burden. Sue found herself stripped of her former sense of abilities; the very landscape of her self had been laid bare.

Deepening her feeling of vulnerability was the external voice of our North American death-denying culture that discouraged open conversation about this incident and that could not provide a context for meaning or avenues of support. As Sue grasped for answers to her deeper questions about this tragic event, society further isolated her for having lost an adult child, especially under such ambiguous and seemingly random circumstances.

I offer this vignette as an invitation to begin to reflect on the power that shame can wield from both the internal voices of our individual past life histories, and the external messages of our culture as a consequence of loss by death. In sharing stories of some of the persons I have companioned as a hospice bereavement worker over the years, I will focus on the relation of shame to grief, and how we can help our clients, and eventually ourselves, to cope when shame undermines the innate capacities that we all have to grieve our losses.

First, let us begin with the question of what shame is. It is a fundamental feeling about one's very self. It can be described as a sense of brokenness or "a lacking," manifesting itself in an overwhelming sense of vulnerability or uncovering. Some might call it the basis of fear or an experience when one cannot defend the self. Gershen Kaufman (1992) points to this, claiming that, "[a]bove all else, shame reveals the self inside the person, thereby exposing it to view. To feel shame is to feel seen in a painfully diminished sense. This feeling of exposure constitutes an essential aspect of shame. Whether all eyes are upon me or only my own, I feel deficient in some vital way as a human being" (p. xix). It may seem amazing that a person with such competencies and confidence in the stability of life, at one point in time, can be reduced, like Sue was, by the death of her son, to feeling she had lacked the capacity for such simple things that came so easily prior to this death. In this case, shame is not the result of having done something to bring on such a feeling. It is more related to the inability or incapacity to do something.

Yet, death brings such a comprehensive shift in all that is familiar, though the basic scenery of life remains the same: same car, job, or house. Somehow all the synapses of a life that were connected and organized around another person are severed dramatically. Sometimes I think of a woven rug in order to describe these strands of connection that, over time, create such powerful designs on the looms of our relationships. When seemingly torn from our place in the other's life we may feel as if we are left like children, unable to find our way for a time. At the extreme, we may feel powerless and alone. There are also the physical, cognitive, behavioral, and emotional changes brought about by bereavement that may lead to self-estrangement and a world that seems unrecognizable.

When I reflect on the challenges that bereaved men and women face in the daunting task of relearning their worlds (Attig, 1996, p. 99), as well as discerning the meaning of witnessing the process of illness and death, I am in awe at the capacity they have to move forward in their lives. Yet, the bereaved seldom recognize their own heroic efforts, or the legitimacy of their struggle. John, a man in his 40s with a teenage son at home, described his situation after the death of his wife as if a tsunami had hit and he stood up to find that most of what he had regarded as familiar had suddenly washed away. In a bereavement support group, a retired grief counselor found himself at a loss to cope with his own spouse's death. All the words he had offered to countless widows and widowers in years past did little at this time to give him a solid footing in the new disorienting landscape after losing his life partner. Yet, it was very difficult for both men to connect the cause of their struggle to the experience of death. Instead they seemed to assume fault themselves. They were ashamed of their incapacities to accomplish, produce, function, and have a sense of agency.

The word *shame*, itself, can have the power to shame. When asking people who are grieving if they feel shame, there is, at times, an initial recoiling at the word. Sometimes the term *embarrassed* is used more easily to describe grief reactions, as if in admitting to shame, you are uncovering yourself, and in a sense you are. Kathryn Royer, in writing on shame and trust adds, "One of the most forbidden words is shame" (2008, p. 6). She aptly points to shame's "hidden nature" (p. 8) that makes it uncomfortable to recognize and work with regarding feelings of incapacitation, weakness, or low self-worth. It seems shame does not want to be found out, making it more difficult to develop a conversation to examine its nature and develop helpful ways to cope and mine what deeper meaning shame has to offer those who are wrestling with it.

Often when I hear the phrase "what is wrong with me," I take it as another clue that the bereaved person does not grasp, at that moment, that his or her situation justifies the behavior, thoughts, or feelings that can feel so vastly out of character. The utter vulnerability and perception of helplessness or loss of control can be overwhelming as one's life story has suddenly lost its coherence and familiar rhythms. Larry, a bereaved spouse, told me in one of our conversations, "All the neighbors are looking at me ... and, even at the grocery store, it feels like everyone has their eyes on me." To him, it was as if others knew that he had lost his wife "reading it on my face." Larry had grown up in a home where both parents drank habitually. He learned early on that he had do things for himself, and he did. Getting through school with no support from home, he landed a good job at a major corporation, got married, and raised a family. His work ethic led him to take overtime and he won awards of excellence on his job. He also was handy around the house and did most of his home maintenance without assistance. Even his multiple back surgeries did not stop him from pursuing his interests.

When his wife, Joan, was diagnosed with brain cancer, Larry used that same drive in his role as a caregiver, particularly when she declined physically and required more personal care and assistance. He retired and insisted on providing the care himself with minimum assistance from his sons and daughter. Finally, he was compelled to utilize our hospice services and allowed other people to help. At a certain point in his caregiving, Larry had a sense of powerlessness; he could no longer effect any change in his wife's condition. Joan was now combative and critical of him due to her mental deterioration. He described to me a desperate moment near the end of Joan's life when she fell in the living room and battled against him, "her arms flailing in the air," when he tried to offer help. For the remainder of her life, and in her dying, there was no further trace of the life they had shared together for 45 years.

After Joan's death, Larry found himself in what seemed to be another world. He suddenly felt alone and unable to do the things that he had so easily done without effort. Due to the strain on his back from caregiving, he was physically unable to engage in many things that had given him satisfaction. When family and friends did not appear as regularly as he expected, he became resentful. As we talked, he reflected on his core value of self-sufficiency that was so challenged by his current experience that he felt great shame. In the past, Larry had led others to believe that he needed minimal assistance and they, too, had left him alone during this time of great need. Larry suddenly smiled in the middle of our conversation and recounted a story about his mother. When he was a little boy, he remembered her saying, "Larry is the one we never worry about; he never asks for help."

Individual narratives like Larry's speak to the dilemmas related to one's core values that may invite shame, but the subject of death alone can evoke shame in our North American culture. An incident brought this home to me one evening while attending a party in a comfortable home in an upper-middle-class suburb. A tanned, middle-aged man approached me in a welcoming and friendly manner. Reaching his hand out to shake mine, he asked what I did for a living. I replied, "I work as a bereavement counselor for a hospice." Suddenly, his faced changed, taking on a look of surprise and absolute disgust. In reply, he exclaimed, "none of us want that" as he abruptly turned and walked away. His behavior, though a bit extreme, illustrates the external source of shame that comes from the way our culture responds to death and, indeed, increases one's interior vulnerability to shame, as is implicit in Larry's story. I will look more closely at this exterior source of shame embedded in our culture in the following section.

OUR CULTURE THAT SHUNS DEATH AND THOSE GUILTY BY ASSOCIATION

Throughout history there have been individuals and groups that removed themselves, temporarily or for a lifetime, from their respective dominant cultures in response to perceived excesses or destructive elements. Such monastic or countercultural community movements or their representative individuals often lent much perspective to the current social mores and customs that negatively impacted their respective societies. American authors Henry David Thoreau retreated to Walden Pond and Thomas Merton reflected from his hermitage on a Cistercian monastery at Gethsemani in Kentucky. Both were prolific writers offering a public argument for self-assessment. Today, such voices that critique a North American culture so singularly focused on youth, material success, productivity, efficiency, and individualism, are seldom heard. They seem to be lost between the barrage of media messages and images promoting pop culture, and the haranguing of reactionary conservatism. Tag lines such as "Life takes Visa and life takes convenience" or "My phone is always on" are emblematic of our society's overblown claims based on image, productivity, and power. The tolerance for downtime is increasingly shortened with the advent of fast-evolving communications technology. For example, when Blackberry went down for 12 hours, people experienced horror at missing something that could have been important. There was such an outcry it was reported in all the major papers. Along with this strong desire to possess real-time information and "make the moment work for us," even God has been appropriated into this ethos. The best selling book *The Secret* is iconic of a spirituality that claims proper intentionality will bring about the blessings of prosperity and health.

These popular culture messages surround those who are grieving as well. In fact the bereaved become the embodiment of the opposing viewpoint. Loss of a loved one by death is not supported by this American dream. Our mental health establishment is also a reflection of this trend. In Allan Horwitz and Jerome Wakefield's (2007) article in the *Philadelphia Inquirer* titled "Sadness Is Not a Disorder," they point out that the *Diagnostic and Statistical Manual of Mental Disorders* "describ[es] anyone who for two weeks suffers from at least five out of these possible symptoms—sadness, diminished interest or pleasure in daily activities; difficulties in sleeping or eating, physical slowing down or restlessness; fatigue; feelings of worthlessness or guilt; diminished ability to think or concentrate; and recurrent thoughts of death or suicide—can be diagnosed as having clinical depression." The only exception is for those experiencing early bereavement. Grievers have a pass for 2 months. Other then that qualification there is no other mention of context explaining such symptoms. In other words, we cannot be deeply sad for more than 2 months, whatever the circumstances of our lives. Otherwise we must be clinically depressed and require medication to restore us to our previous optimism.

The media's take on death is consistent with the American culture's desire for speed and entertainment. We witness death in fast motion and lean to the spectacular whether it is murder on our local news, coverage of war, or portrayal of violent deaths on our most popular television series such as *24* or *Lost*. Death is speed, action, adrenaline, and violence. For most of the bereaved who have experienced a hospice death, this is not the case. It is more likely their role to witness the slow decline of the person they have cared for punctuated by crisis, transition, and then, waiting upon death at bedside. For many this can be a very tedious, slow, and stressful experience that meters out slowly, requiring great patience and endurance.

Responding to this most common manner of death, the hospice movement in the United States began during the early 1970s and sought to address the shame of death prevalent in this culture. Earlier, in 1963, Cicely Saunders, the founder of the contemporary hospice movement, who, at that time, was paving the way in the United Kingdom for comprehensive end-of-life and bereavement care, came to speak on that subject at Yale. Attending that lecture was a group of grassroots activists from New Haven, Connecticut that established the first non-profit hospice organization, Hospice, Inc., to establish end-of-life care that would meet the spiritual, social, physical, and emotional needs of the terminally ill and their families. The time was ripe in the late 1960s for Dr. Saunders to bring the message of hospice to America. In 1969 Dr. Elisabeth Kübler-Ross's book *On Death and Dying* exposed the shunning and neglect that relegated dying people to private rooms at the ends of hospital wings. The dying received little attention and inadequate symptom management. Death was kept out of sight to the extent of abandoning our dying and their caregivers; allowing great suffering as the cost of hiding the shame associated with death.

Also responding to this injustice in service of secrecy, at that time, was a robust euthanasia movement that took another route to counter the lack of control one had over one's care in the last chapter of life. Robert Fulton and Greg Owen describe these times in their chapter "Hospice in America":

> Responding to the loneliness, isolation, lack of family involvement and
> unrelieved pain that came to be synonymous with individuals dying in

acute care hospitals, concerned persons in the euthanasia movement
advocated the right to die either by assisting the patient to end his life
or her life, or by the discontinuance of treatment. Robert Veatch of the
Hastings Center reported in 1977 that forty pieces of legislation were
introduced into state legislatures during this period in an attempt to
legalize one or another aspect of euthanasia. (1981, p. 10)

Yet, the euthanasia movement did little to address the more global
problem of death and shame that seemed to deny those who were dying,
or the bereaved, an esteemed place in our society. In fact, I believe
this movement was an extreme manifestation of that shame. Why not
attempt to eliminate dying altogether and seek to control the end by
preempting death itself by somehow controlling its timing? This seemed
to be more akin to Somerset Maugham's adaption of an ancient Arabic
fable, "The Appointment in Samarra." In the fable, a servant sees Death
in the Baghdad marketplace in the form of a woman. Seized with terror,
he mounts a horse and flees to Samarra to hide. His master questions
Death as to why she threatened the servant. She remarks that she had
not meant to be threatening, but was surprised to see him there in the
Baghdad market as she had an appointment with him that evening in
Samarra. The euthanasia movement, like the servant who assiduously
seeks to undermine death's inevitable grasp, only is fooling itself through
a futile charade. Granted, those who advocated euthanasia presented a
valid argument against the indignity and suffering related to inadequate
symptom management and the isolation associated with the dying process of the times, but the movement did nothing to address society's
crusade to hide death, or the shunning by the community of the dying
and bereaved. Instead, it colluded with those tendencies to cover up the
reality of death and its implications.

The hospice movement, on the other hand, sought to shine a light
on death, dying, and bereavement and bring them into a national discussion on a more comprehensive level. It attempted to open a conversation to bring death out of the closet thus making the needs of the dying
and bereaved known so they could be addressed. Saunders's philosophy
made an audacious claim without romanticizing death; if certain physical, emotional, and spiritual needs were addressed openly during the
dying process, as well as in bereavement, there was a potential for an
experience of growth, intimacy and meaning for the patient as well as
for his or her caregivers. She learned this lesson from her first dying
patient, David Tasma, a Polish refugee, who made the first monetary
donation to her movement (Saunders, Summers, & Teller, 1981, p. 4).

THE GRIEVER AS CASTAWAY

It has been more than 30 years since Kübler-Ross wrote *On Death and Dying*. Her publication pioneered the death and dying movement, which attempted to present death as a natural part of life and free it from its shadowy place at the margins of society. No longer would people feel sequestered by the culture when they traveled through the "dark valley"; this subject would no longer be spoken uncomfortably in whispers. Organizations such as the National Hospice Organization (later known as the National Hospice and Palliative Care Organization) and the Association for Death Education and Counseling advocated for further research and understanding regarding death, dying, and bereavement, and created an open forum for cultural discussion on the subject. Subsequently other bereavement education organizations were founded and programs of thanatology and death studies appeared in colleges and universities. Those who worked with the dying and bereaved understood the isolation and pain that people experienced as a result of this great divide and worked as a part of this movement to alleviate the suffering caused by it. Many of those professionals and volunteers in related fields believed the death and dying movement would be the antidote to the shame that was evident in the silence, secrecy, and distraction that North American society employed to cover death's trail.

So now, 30-plus years later, where are we? Well, we have come a long way as far as our research and practice in regard to supporting the dying and bereaved. Our legislation regarding advanced health care directives and the right to adequate hospice care including bereavement services is available to all. However, are we any more comfortable with death and dying? When I reflect on this question as a hospice worker I compare the death and dying movement to the civil rights movement. Much legislation has been passed to provide legal rights for minorities to achieve equality and equal opportunity in the society. Yet, I wonder if these important steps really changed basic attitudes about race or the deep unconscious roots of racism. Though the number of bereavement counselors, educational programs, and conferences addressing end-of-life issues continues to grow, the general public still seems fairly unmoved. In the end, we remain divided; end-of-life care and bereavement professionals companioning the dying and bereaved, as well as those directly affected by loss, while the society at large continues to distract itself from the thought of death or its profound lessons. Many bereaved people would still confirm C. S. Lewis's statement from his classic memoire of loss, *A Grief Observed*, published in 1961, saying, "an odd by-product of my loss is that I am aware of being an embarrassment to everyone I meet.... Perhaps the bereaved should be isolated in special settlements like lepers" (p. 64). I cannot think of a more powerful image of shame then that of the leper. I do not imagine the leper simply feeling embarrassment, though embarrassment seems to be a word more comfortable to use then the powerful appellation, shame.

It is for this reason that I offer the metaphor of a castaway to describe the experience of many bereaved persons. Loss can evoke a sense of isolation as the first wave of caring attention recedes after the funeral and those few weeks after a death. Many bereaved people will share then, "I haven't heard from anybody," "People won't mention Helen," "It's been 6 months and my friends think that I should be moving on" or various other admonitions or advice along the same lines. A distraught adult daughter called me recently saying, "It's been two weeks since my mother's death and my father is acting bizarre. He keeps confusing things and keeps going over and over stuff." When I asked if he had any friends, she replied, "That's it, they used to do everything together for the last 62 years ... she was his world. I don't understand it ... I took all the pressure off him caring for her while she was sick so he could just sit there and hold her hand." After those words had just come from her mouth, I found it ironic that she that she still could not fathom why he was behaving in ways that were so out of character for him. It is no wonder that there is relief for new attendees of bereavement groups as they respond to fellow participants' comments saying, "me too," "you mean that is normal?" or "I thought I was the only one." Often, the bereaved are disappointed by friends or family that fall short of their expectations for support and understanding, or sometimes they are surprised by those they had not known well or had not thought would be there for them, but stepped up to the plate.

Yet, why do those who grieve feel so alone? I believe they embody what so many people fear for themselves, such as vulnerability, powerlessness to control external circumstances, loss of direction, anxiety, unanswerable questions, and death itself. It seems that our contemporary culture, along with its institutions, leave us woefully unprepared to discover meaning in death and grief, or simply to discuss them. Therefore, we are left to fend for ourselves. What has occurred in response to this lack of understanding and support has been a proliferation of bereavement groups. Some are focused on grief and some are simply means for social connection for those who have experienced loss by death. A subculture of support in the community has been created where people can discover they are facing some of the same challenges and sharing many similar responses to their circumstances of loss. They also are free to share alternative possible meanings related to the grief that they may be wrestling with. As they do so, the shame that grievers may be experiencing is ameliorated as they, over time, are more free to discover and accept the deeper implications for themselves of having been a caregiver and seeing death play out in their homes. They do, however, have to possess resources that counter the pervasive voice of the culture that would rather sequester them than bring mortality into the mainstream.

I run a monthly bereavement group for those who are past the first year postdeath and they continue to complain that others do not understand that they are still affected by their losses past prescribed timeframes. Just because we have learned to run the mower, service the car, cook, do laundry, cope with the holidays, pay bills, or eat out alone doesn't mean we are through grieving. For many, a different question arises, "who am I now" or "where do I go from here," now that they possess this life-changing experience. The new challenges and tasks of life invite them to redefine themselves, which brings with it both opportunity and pain. My group members comment that this process is extremely difficult in that as they grow into a newer sense of identity, they are moving further away from the familiar life that they lived when the deceased was physically in their world. I often hear the word betrayal to describe this movement, in that it can bring its own mix of shame and guilt. These challenges of later grief are unacknowledged and can lead the bereaved to wonder, "I am well into the second year, why am I not further along? Why am I not over it?" There again, it comes back to "what is wrong with me?" The experience, however, of sharing in a group or individually where the great duration of grief is acknowledged as natural, and a model of agency is offered amid the common feelings of powerlessness, can invite grievers to finally begin to accept the profound life-changing nature of what one has experienced as a hospice caregiver. This, in turn, can invite bereaved persons to enter into discovering the meaning of the struggle and duration of their grief. It is not surprising that when effective grief groups connect, there is a corporate realization of the inadequacy of the culture to support the journey they are walking on though a misinformed notion of grief and a taboo against speaking openly about it. When this occurs, the power of the culture to stigmatize is lessened and this exterior source of shame can be robbed of some of its power.

Another aspect of the dominant culture that contributes to alienation among the bereaved is our value attached to speed and efficiency. We are a people that happily reply to the familiar query "How are you doing?" with "I am very busy." Furthermore, we seem to have a sense of entitlement to expect that all things can be made to move along smoothly given the right attitude, technology, or system. Waiting is something that is seen as an obstacle to be solved by the newest upgrade. Even though many of us North Americans may have come to believe in our fast-paced, efficient, and optimistic view of the world, the one who wrestles with grief reminds us of our finite humanity and connection with all living things that have a beginning and an end; that not all things have a solution. The consequences of this assumptive worldview are that the griever who may struggle to perform simple tasks, feels lost, and has few discernible goals or direction is often misunderstood, dismissed, or avoided. This can compound the interior sense of shame that one may feel when things that came easily to them such as eating, sleeping, decision making, and confidence have mysteriously vanished or have become "hard work" as a result of the dramatic rearrangement of life impacted by death. It also can exclude them from the social networks that create the holding environment needed to support their natural capacities to navigate through the uncharted territory of grief and address the many challenges of rebuilding meaningful lives.

A MAN'S SENSE OF SHAME

Men may be particularly vulnerable to shame when grieving. John's wife died of cancer at home under hospice care in her early 40s. They had two teenage children whom he was trying to raise without having a mother at such a crucial developmental time in their lives. As a parent he was under the stress of managing his own grief, parenting his son and daughter, and helping them with their own sense of loss. Three months after his wife's death I made a second visit to John in response to his frustration with himself that no matter how hard he tried, he could not "get back to the way I used to be." I heard him say, "Why does everything need to be such work?" and "I can't seem to get anything done." "When am I going to stop using this [meaning the illness and death of his wife] as a crutch ... why am I such a wuss?" John conceded it was a horror to witness his wife's deterioration over the course of months "from being a good-looking woman to a corpse." Despite this, and the subsequent challenge of single parenting grieving children, working full time, and adapting to an entirely new life, he still expected himself to handle the situation better. As he told the story that spoke to the gravity, pain, and great challenge of caring for his wife and coping with life after her death, he was yet not able to see this life-changing event as cause enough for his fatigue, lack of motivation, and inability to function as he had before this horrendous experience. When I offered the word shame to describe some of what he was relating, John paused and continued to try to articulate his frustration. Then he came back to it and said, "When you said the word, shame, I felt a lump in my throat ... yeah, that is just what I am feeling ... ashamed of myself because I don't have what it takes to get over this thing." I visited John 2 weeks later. He had his laptop open on the coffee table with a picture of his wife on the screen saver. He invited me to look at a slide show that her girlfriends had put together of her life for a benefit party to support her treatment. As we sat on the couch together we watched a story unfold of a lovely young woman who was engaging in the ordinary things of life, such as parties and celebrations with friends and family, slowly change, the signs of chemotherapy and radiation as well as steroids altering the contours of the once familiar face, frame by frame, belying the thresholds they had crossed as well as the thresholds to come. As we watched, John's eyes welled up as he spoke of the last chapter of Marie's life. I used this unplanned opportunity and explored his experience of bearing witness to his wife's dying. From this sharing began an acknowledgment of his profound experience of loss; one that shifted the sands under his feet so irrevocably as to jar his confidence and disrupt the familiarity, predictability, and meaning of his life. On a later visit, John related to me that he was asking himself the question once again in a most critical voice, "What is wrong with me?" He answered himself, "Oh yeah, I am grieving," humorously alluding to my returning to this point on most of our visits.

In my experience, many of the men I have worked with struggle with shame. Their response to loss so conflicts with much of their expectation of themselves and that of the American culture that surrounds them. Like John and Larry, who were accustomed to taking care of their families and had solid work ethics that made achieving goals and solving problems a part of their identity, many who have been hospice caregivers suddenly find it difficult to explain the dilemma between who they once were and who they find themselves to be after the death.

Other variables in addition to societal expectations imposed on men from the culture can make men more vulnerable to an interior source of shame. Men who had experienced parental loss in childhood that I have met with when their spouses died contended with what they described as a feeling of abandonment again as they had felt when they were children. John's mother had died when he was 12. He shared with Larry the value of self-sufficiency that he constructed out of his early life experience, but also was overtaken, he related, by feelings of abandonment and vulnerability that he had experienced so acutely years ago when his mother died. Such experiences of fear or vulnerability for men, in my experience, are so acute for those who have embraced values of autonomy and self-sufficiency, and find themselves, again, in the context of helpless childhood. Shame is the likely outcome.

HUMILITY VERSUS HUMILIATION

Can loss bring with it a sort of humiliation? When I visited with Stan, who had lost his partner of 10 years, he looked up with his eyes full of tears and said, "I gotta get by this, everybody will think I am an idiot." He went on to say that he didn't want people to see him "cracking up like that." Our confrontation with death (in hospice it comes into our very home) as caregivers can strip us bare of our security and defenses. The composure, meaning, and familiarity of our world have been pulled out from under us. Thelma exclaimed, "I just want my mind back," as she struggled with her fourth loss in 3 years. With a deep heaviness she sighed, "I am ashamed that I do not have any strength left to do anything"; this coming from a very tenacious woman with her own business and a history of dealing with adversity. In our culture, humility is often confused with humiliation, or, you might say, "eating humble pie." It has lost its place as a human virtue in a culture that glorifies upward mobility and denies life's inevitable physical diminishment. Therefore, when we are confronted with our reactions to loss, it may be hard for many of us to accept ourselves as dramatically changed and diminished in our capacities to function as we once did and, consequently, we may, like Thelma, feel ashamed. Since there is little popular cultural support or collective wisdom for finding a "different kind of strength" or value in the griever's struggle, or simply to honor it as a normal, though profound, experience in the cycle of life, the bereaved may feel that they have not lived up to the expectations that surround them. This can be particularly painful, as I have mentioned, for people who have internalized the cultural messages lauding productivity, materialism, autonomy, and control due to their parenting or circumstances growing up. Core values such as individualism, self-reliance, or the unlimited power of will to accomplish anything are ultimately challenged by the hospice experience of caregiving and death.

During a regional meeting of hospice bereavement professionals on the topic of the popular culture and grief, the members present determined that an important part of our vocation was to assist those who grieve to discover a "different kind of strength" or meaning in their experience of facing a new life without their loved one, while exploring the deep questions that witnessing their illness and death invites. The materials for such meaningful conversations are embedded in the caregiver's stories that are often replete with instances of courage, endurance, compassion, and commitment mixed in with exhaustion, irritation, fear, and regret that can also be used to make parallel analogies to their current grief narratives. For example, Jean mentioned the time when her husband had called her to his bedside for the third time in the middle of the night: "I can't believe that I yelled at him ... he didn't know what he was doing." She felt shame that she was not able to control her anger for having been called out of bed, yet again, while she was extremely sleep deprived. I invited her to visually picture what she was going through at the time of the incident; to recall her emotional, physical, and spiritual exhaustion. Then I asked what her husband's greatest wishes were. Jean responded, "He didn't want to go to the hospital anymore, and he wanted to die at home." We agreed that she had made that possible for him. She also discovered though sharing her story, moments that she had displayed great strength though she did not feel strong, and had acted courageously despite her fears. None of this was obvious or dramatic on the surface. Her story was set in a context of being powerlessness to change the situation, and constrained by her physical and emotional limits. Jean and others may be disoriented and dismayed by their perceived incapacities during bereavement, and thus may hold on to those events in their caregiving stories, constructing narratives that are consistent with a sense of failure. In our subsequent conversations, however, Jean began to appreciate herself as having accomplished something significant despite her limitations. In fact, it was her limitations that made them significant. This revelation continued to unfold in the months following the death of her husband, giving her freedom to revision her perceptions of both her caregiving and bereavement. The word *agency* may be more helpful in terms of pointing out this paradox. That one can be still have authority within a life that is well beyond changing the hard circumstances surrounding it, yet within its agency to respond in ways that could be called extraordinary. Again, I believe it is this sense of lacking agency and capacity that brings on shame, a nakedness before the unremitting forces of death, and diminishment that is reinforced by our culture's insistence that power be defined in such narrow, superficial, and conventional terms.

I propose, instead, that it is in the process of accepting our own finite humanity that we can begin to allow ourselves to feel the pain of our loss and its implications without embracing shame. I call it practicing humility. The Latin stem *hum-* is the foundation for the words *human, humane,* and *humus.* These words speak to the quality of being human and of our connection to the soil or earth. The earth speaks to our mortality, from where we were formed and will return to, following the great rhythm of all living things. This is, however, not a small task given the countercurrent of an entire public information machine working with our innate resistance to keep this avenue closed. Buddhists practice daily, as mentioned later in this chapter, the discipline of the Five Remembrances that point to our contingency and our relationship to all things that have a beginning and an end. But it is also possible to be mindful of these principles unfolding before us all the time in the world around us. It is as simple as the once towering poplar tree that I noticed now fallen across a familiar path in the woods where I regularly walk, its rotting trunk laying on the ground that was now surrounded by the new undergrowth. By intentionally moving in this direction of awareness of our finite nature, and that of all things, we can also come to accept ourselves with greater compassion and, perhaps, to see the depth of spirit that we possess despite our limitations in the face of death and loss. For me this is a more helpful conception of humility that can assist us in navigating the territory of grief. In my experience, this active process of acceptance is found in community with others who are also willing to risk this challenging but rich path. Without the support of a community that reinforces an affirmation of the natural challenges and movements of birth and death, it seems improbable that we can face our own and others' mortality, or have the courage and resources to find greater purpose and meaning in the face of death. Without this kind of humility, I would propose that we cannot hope to fully grieve our losses or live with the anxiety inherent in being a finite being. The alternative position is to collude with our North American game of hiding death by distraction. In this case it may be easier for some to live with shame than come to grasp the tragic wisdom of our nature to grow, become ill, and die.

OVERCOMING SHAME

Jean exclaimed, "I should have been able to save him." After some years of her husband struggling with an aggressive cancer, she had not believed he would die so soon and grasped at ways she could have averted this tragedy that had so transformed the landscape of her life. Bill remembered the last few days of his wife's life in the hospital and said, "I could have insisted that the doctor pursue any kind of treatment on Thursday; Friday she could no longer talk, and Monday she died." Bill struggled with shame, believing that he should have been able to change the course of her illness and death. Furthermore, his inability to battle a sense of helplessness against the tide of his grief reinforced this feeling. Being a long-time Roman Catholic, he considered seeing a priest for confession. As we explored this further, he related with great emotion, "I really need Vickie's forgiveness." In other words, Bill assumed some responsibility for allowing her to die due to his inability to think clearly enough to act. He was attempting to find a way to offer contrition. He may have felt guilt in that he was indirectly accountable for Vickie's demise, therefore needing forgiveness. But I think that shame is a more accurate term in that Bill struggled with some lack or incapacity in him that lead to the loss of his wife and his world. Absolution may only go so far in releasing Bill from this dilemma.

Shame may function to stave off the reality that death is inevitable and that we are unable to avoid its painful implications. Bill's cry still implies that he could have chosen a different course of action to prevent death. Jean, Bill, and others mentioned earlier in this chapter illustrate an assumption that they should have had the capacities to control the extremity of their mental, physical, spiritual/existential, and emotional reactions to the life-changing experience they have encountered. It seems that although these hospice caregivers have walked this rugged path step by step, he or she has not grasped its heights and depths, or acknowledged its most powerful implications.

In the end we are powerless over death and the debilitating chapters leading toward its entrance in our lives, though we are not powerless in our responses to it, as countless caregivers have taught us. There is, however, a way to navigate through this uncharted territory called grief. It requires much risk and endurance as we are invited to engage in an innate trial and error process of adapting and responding to the challenges of changed daily life patterns, relationships, an evolving sense of identity, as well as the reflection upon the journey of illness, death, and its unfloding personal meaning.

Through practicing this human process of realignment of self, other, and the world, grieving invites us to overcome the protective function of shame; a purpose, I have come to believe, that allows the griever time to assimilate death's meaning as well as its particular impact on one's life story. My friend and colleague Bob Niemeyer likes to say "feelings have functions" (Neimeyer, 2000, p. 94). I think that the pain of shame asks us to consider its purpose, to answer the questions it asks of us: What are you ashamed of? How can you respond? These questions can invite a deeper examination of the ways that we are struggling against the power of death, change, and what are our possible responses to such a reality. Our answers, given assistance from supportive others and other resources, can help us to gain greater acceptance of our own mortality as well as the impermanence of our world sufficient enough that we can continue to live with purpose and develop notions of hope. Our hospice patients often come to redefine hope in the goals they discern are important to them based on their unfolding realization of their own impending deaths, and those goals are usually related to their relationships, the meaning of their lives including spiritual or existential concerns, or such things that they have always wanted to do and desire to still experience. It is a gradual process to accept the truth that death is certain and we are unable to thwart it. Shame may, indeed, be the last holdout against the reality of death. Perhaps shame insists that we somehow have some power over death, but for some fault of our own, we are vulnerable and powerless against it. As the movements between the new challenges of life and the construing of meaning that we give to our experience of illness and death (Stroebe & Schut, 2001) continue to draw us forward, we are invited to begin to let go of shame. We can come to accept that those we have been attached to and the predictable and familiar life we lived has slipped irrevocably beyond a former threshold. We then can discover that the fault does not lie in us.

Shame may be a more preferable experience than that of accepting death, as well as the fact that the life that we have come to know has ended. Again and again this phenomenon seems to present itself to caregivers in very symbolic ways. Sarah met with me individually and then attended a hospice bereavement group after the death of her mother. She shared privately that she was the one in the family that others depended on, that her mother, siblings, and daughter leaned on in times of trouble. Sarah and her daughter participated in a mother and daughter sports activity where she demanded excellence of herself as well as of her daughter. Her now deceased mother had been a constant presence in the bleachers cheering them on. After Sarah's mother's death (her father had died 8 years prior), she found that she no longer could count on her self-assured identity. In our first meeting, she expressed bewilderment at the changes going on inside her. Why did she "feel so weak" and unable to "snap out of this." She felt shame that she could not perform with her daughter as well as before, and imagined her mother looking on from the bleachers with disappointment. Nearing the first anniversary of her mother's death, Sarah had not yet completed some necessary tasks as executrix and was both distressed and perplexed. She complained that her confidence was nil and she had begun to slur her words on occasion. A school graduation program for her daughter had proven to be more emotionally difficult due to the deep sense of her mother's absence. Although Sarah expected to sense her mother's presence during this important family milestone event, all she felt was utter emptiness and sorrow.

As she continued her story, Sarah spoke about a sweater that she had rolled up to prop her mother's head up the day of her death. It was in a bag at her home, and she could not bring herself to wear it or even take it out of the bag. She wondered out loud, "I wear my dad's old shirt and it gives me comfort, why can't I do the same with this?" Her mother had also left a necklace and ring that remained in the safe at her old home. "I know they are in the safe, but I can't bring myself to getting them out," she related. Sarah had both a strong intuition that she needed to attend to these things and a strong resistance against proceeding ahead. Being caught somehow in the vague land between her past life and the one that would draw her forward, she found herself weak, vulnerable, and ashamed that she would feel so unfamiliar with herself. Even the values and role that made her feel such a sense of strength and gave her an important place in the family seemed to have vanished. I asked Sarah what would happen if she were to take the sweater out of the bag and put it on; the jewelry out of the safe and wear it? Tears came in response to my question. I believe at a deep level, she already knew that she was at the crossroads of beginning to accept that both parents had died, and she would be shouldering a new sense of mortality, living with that deeper awareness. This new understanding could give her the ability to set aside the notion that she was somehow intrinsically broken, but rather justified by the life-changing forces of death to be, for a time, disoriented and uncharacteristically vulnerable.

How, then, does the bereaved person come to understand and accept their finite nature and live purposefully? Grievers over the years have taught me that we have the innate capacity to integrate our mortality and learn to live meaningful lives again with adequate support from our communities. I use the metaphor of a grief compass that sits at our core to describe this phenomenon. At first the needle loses its familiar true north and seems to swing wildly across the compass rose in alternate directions, many times, along with chaotic thoughts, feelings, and behaviors. Over time, however, becoming more attuned to our emotions and the deeper questions associated with them, as well as beginning to trust our own instincts of what may be helpful to us, there begins a trial-and-error process of rebuilding of our worlds. Like a scientist or sleuth, one learns to test and follow up hunches on which trail to take next in the unfamiliar forest of grief. It is only by living through our mistakes and building on our successes, while practicing discernment based on the results, that the needle of our compass begins slowly to find new direction. All of us have the inner capacity to grieve. However, some who grieve may need assistance to identify and unblock some of the detritus of unhelpful past experience as well as the cultural messages that obstruct those innate tools. All of us who companion the bereaved can encourage and support these processes.

Though the veil of mortality has been cast aside for bereaved hospice caregivers who have witnessed the physical diminishment and death of their loved ones, they are not always able to grasp the gravity of death when thrown into this unfamiliar territory bereft of the patterns, habits, and commitments that were inextricably connected with the deceased (Attig, 1996, p. 144). It is in this long process of redefinition of our selves and all that is around us that we may begin to consider what meaning mortality has for us. Unfortunately tools or alternative meanings for this journey are sadly lacking in our North American culture and we have to look for resources elsewhere. The antidote to our cultural messages regarding illness and death might be summed up in the Buddhist Five Remembrances that are a part of daily practice in that tradition. These are daily reminders that we humans are of the nature to age, become ill, and die; that all things change, and our most cherish attachments will pass from us. However, it also affirms that we can learn from all our experiences and gain wisdom; that our true belongings are our actions, especially those of compassion, kindness, and generosity. This is also expressed in a verse from Psalm 90:12 in the Hebrew scriptures (New Revised Standard Version): "So teach us to count our days that we may gain a wise heart." In contemporary thanatology this is called posttraumatic growth.

CONCLUSION

In this chapter, I have sought to articulate some of the ways I have come to think about shame in the context of my hospice work. However, the meaning and function of shame as it relates to death and grief remain mysteries in many ways. I have journeyed with many grieving families over the years at Delaware Hospice, and they continue to open up those mysteries for me. My hope is that this reflection from a hospice perspective, along with the other contributors, can offer a substantive exploration of the challenge and opportunity that shame poses, in service of those who are most affected by it: the bereaved. I am grateful to have been able to work as a part of a movement that continues to struggle against the shame associated with death in our culture. The hospice movement seeks to bring both the needs of the dying and bereaved to light, and attempts to introduce what they have to teach us about life into social discourse. This is unlike the euthanasia movement that attempts, ironically, to circumvent the shame of death by attempting to somehow erase it with death itself. It seems like a futile way of grasping at control of this last frontier that humans want to defend against and defeat. This only elevates shame by continuing to cover up death and its associate, bereavement. This stance leaves few alternative meanings to assist us as we walk through the most natural occurrences in life, as is birth, or to mine the profound questions and challenges that death poses to us as human beings. Despite these obstacles, bereaved persons have taught me the great potential for growth and development as a result of this mysterious process called grief, given the support from the community and resources that offer elements of affirmation and hope for this arduous trek. I also have personally experienced this with the dying, who are often written off by our culture as out of the game. I have observed tremendous growth and transformation in those able to share their experience and receive assistance in life review, discern elements of hope, and discover roles that support a sense of agency within a culture that offers them only that of victim.

Though shame has an interior voice based upon our individual histories and the nature of the self, any conversation about shame needs to include the significant part that our dominant North American cultural messages play in the imposition of that feeling on those who may be vulnerable due to their life experience and meaning making in the face of death and bereavement. Being aware of the power of culture as well as our personal vulnerabilities reveals the exterior and interior structure of shame that can reinforce each other. In hiding death, our culture misses the rich lessons that are taught by those who are dying and their bereaved family and friends. Acknowledging and honoring this hard-earned wisdom can lead to a more inclusive community and create the diversity of meaning and compassion necessary for supporting us all through the necessary transitions in the human life cycle. Paradoxically, our culture sets itself on a destructive course as it neglects, or outright denies, end-of-life issues. If not addressed, this will continue to bring great suffering to our society as increasing numbers of us are aging and may lack the humanity and wisdom to cope. Popular culture's use of distraction and illusion disenfranchises many, and creates an environment of attachment, competition, and fear that fosters far more problems than there is room to explain in this work. In a sense, society's own shame and subsequent denial can bring about the death of its soul.

EPILOGUE

I have a particular interest in the experience of shame as it relates to life-threatening illness, death, and dying through my own experience of being twice diagnosed with cancer. This first diagnosis of Hodgkin's lymphoma occurred when I was 17 and the second came 30 years later with a gastric cancer. As an adolescent, I was ill prepared for the manifold feelings and experiences of being diagnosed with a life-threatening illness. It seemed that, almost immediately, I fell out of my normal teen life and started to lead a surreal life with little precedent. My treatment led me to Memorial Sloan-Kettering Cancer Center in New York City, taking me out of my familiar surroundings and high school in a small suburban town in New Jersey. Instead, I found myself riding the subway to the hospital from an apartment in Murray Hill, Manhattan. I can easily remember the walk down from the subway to the hospital thinking to myself, "You are an alien being, who would want you ...

you will never get married, you will never travel." I felt shame for being the cancer patient that I was and became overwhelmed by the many forces that seemed beyond my control. My body itself began to change with the effects of radiation and chemotherapy. However, in this major cancer center, where we all were visible signs of the struggle of coping with cancer treatment, not a word was breathed from either patients or health care professionals about what we were all experiencing. All the images of mortality and the courageous daily steps that were being taken in spite of those images were not mentioned or invited into words. After nearly a year of treatment, celebrations were had, accomplishments acknowledged, but little said about the gravity of the experience. When I look back on it now, I think that I carried that shame well on into the future without a context to think about it. As a 17-year-old, I was supposed to be becoming a man. With the constraints of the disease and treatment, I had very little autonomy or choice in the midst of such an important stage of development and little help from the surrounding culture or professionals to discern any greater meaning relating to my treatment and recovery, or a role that would have empowered me other than a superficial positivitism that resembled more of a denial than assumption of the gravity of what had become of a 10-month sojourn through chemotherapy and radiation.

Thirty years later, I was diagnosed with gastric cancer and my second experience in treatment reminds me of the hoped-for goals and outcomes of the death and dying movement. Despite the progress in speaking about life-threatening illness such as cancer, there has been little progress in dealing with the basic attitudes toward mortality and agency for those with life-threatening illness. The culture still divides treatment into failure and success without regard to the extraordinary things that those who are ill and their caregivers accomplish despite their prognosis and outcomes. Unfortunately, we are still stymied by a diminished cultural expectation or alternative roles that may confer authority on those persons with life-threatening illness who are learning life lessons that will eventually be relevant to all of us who will, most likely, cope with physical diminishment and life-threatening disease (not many of us will be hit by a bus). Without such roles or meanings, shame fills the void leading to the hiding of illness, mortality, and its effects from those around us, just as it can in relation to grief.

My 8 years of running a specialized group for those who want to explore issues of their mortality for the Wellness Community, a national nonprofit organization designed to support those with cancer and their caregivers, have taught me much in the way of transcending the boundaries of culture, through open mutual thought and dialogue about the meanings of living with late-stage cancers. Some of our group members have survived several years before dying and continue to be a powerful teaching presence for us surviving members. Being able to speak frankly about living with a real sense of mortality and being able to share its implications and choices of response have diminished that sense of shame and isolation that members have experienced within the mainstream. In coming to accept the progression of their disease, many of our members are forced to redefine hope and purpose in innovative ways that are more based on goals relating to their relationships, values, the arts, and spirituality rather than treatment outcomes and survival. Over the years I have observed great developmental strides in maturity and wisdom as group members reached more deeply into their resources, demonstrating their courage, honesty, and authority to teach despite the circumstances of their cancers.

It is in great measure due to the group members' pioneering work and risk-taking conversations that I live as well as I have with my cancer. Many of those members have died, but I consider them my "balcony people," those who are no longer physically present, but by their example and wisdom, continue to inform and support my journey, as I seek to live fully with the knowledge of my connection with all things that have a beginning and an end. The greatest gift they continue to give me is the encouragement to live intentionally with the knowledge not only of my contingency, but the power of even my small responses to give of myself purposely and to contribute to my community despite the circumstances of illness that we humans have little control over. Their example of setting aside shame creates a vast space for a fuller and more satisfying version of the human story; one that supports us all through the entire life cycle.

REFERENCES

Attig, T. (1996). *How we grieve: Relearning the world.* New York: Oxford University Press.
Fulton, R., & Owen, G. (1981). Hospice in America. In C. Saunders, D. Summers, & N. Teller (Eds.), *Hospice: A living idea* (pp. 9–18). London: Edward Arnold.
Horwitz, A. V., & Wakefield, J. C. (2007, December 9). Sadness is not a disorder. *Philadelphia Inquirer*, p. C1.
Kaufman, G. (1992). *Shame: The power of caring.* Rochester, VT: Schenkman Books.
Kubler-Ross, Elizabeth. (1969). *On Death and Dying: What the dying have to teach doctors, nurses, clergy, and their own families.* New York: Scribner.
Lewis, C. S. (1961). *A grief observed.* New York: Harper.

Neimeyer, R. A. (2000). *Lessons of loss: A guide to coping*. Keystone Heights, FL: PsychoEducational Resources.

Royer, K. (2008). The bridge of trust can heal the power of shame. *Presence: An International Journal of Spiritual Direction, 14*(2), 6–16.

Saunders, D. C., Summers, D. H., & Teller, N. (Eds.), (1981). *Hospice: The living idea*. London: Edward Arnold, Ltd. and Philadelphia: W. B. Saunders Company.

Stroebe, M. S., & Schut, H. (2001). Meaning making in the dual process of coping with bereavement. In R. Neimeyer (Ed.), *Meaning making and the experience of loss* (pp. 55–73). Washington, DC: American Psychological Association.

SECTION 4

Cultural Differences

CHAPTER 7

Shame and Death in
Cultural Context

Paul C. Rosenblatt

SHAME IN CULTURAL CONTEXT

In What Ways Is Shame a Human Universal?

Richard A. Shweder, an anthropologist well known for his research on shame and culture, wrote that unlike a number of other emotions "shame is shame wherever you go" (2003, p. 1109), by which he meant that "deeply felt and highly motivating experience of the fear of being judged defective ... are probably found everywhere in the world" (p. 1116). He went on to say that despite what he saw as the invariant essence to the feeling of shame, there are quite diverse ways, even within a culture, for defining shame; quite diverse conditions for experiencing it, recognizing it, and communicating it; and great diversity in the meanings it is given. Thus, in Shweder's view, even if the core feelings and social relationship aspects of shame are more or less the same from one culture to another, there is also much that varies. And other anthropologists who have written about shame have emphasized how across and even within cultures the context of shame, the social positions linked to various forms of shame, and the ways that people become shamed or are made aware of their shame vary and change from time to time (Lindisfarne, 1998; Rasmussen, 2007; Rosaldo, 1983). So shame must be analyzed in sociocultural as well as psychological terms (Kilborne, 1992; Rasmussen 2007; Rosaldo, 1983). And if one thinks of shame as Shweder and other anthropologists have, then shame is actually not a simple, unitary feeling/thought/experience that can be recognized and interpreted in a straightforward way no matter what the cultural context. Instead shame is a mix of feelings, thoughts, awarenesses, wants, values, and beliefs that vary considerably from culture to culture, because cultures create, support, reinforce, and define different feelings, awarenesses, wants, values, and beliefs. From that perspective we are challenged to discover and understand the differences among cultures in the form, expression, context, and meaning of shame as it relates to death.

Building on this line of thought, the anthropological perspective on shame warns us that it is too easy, and very much a mistake, to take the particulars of shame as it relates to death in one culture (for example, middle class, white U.S. citizens in therapy) and assume they apply everywhere, or to force the differences from culture to culture into a frame that eliminates or rounds off differences. It would be a mistake to make a single cultural reality the norm against which other cultures are evaluated. In fact, if we take that tack toward how other cultures do shame as it relates to death, other cultures will often be found to be deviant and wanting, rather than understood in their own terms. Related to this, trying to translate the English language term *shame* into another language or to translate a term from another language as though it could be glossed simply as shame in English is risky. A term in one language has implications, connotations, metaphoric links, and overlaps with other emotion terms that would be obscured if it were to be glossed with a simple term from another language. For example, Macdonald (2007, pp. 129–130), discussing translation of terms used by the Palawan of the Philippines that might be roughly glossed in English as shame, wrote that simply glossing the Palawan terms related to the English-language term shame as shame obscures as well as enlightens. Palawan shame is not quite the same as what might be the typical usage of the word shame for English speakers. For example, the Palawan word for shame "refers to a wide spectrum of affects, from a social construct akin to dishonor, loss of face, and shame, to a subtle feeling of embarrassment or awkwardness; it applies to the special feeling of being belittled by someone who is behaving disparagingly and arrogantly ... towards one, and also to a sense of shyness or of being socially inappropriate" (Macdonald, 2007, pp. 129–130). Similarly, Berndt (1962, pp. 195–198) discussed the challenges in glossing a term in the four New Guinean language groups that he studied that could be translated into English as shame but also could be translated in a number of related but different ways. The term could be translated to include "real or assumed shyness," a "shame that leads to anger," and a "shame that is something like wanting to escape." Also, to take the New Guinean term that could be glossed as shame in English as though it applies simply to the feelings of a specific individual would miss, among many cultural differences from the English speaking world, that felt shame and the shaming engaged in by others often apply not only to the individual but to the individual's kin (Berndt, 1962,

p. 372). In short, to take a word from another language and culture and gloss it as the English language term shame could tell us something, but we would miss the ways that the word refers to emotions, senses of self, social situations, and cultural meaning systems that are not what most English speakers have in mind when they use the word shame.

From a somewhat different perspective on the challenge of translating shame-related concepts from one language and culture to another, for the Maori of New Zealand, at least in the past, the term applied to the dead ("mate") was also applied to men who were in some way weak, men who were, among other possibilities, overcome with shame (Smith, 1981, p. 154). Thus for Maori men, feeling shame was a kind of death. From a somewhat different perspective on translating the term shame from one language to another, for Tagalog speakers in the Philippines (Palmer, Bennett, & Stacey, 1999), there are terms that can be translated into the English term shame, but the metaphoric roots of the terms are rather foreign to English speakers, for example, "debt of the inner being." So even if Shweder is to some extent correct in saying that shame is shame wherever you go, perhaps there are a few languages and cultures in which there is a term for shame that means precisely what it means in U.S. English. In fact, it can be argued that the more detail one has of a situation in another culture where shame and death are linked, the more one knows of what is said and done in that culture regarding shame, and the more one knows of the circumstances in which shame is relevant, the less confidently one can write as though a simple understanding of the shame–death linkage is appropriate and the less one can offer an understanding that is unambiguously intelligible to English-speaking people in middle-class U.S. culture.

Cultural Differences in Meanings, Contexts, and Consequences of Shame

In Western psychology, shame is an individual disposition. One feels shame in one's own self and psyche. There are writings in the Western psychological traditions that depict shame as interactional. One feels shame in relationship to another or because one is seen by another or one thinks about the standards of another; but even in these cases, shame is the feeling of an individual, not a shared feeling. However, in some cultures, shame is familial, not individual. For example, in Korea (Yang & Rosenblatt, 2001), the whole family experiences one's failing, one's loss of face, and one's public humiliation. One of the links of shame to death in the case of Korea is that certain causes of death are seen by some Koreans, perhaps particularly in the older generation, as shameful

(Yang & Rosenblatt, 2001). And the whole family is shamed, with one manifestation of that being that anyone in a family that has experienced that kind of death, cancer, for example, may have more difficulty finding a partner to marry, since when marriage is being considered attention is paid to the pedigree of a potential partner, and shameful things anywhere in the other's family background are problematic.

There may often be a sense in Western society that shame is an undesirable feeling, that one should be able to get past it, and if counseling or therapy can help, by all means seek that kind of help. However, in some cultures, shame seems to be valued as a sign that one has a sense of honor, that one understands and respects cultural values, and that one is a proper member of one's family and community. Shame also is seen as reinforcing cultural values. Thus, even though continuing to experience and express shame can be uncomfortable, in some cultures shame also has positive meanings, for example, that one has an assured and respectable place in the family and community or that at one's core one supports the values of the culture.

There are also cultural differences in what people might do who feel intense shame. In some cultures, shame is intolerable and might lead to suicide, immigration, or some other flight. But in other cultures there are ways to remove shame, for example, by ritual or by making amends.

In the United States, some people go on television to talk about the shameful things they have done and their feelings of shame. And perhaps that is cathartic or a way of honoring such cultural values as honesty and objective reporting of the news. But from the perspective of people in some other cultures (Korea, for example, as described in Yang & Rosenblatt, 2001) public openness in the United States about shame is seen as almost insane. The openness adds to the shame of oneself and one's family, both because it becomes more public and because it is shameful (a second shame) to publicize one's shame. It invites everyone to be critical of one, to think contemptuously of one, to sneer at one, and to exclude one.

Linking Shame and Death Cross-Culturally

In the cross-cultural literature on shame, links are rarely delineated between shame on the one hand and dying, death, and grief on the other hand. In the cross-cultural literature on dying, death, and grief, shame is often not mentioned. However, both literatures offer readers a scattering of valuable and interesting links between shame and death, and those links are the focus of this chapter. But it would be a mistake to take the matters discussed in this chapter as cross-cultural universals. Although there are certainly links in some cultures between shame, and dying, death, and grief, there are many cultures that apparently do not offer social scientists compelling and highly visible linkages between shame, and dying, death, and grief. And then some of the cultures that do have such links are cultures where shame is linked to absolutely everything in the culture (e.g., the Orokaiva of New Guinea, Sharpe, 1987). So in those cases, the linkage does not mean that there is anything unusually shameful about dying, death, and grief. The literature discussed in this chapter offers cultural insights, ideas about cultural and psychological possibilities, and hints of what might be applicable in a diversity of cultures, but the literature is so sparse that it would be a mistake to make claims about anything approaching human universals. Even if one agrees with Shweder that there is a human core to shame, it is difficult to generalize on the basis of cultural variations in shame or on the basis of the cross-cultural literature linking shame to death, dying, and grief.

DYING AND DEATH AS SHAMEFUL

In many cultures, the issues that come up again and again that relate to shame have nothing directly to do with death. Often they are about honor in the community, sexuality, behavioral and social proprieties, physical appearance, or fitting into the community and meeting appropriate standards (cf. Rasmussen, 2007). But in some cultures, these matters at times become entangled in issues having to do with death, and in a few cultures, death is central to considerations of shame.

Shameful Fatal Illnesses

In some cultures, dying and death are not shameful, but certain kinds of dying and death are. For example, in many cultures in Southern Africa, dying from HIV/AIDS is considered shameful (e.g., Rosenblatt & Nkosi, 2007, writing about the Zulu of South Africa; Stadler, 2003, writing about Sotho and Tsonga speakers in South Africa). People in such cultures so want to avoid the shame associated with HIV/AIDS that they may deny that someone in their family is ill or dying, or they may mislead others (and perhaps even themselves) about the cause and likely trajectory of the illness. Practically speaking, feeling considerable shame about a fatal illness may mean that people do not seek treatment or adequate treatment or fall short of following the proper treatment regimen. In the case of HIV/AIDS, denial of what is considered in one's culture to be a shameful illness may lead to a failure to protect others (sexual partners, for example, or a fetus about to be born). And if there is a stigma attached to certain fatal illnesses, the stigma attached to the illness of one family member may spread to other family members and may affect their status in the community or their chances for marrying the proper kind of person.

Perhaps grief counselors will rarely see people from a culture other their own, and perhaps it will be even rarer that they see someone from a culture other than their own who has shame issues connected to a loss. Counseling may not be meaningful to people from other cultures, and shame issues might preclude the issues ever being voluntarily brought to the attention of another person. But for any counselor, sometimes very surprising clients come through the doorway, so let us imagine that a grief counselor will have the opportunity to help someone from a culture other than the counselor's and that the person has loss issues connected to a culturally shameful illness. For a grief counselor trying to help someone who has a culturally shameful illness or who carries the shame of having had a family member die of such an illness, it may be useful to learn circumlocutions appropriate to the client's culture rather than to name the illness. If the shame is linked to central values and beliefs in the client's culture and is a very substantial part of the client's feeling and thinking, working around it with circumlocutions will be challenging, because so much of what might be talked about will link to the topic of shame. But then there is also a possibility that one could make the counseling session a time when shame can be put aside. If one is a cultural outsider with regard to the person whose shame issues are prominently connected to the death, one may have the advantage of not being seen as part of the devaluing audience that many people think about and experience when they feel shame (cf. Hahn, 2009). A cultural outsider may—with sufficient time, trust, and work at moving the discussion some distance from the cultural shoulds, values, and beliefs that lead to the shame and to the intolerability of speaking about the shameful illness—find it possible to talk directly and helpfully about the shameful illness and its consequences. Among other possibilities, being able to talk about it may make it possible to normalize what millions of people suffer from and die from, for example, HIV/AIDS or cancer. Also, it may be important and useful to directly explore the consequences of the shameful illness for the client, for example, in community reputation, the spread in the family of the dreadful illness, or the consequences of the illness for marriage prospects for family members.

Shame can also be understood as about disrupted ties in one's community (Hahn, 2009). From this perspective, working on shame issues connected to a certain mode of dying with a cultural outsider is of limited value. The relationships that are disrupted are with cultural insiders.

So a cultural outsider working with someone experiencing shame issues connected to a death might need to find ways to help the person to rebuild connections with cultural insiders. Support groups of cultural insiders who have had to deal with more or less the same kind of death might be one route. Helping a client to find a culturally insider religious congregation or other organization of people who are accepting, rather than shaming, of someone who has dealt with a shameful death would be another way. Sometimes there are cultural rituals for neutralizing shame or in some other way restoring relationships that have been damaged by a shameful illness. If such cultural rituals exist, it may be productive for a culturally outside grief counselor to encourage the performance of such rituals and the client's involvement in them.

THE SHAME OF REMAINING ALIVE

There are cultural situations where people are shamed for existing, for remaining alive. One prominent force for that kind of shaming is racism. For example, in Australia, White people shame people who are of mixed Aboriginal and White parentage for existing, for living while carrying the stigma of mixed ancestry (Dalziell, 1999, pp. 113–114). Similarly, one can see many forms of racism in the United States directed at African Americans as, in part, shaming (Rosenblatt, 2010), and in some instances the shaming may be so attacking of a person's inner core that it can feel that one is being shamed for existing. For a grief counselor working with someone who has been shamed in this way, not only is there the challenge of dealing with someone whose shame issues may block self-disclosure and may make being with the grief counselor or anyone else painful, but there are also the challenges of affirming the worthiness of the person being counseled and of the person's right to continue living. And if the counselor is White and the client is not, and the shaming has been done directly or indirectly by White people, that will mean that part of the support will have to deal with what it means to the client for the counselor to be White. Without attention to that, there may be issues of trust that make any kind of help impossible.

Among the Bariba of Benin in West Africa, a war leader who remained alive when the warriors he led were killed would be so shamed that he would kill himself and be expected by other Bariba to do so (Sargent, 1984). Then there is the literature on survivor shame, that having survived something (for example, the Holocaust or an automobile collision) that killed others can lead to feelings of shame (as well as feelings of guilt). Survivors can feel shame for still being alive (Leys, 2007), for having not found a way (even if there was no way) to save others who died, or for having acted in ways that enabled them to survive when others were unable or unwilling to act in that way or did not know that acting that way could be life saving. The shame of a survivor may not be something that can ever be removed. It may be part of everyday existence, permanently attached to the memory of those who were killed when the survivor was not, something that comes up whenever the survivor is aware of existing and of the nonexistence of others.

Perhaps any of us who have lived long enough—outliving colleagues, friends, schoolmates, and family members—can feel survivor shame. But there are cultures where survivor shame has particularly great weight as a result of the cultural meanings of surviving and of still being alive. Thus, for a grief counselor confronted by survivor shame, the cultural context is important to understand. A Bariba war leader who has not killed himself may have to feel and express survivor shame in order to maintain any self-respect and to be a good Bariba. Since none of us is without culture, even if a grief counselor is working with a shamed survivor from her or his own culture, it is important to know that culture at it relates to issues of surviving and of shame. Perhaps for many Euro-Americans, survivor shame is in part an expression of love and of a belief in personal efficacy: "I would not feel this shame except that I so loved this person and I did not do what I might have been able to do to save the person's life." If that is the kind of thinking a person feeling survivor shame is living with, it might be best to acknowledge the thinking and validate it. Rather than trying to somehow dispel the shame, it might be better to accept it and then help the client to use the love and feelings of efficacy to move to other places than shame. What would be an expression of love of the person who died? What would she/he want? As a person who is still efficacious, what can you now do that in some way will make a difference, not, or course, in the life of the person who is now dead but in memory of the person or to honor the person or so this thing is less likely to ever happen again?

THE SHAME OF TAKING CARE OF OR NOT TAKING CARE OF THE DYING

There are cultural settings in which providing care for people who are dying of certain illnesses is shameful. The shame may be linked to the shame of the illness from which a person is dying. If one cares for someone who has a shameful illness, one may be seen as acquiring some of the shame of the illness. This seems especially common cross-culturally in providing care for people dying of HIV/AIDS (e.g., Kittikorn, Street, & Blackford, 2006, writing about Thailand; Li et al., 2007, writing about

China). In such cultures, there are standard evasions available to those who have provided care that is considered shameful. For example, people do not admit that the person they have cared for or are caring for has or had a shameful disease. It could be tempting for a grief counselor who comes from a culture where such care is not at all shameful to say that there is nothing to feel ashamed of. But I think it is not necessarily helpful or even relevant to use one's own culture as a basis for offering support to someone from a different culture. Perhaps it could be worth a try to say something that moves the discussion to the counselor's own culture, something like, "In my own culture, providing that kind of care is not shameful. In fact, I have provided such care for a friend." But it might be more productive to learn to do what fits the person's culture, for example, to respect the evasions and never to actually name the disease or even perhaps to speak directly about providing care.

There is also the possibility of shame from *not* providing care for the dying. For example, in cultures and ethnic groups in which there are strong expectations that when someone is terminally ill, family members provide the care the person needs, not providing such care could be experienced as shameful (for example, in some African American families it could be shameful to not provide family care to a dying family member; Turner, Wallace, Anderson, & Bird, 2004). As with any other shame topic, this one could be challenging to address because people might not want to speak about matters of shame and because the shame could be linked to matters they would not want to give up, for example, love of the person who died. However, it might be helpful, if the opportunity arises, to go back to the time when the decision not to provide care was made. Did the person who was not cared for say that she or he did not want family care? If so, not caring for the person was an act of respect for the family member's wishes. Was the client in a place economically, geographically, psychologically, or in terms of other responsibilities able to provide the care? Sometimes reviewing the processes that led to care not being provided takes some of the edge off of shame about not providing care in a culture where there is something of an expectation that one provides end-of-life care for a family member.

THE SHAME OF IMPROPER MOURNING

One can argue that the rituals and mourning activities surrounding death have deep meaning and can be helpful in dealing with the emotional, cognitive, social, spiritual, economic, and other challenges of a death. However, rituals of mourning also have the potential to create shame problems for bereaved people. If rituals of mourning have a strong presence in a culture, the rituals create standards by which the bereaved are judged, and bereaved people who are wanting by the mourning standards of their culture and community may feel shame. For example, in Taiwan there is an expectation that at a husband's funeral, the new widow will cry, and if she fails to (perhaps because she feels numb or is distracted by all the other ritual requirements at that time) some community members will look at her critically and she may feel shame (Hsu, Kahn, & Hsu, 2002). Perhaps fear of shame is part of what makes many people carry out any specific mourning ritual properly. Also, the belief that some people fail to meet the standards and feel shame is in a sense an endorsement of the ritual standards. That is, if people are seen to feel shame for not meeting the standards and are believed to feel shame for not meeting the standards, that says to everyone that the standards are important and presumably worthwhile. Of course, from another perspective, rituals that demand a great deal from widows and other bereaved people who may be struggling, stunned, shocked, anxious, overwhelmed with sorrow, and distracted could be seen as burdensome.

In the Taiwanese example, shame comes from not grieving enough at a certain time. But in some cultures proper mourning may require limiting the public expression of grief, that is, not grieving too much. An example comes from southwestern New Britain (an island in the South Pacific and part of the country of Papua New Guinea), where Maschio (1992) reported that all his informants said or implied that they would feel shame if they grieved publicly for a loved one too long after the person's death. As one of his informants said, "We hide our hearts from others" (p. 412). Here again a link between shame and death seems to be that the discipline of mourning requirements is maintained partly by people not wanting to feel shame, and then if they do feel shame because, in the case of southwestern New Britain, they cried inappropriately, that is an endorsement of the mourning requirements. They may grieve intensely in private, and then they will not feel shame, but it is shameful to grieve in public too long after a death. So grief is made a "private possession" for people in southwestern New Britain (Maschio, 1992, p. 413). Others in the community may know that a person is feeling grief, for example, if they see the person sitting alone in his or her garden, and they will leave the person alone and feel sympathy for him or her. Maschio (1992, p. 413) wrote that the mourning requirement, reinforced by feelings of shame if violated, pushed people to accept a death. So in a sense the mourning requirement put a time limit on the mourning of people in southwestern New Britain. In fact, there are many cultures with ritual ways of time limiting mourning (Rosenblatt, Walsh, & Jackson, 1976). But time limiting may accomplish many other things beyond or alternative to pushing people to accept a death. It may,

for example, free a bereaved person from restrictions that are onerous (for example, restrictions on necessary work). It may free others
in the community from onerous interaction requirements, for example,
having to avoid the bereaved or to interact only in specific, ritual ways
(Rosenblatt & Nkosi, 2007, writing about the Zulu of South Africa). It
may free the spirit of the dead in some way—perhaps to move on from
proximity to the bereaved to something like a distant heaven. So time
limiting mourning may be about many matters that have no obvious link
to shame.

Improper mourning is common for people who have been caught
in warfare. In the Congo, Liberia, Sierra Leone, Rwanda, Cambodia,
and other countries that have experienced dreadful, bloody wars, it may
have been impossible for survivors of millions of people who died as a
result of warfare to carry out proper mourning. So for surviving family
members, there may be a lifetime of shame in not having carried out the
proper mourning. And the shame may be complicated by such cultural
beliefs as that the dead cannot be at peace unless the proper mourning
is carried out or that the spirit of the deceased may bring misfortune
on family members unless proper mourning is engaged in. For a counselor working with someone who has lost family members in a war, the
trauma and grief stemming from all the deaths and other losses of the
war can thus be complicated by the shame and other consequences of it
having been impossible to mourn properly. These issues are worth airing
in themselves in grief counseling with someone whose family has been
caught in a war, and perhaps with some people it might be possible to
arrange a belated and not-quite-proper mourning ceremony or series of
ceremonies years after the death and without the body present. Friends
and family might gather, prayers might be said, sacrifices might be
offered, the proper things might be said, and the dead might be asked
for forgiveness for the delay in mourning and for a mourning ritual that
is unusual. And this may help to address the shame of not having performed the proper rituals in the proper way at the proper time.

SHAME THAT CAN CAUSE DEATH THROUGH SUICIDE

Perhaps it is never completely clear what a person's motives were for
suicide (Berndt, 1962, p. 181). In many instances there may be a blend of
motives, cultural shoulds, and odd circumstances. But if we can assume
that the substantial ethnographic literature connecting shame and suicide can be relied on, there is much that can be said about the links of
shame and death by suicide to culture. To begin with, there are cultural
contexts where the people of a culture say that death by suicide can (and

perhaps even should) result from certain kinds of shame. For example, in some Arctic cultures (for example, the Chukchee and Gilyaks) certain kinds of shame may call for one to commit suicide (Pentikainen, 1983, reviewing ethnographic literature on 71 different cultures). Some kinds of shame can be so intense, so horrifying to self, so horrifying to others, or so polluting of one's family, kin group, or community that the shame seems to call for the person on whom the shame centers to die. The death may be an escape from the pain, a way of paying back or compensating others, a way of cleansing oneself or one's social group, a way of removing the shame of family and community, or a way of restoring or claiming honor.

There are cultures where one may become so ashamed of how one has declined physically that living seems to no longer be worthwhile. For example, in the Northern Territory of Australia, where euthanasia has been legalized, some Australians who request euthanasia do so because of shame over loss of bodily functions or deterioration in physical appearance (Street & Kissane, 2001). And there are instances when a person who was denied euthanasia committed suicide, possibly because the shamefulness of the deteriorated body was intolerable.

There are cultures where one may come to feel shame at being worthless by cultural standards and see no way out of the situation except to kill oneself. For example, in rural areas of the People's Republic of China, suicide rates for women can be quite high, and possibly this is in part due to a lack of social and economic opportunities. This lack creates conditions of intolerable pain and shame (Shiang, Barron, Xiao, Blinn, & Tam, 1998). Among the Orokaiva of New Guinea, young women in a community were committing suicide in a context in which young men of the community had gone far away to find work and were rumored to engage in infidelities there (Sharpe, 1987), which, in a sense, made the young women feel the shame of being worthless by the standards of the young men of their culture.

There are cultures where family conflict can be so shameful and so beyond hope of remediation that people choose to escape it by committing suicide. In the Micronesian island group of Truk, suicides are common and are often linked to anger and shame about family conflict, with suicide being an extreme expression of a cultural pattern of withdrawal from conflict (Hezel, 1987). Also Trukese suicide is a way of restoring a damaged reputation and protesting one's innocence (Hezel, 1984), both of which may be in reaction to a situation that causes a person to feel shame.

There are cultures where one is expected to commit suicide if shamed, but it is not clear that the person who was supposedly shamed and who committed suicide felt shame or wanted to commit suicide. That is, sometimes the suicide may be an act of social obligation and of conforming to cultural standards. One example, though it is outdated, is that some Korean women in the past were expected to kill themselves if they experienced the shame of rape, and in fact women were expected to carry a dagger to quickly dispatch themselves should they be raped (Yang & Rosenblatt, 2001). Women who committed suicide may not have wanted to and may not have even felt shame, but in the surrounding community and in the culture the women were defined as shamed and were expected to commit suicide.

Suicide in some cultures is an act of a person desperate to escape from the pain of having been lowered in the eyes of kin. Suicide might not be the only escape, but it is one way out. For the Maori of New Zealand, at least in the past, having been lowered in the eyes of one's kin group led a man to commit some desperate act such as suicide, revenge taking, or going into exile (Smith, 1981). Similarly, among the Bariba of Benin in West Africa, people said that suicide was preferable to continuing to exist in shame if one led troops into battle and they were killed, if one were a thief, if one were accused of a crime even if one did not commit it, if one had acted cowardly, or if one were a man whose wife committed adultery and she did not return after he sent her his severed finger (Sargent, 1984). However, Sargent, whose ethno-graphic account of the Bariba is cited at several places in this chapter, had no direct evidence of such incidents of suicide, so it is possible that the Bariba were linking suicide and shame at a metaphoric, rhetorical, or mythological level, rather than at the level of actual action. On the other hand, Sargent seemed to have had plenty of direct evidence that the Bariba were remarkably stoic in the face of physical and emotional pain, and so there was a sense that the loss of resistance to pain or to expressing pain, a loss of control, could be very shameful to a Bariba, and suicide was one way out of the shame. But then she also mentioned in passing two other responses to shame: (a) in the case of having been a thief one could migrate elsewhere, and (b) in the case of a man whose wife committed adultery, the man could diminish the value of the wife and of all women in his mind, so his wife's adultery was then not so shameful.

So far, in many of the examples of the link between shame and sui-cide, suicide has been seen to be entirely or in part an escape from shame. But there are cultures where suicide, while an escape, is also a way to make things difficult for others who caused the shame (in effect making them one's murderers). With the Kaliai of northwest New Britain, when suicide makes others one's murderers, the "murderers" must compensate the family of the person who committed suicide and they live in fear that they might be killed by vengeful relatives of the deceased (Counts, 1980). Besides, the suicide would remove the shame of the person committing suicide, by communicating to others how much the individual had been in pain and humiliated and wronged. Marshall (1979, pp. 78–79) observed a similar pattern in Micronesia of those who feel intense shame killing themselves in order to take revenge on those who they feel are responsible for their shame. Although in Micronesia, many of the revenge suicides are male, Counts said that around the world such suicides are more commonly women (1980, p. 336), and she argued that the reason for this is that in many of those societies women are relatively powerless and do not have other recourse to deal with their having been shamed. Also, in a sense, revenge suicide can be a way of shaming those whom one sees as responsible for one's own shame (Counts, 1980, p. 337, citing Strathern, 1968, 1972, pp. 142–152, who was writing about a New Guinea culture). Similarly, Meng (2002) has written about the suicide of a rural woman in China, whose death exerted revenge on her husband and in-laws, and included in that was that her mother-in-law had to live with the shame of being perceived in the community as having caused the suicide.

According to Counts (1980), shame-linked suicide among the Kaliai is culturally shaped. That is, there are culturally defined and expected ways to kill oneself. So even in the depths of shame and despair, one generally follows a culturally approved path. And if one is committing suicide as vengeance against others who have shamed one, it may be extremely important that everyone in the community understand that one has committed suicide and why, and that is communicated during the suicide process.

Perhaps grief counselors rarely have the opportunity to work with a person from a culture different from the counselor's and whose cultural logic leads the person to be intending to commit suicide. (One can imagine that people from many cultures have no concept of counseling, that people feeling shame are not likely to want to talk to someone about their shame, and that if one's cultural logic pushes for suicide one would be intent on committing suicide rather on seeking professional help.) But assuming that someone from one of the cultures described in this section of this chapter comes to a grief counselor, there will be ethical issues for the counselor. The counselor may be pushed by professional and culturally based personal values to want to do the utmost to prevent the suicide, but it is also conceivable that the counselor may be pushed by respect for the other person's cultural value to understand the logic that leads to the person thinking of committing suicide. But let's say that the counselor decides to try to stop the person from committing suicide. Interventions with suicidal people are challenging, and cultural differences can add to the challenge. Here it may be especially crucial to understand the cultural meanings and contexts of the shame and the possible suicide. And as part of that, it may be very important to explore whether there are culturally appropriate alternatives to suicide, for example, apologies from someone who has shamed one or moving to a new community. Another possibility arises from the fact that many people on the planet are in a sense bicultural. For example, they may be Kaliai but also have picked up aspects of Christian religion that represent Protestant U.S. or British religious culture. If that is so, it may be possible to make the counseling a process of making the values of a person's alternative culture more salient. And part of that may be to elicit approaches from the point of view of a second culture to deal with a shaming situation, for example, prayer or some form of turning the other cheek.

A grief counselor working with someone who has lost a relative to what apparently was a shame-based suicide might do well to explore with the person what messages, if any, the person who committed suicide might have wanted to communicate to them with the suicide. The grief of someone who has lost a family member to shame-based suicide might have dimensions of acceptance, because the suicide might be seen as culturally proper, but the person may also be feeling guilt, anger, pain, shame, and an assortment of culturally unique feelings as a result of the suicide (Rosenblatt, 2008). As with all other instances of cross-cultural grief counseling, it could be a mistake for a counselor rooted in a culture alternative to that of the client to transfer her or his own cultural meanings and understandings to a client dealing with a shame-related suicide. Indeed, a useful part of the grief counseling might involve the process of eliciting from the client the culturally rooted meanings, understandings, and feelings related to the suicide death. For the grieving client, it is possible that the process of explaining her or his culture to the therapist will provide a certain emotional distance from the most toxic feelings and thoughts, and may also bring up culturally meaningful alternatives for understanding what has happened and for processing it.

SHAME CAN CAUSE THE PERSON WHO IS FEELING SHAME TO DIE BY PROCESSES OTHER THAN SUICIDE

In some cultures shame is seen as a cause of death. For example, among the Hopi a young woman who was raped and had an illegitimate baby as a result was said to have died from the shame of what happened (Brandt, 1954, p. 47). This was in a context where unmarried mothers feel so much shame that they avoid being in public and may even kill their babies (Brandt, 1954). The mechanism of death might have cultural meanings, for example, someone dies of not caring to live, dies of a broken heart, or dies because the future that is available is intolerable.

Providing grief counseling to someone who says a relative has not committed suicide but has died of shame, it might be useful to explore the client's understanding of what has happened. And in doing so, it might ordinarily be unhelpful to challenge the cultural understandings. The client's culture-based understandings are what they are, and often the best help one can provide is to accept the client's reality and work with the client in doing whatever might be culturally appropriate for the client in coming to terms with the death. In fact, with almost any client from any culture the grief counselor generally would do well to accept the client's account of how the death came about.

SHAME AND KILLING OTHERS

There are cultures in which feeling shame can be linked to wanting to kill others. Perhaps that is a widespread human phenomenon. For example, the so-called war on terror engaged in by the United States may so shame people in various countries that they are motivated to kill people from the United States (De Zulueta, 2006). But then the United States may carry out warfare in order to avoid shame (Armstrong, 2006). And of course the killing, mutilation, and other products of United States warfare may lead many in the United States to feel shame (Iyer, Schmader, & Lickel, 2007). If shame so underlies wanting to kill and the consequences of killing in the United States, that does not mean that the links of shame and killing others are cross-culturally universal. The dynamics underlying shame that can lead to killing, the psychological transformations produced by the killing, and cultural meanings given to shame and killing may vary enormously across cultures where there seems to be some kind of link of shame and killing others.

One of the anthropological classics dealing with the links of shame and killing is Rosaldo's (1983) account of Ilongot headhunting. Among the Ilongot of Northern Luzon in the Philippines, there are times when a man feels shame (or some other "weight" in the Ilongot emotional schema) and can feel the satisfaction of lifting the weight of the shame by killing someone. In particular, youth who feel the heavy weight of shame can reach lightness and joy through successful headhunting. Killing does not make shame go away, but it transforms the shame of being less than others into the shame of mature men, whose shame is linked with respect for kinsmen and community members, humility, and efforts to maintain good relationships with them despite feelings and events that could undermine the individual and those relationships.

There are also cultural instances when a family member seems to other family members (if not to the self) to have brought shame on the family, and family members will kill their relative to in some sense neutralize the shame. So-called honor killings throughout the Middle East illustrate this dynamic (e.g., Abou-Zeid, 1966, writing about Egyptian Bedouins). But the killing (and the threat of it) can be seen to be as much about male control and lack of options and protections for women as it is about shame and restoring honor (Shalhoub-Kevorkian, 1997). Perhaps that is why it is not unrealistic to imagine a grief counselor dealing with grief and shame of a family member whose sister, daughter, or other female relative has been killed by one or more male members of the family. Although the killers may feel that they have reduced the shame of the family, others may feel that the killing itself is shameful, but they may also feel shame that they feel this way. Of course, in any counseling situation where shame is involved, a person may be reluctant to talk about what is shameful, but it is possible that the reluctance is even greater in a situation of multiple shame—shame over what the woman relative allegedly did, shame over the killing of the woman, shame over not conforming to the killers' sense of what is honorable, and perhaps shame over the arrest and prison sentence of the killers. Plus, if the counseling involves use of a translator, there may be additional shame in having a culturally knowledgeable translator know what has gone on and what one has done. However, one thing that may help to make the grief counseling effective in dealing with multiple shame issues is that the client already has two realities—the reality that says honor killing is proper and the reality that says it is not (because honor killing is a crime in all countries where it occurs). Effective counseling might focus on the dual realities and make it the starting place for talk about feelings, beliefs, relationships, the past, and the future. In some ways, working with issues that way may get around the ways that shame may make the person reluctant to talk and also may make the person stuck in dealing with the issues. That is, focusing on the dual realities may make the issue one of how can you resolve the conflict, not how can you function while feeling so much pain.

In the Middle East, South Asia, and Southeastern Europe there are a number of cultures in which a child conceived out of wedlock brings great shame to the mother and her family, and in some instances the shame is addressed in part by killing the child (e.g., Dumencic, Matuzalem, Marjanovic, Pozgain, & Ugljarevic, 2006). There are even regular news reports of such killing in the United States. Who might be the client of a grief counselor in such instances? It might be the mother, who might well have been the killer. It might be another family member. Here, too, there might be multiple levels of shame, shame at the unwanted and shameful pregnancy, shame as a result of the killing, shame at having events known to others, and so on. A challenge for counseling in such situations is that the publicity of the killing may so focus the counselor and others on the killing of the infant that grief and shame connected to the events are overlooked. But the heart of the matter in providing help may be to go there, and so grief counseling that acknowledges the pregnancy and infanticide and then turns to feelings of loss and shame connected to the events may be the path of greatest help.

THE CULTURAL CONTEXT OF THIS CHAPTER

How does the culture in which we write the essays in this volume make shame and its links with death, dying, and grief issues for scholarly examination? How does it make "shame" a thing that is so well defined that a group of scholars can write about it confidently as individuals and enough in concert so that it seems that we are writing about rather the same thing? In writing about shame and its links to dying, death, and grief across cultures, this chapter can be a contribution to this volume because the cross-cultural material can illuminate and lead to a sharpening of understandings coming from the English language and the culture(s) academics who write about grief and shame typically focus on. But it is also possible that the blurring, questions, and complexities that the cross-cultural material raises can lead to a tone of uncertainty and doubt that makes it more difficult for readers to think and speak with assurance about the nature of shame and its links to death, dying, and bereavement. One might ordinarily think of scholarly work leading to greater insight and depth, but what if this chapter led to readers who doubt and are less confident about what is true? If that is the outcome, I hope that it is a desirable outcome.

A chapter like this, and this entire book, could conceivably challenge and threaten culture-based ways of dealing with shame because readers are pushed to think about what they would rather not think about. Scheff (2003) argued that in everyday life in the United States (at least for dominant culture(s) in the country), shame is a taboo topic. That makes sense. One can think, for example, of the apparent obliviousness of many White people in the United States to the ways the legal system, government policy making, and many other aspects of the culture are set up to privilege White people in relationship to others (see Rosenblatt, 2009, for an overview of this literature). To the extent that White people have some inkling of the system that advantages them, it makes sense that for that reason alone shame might be a rather taboo topic. Many people might be disinclined to focus on and think about what makes them feel uncomfortable. Similarly, being a citizen in a country that arguably has been responsible for millions of deaths in recent decades around the world from war and economic oppression, again it would not be surprising that shame is a relatively taboo topic in the United States, because there is potentially great shame in thinking about the death and misery the country has produced around the world. Similarly, with a government responsible for torture and assassination around the world, it might be best to avoid the topic of shame. If shame were a topic that all in the United States talked about openly, fluently, and with insight, there might be enormous pain to deal with. One is reminded of the Germans following World War II who avoided facing the shame of what they, their relatives and neighbors, and their government had done during World War II (see, for example, Hecker, 1993).

But there are other cultural contexts for this chapter to consider. One is the cultural idea of healing, and another is the cultural idea of going to a professional healer to be healed. In the culture that gives rise to and publishes a book like this, it makes sense to think of people healing in some sense from emotional pain connected to loss and shame. And in this culture there are paid professionals who perform such healing. However, in many other cultures, there is not the concept of healing from emotional pain and there are no paid professionals or even unpaid healers whose job it is to help people to heal from or deal with emotional pain. So a grief counselor who wants to help people who do not have the concept of healing or the concept of a psychological healer must do considerable teaching with a person who may seem to need healing and who comes from a culture where the healing concept does not make sense and there are no healers. The grief counselor must teach the person the basics of how to understand what healing might be and why it might be necessary and also to teach the person the basics of what grief counselors do. Those are not impossible tasks, but they are difficult, and part of the difficulty is that the grief counselor must understand the other person's culture well enough to know how to make what the counselor wants to say be meaningful and persuasive to the person.

FURTHER THERAPEUTIC IMPLICATIONS

One issue this chapter raises is about the desirability of privileging a counselor's culture-based realities in relationship to the client's culture-based realities. If a client's cultural background leads to different meanings or implications for shame, might it better for the counselor to learn from the client what the client's realities are, rather than to assume the counselor's own realities are the only correct ones? And if the counselor must learn what the client understands about shame, death, dying, and grief, that puts a premium on the counselor's learning processes. Learning from a

client might have its therapeutic elements for the client, but still the flow
of counseling sessions in which the counselor is working at acquiring sufficient cultural knowledge from the client might be quite different from
standard counseling sessions. And in the case of learning about shame
and what is connected to it there can be great difficulty in drawing a client into discussing what is so painful and what might even be a matter
that could lead to flight or suicide. However, it may be easier for a counselor who is a cultural outsider to draw out shame material from a client,
whose shame might be most intensely and overwhelmingly experienced
in relationship to a cultural insider.

Some therapists specialize in working with people from a particular culture other than their own. For example, I know European
American therapists who specialize in working with the local American
Indian community or with recent immigrants from Mexico and Central
America. Perhaps such specializations are partly a matter of acquiring
a reputation in a community, and that brings one many referrals. But
cultural specialization is almost certainly also about how much one
needs to know to be an effective counselor with people from a particular culture. If it takes years of learning to become well grounded in
what is initially an unfamiliar culture, there should be no surprise that
some counselors have a cultural specialization. On the other hand, we
desperately need counselors who are generalists in working with people from other cultures. There are so many cultures in the world and
there are so many cultures where the opportunity to work with people
needing grief counseling would be so unlikely that the rare person
from the culture who needs help almost certainly would have to have
help from a generalist. Practically speaking, it would be impossible
for there not to be a need for some people to be generalists in working
with diverse clients.

Of course, being a counselor who works with clients from a diversity
of cultures on shame issues linked to death could be quite challenging.
There are cultures, Bali, for example, where it is shameful to reveal your
inner feelings and thoughts to anyone other than close family members
(Wikan, 1990, p. 49). Trying to provide therapeutic help to someone
whose cultural background demands that one be closed would be difficult (see, for example, the various essays in Heimannsberg & Schmidt,
1993). But there are ways to indirectly get to some of what is inside or
to use one's cultural ignorance as a resource. In fact, modern counseling
has many techniques for clients to communicate about the unspeakable,
including projective tests, art therapy, dance therapy, sand tray therapy,
play therapy, and bibliotherapy.

Then there are the special problems of multicultural couples and
families. Members of multicultural couples and families can challenge

one another with their different ideas of emotionality linked to death, dying, and grief, and so of course they can challenge a grief counselor who is potentially in a position to help them. Imagine a couple in which one partner comes from a culture in which it is shameful that she lived far from her dying mother, did not provide care for her dying mother, and was not even able to be present at the funeral, and the other partner comes from a culture in which it is perfectly acceptable to live far from a mother, to not provide care in the mother's dying, and not to be able to attend the funeral. Can a counselor help each of them to understand and accept the other? And can a counselor do it without taking sides and alienating one of them if the counselor comes from and is embedded in the culture of the other? One possibility is for the counselor to inform and model for one partner how to understand and accept the other partner by asking good questions about the person's cultural obligations and feelings and accepting what is told in a respectful way.

It is also possible that working with culturally different clients about issues at the intersection of shame, and dying, death, and grief can make one a better counselor with people from one's own culture. It may, for example, lead to habits of more careful questioning, more caution about making assumptions, and more openness to client realities in ways that could benefit any client.

Finally there is the possibility of a grief counselor becoming open to many ways of healing and dealing with death and grief as they link to shame that are outside the scope of what is conventionally understood as therapeutic practice. Although conventional thinking and therapeutic ethics make therapy about helping the client, the helper can be helped by providing therapy (Rosenblatt, in press). Working with diverse clients can be an educational experience that can make a grief counselor a better counselor and can also produce personal transformations of many sorts for the counselor, including becoming open to diverse ways of understanding and dealing with difficulties in her or his personal life. Imagine the possible professional and personal transformation that could come from working with clients from a culture where the way to heal from shame connected to loss is to hold a cleansing ceremony in which one is symbolically cleansed of shame. Or imagine the possible professional and personal transformation from working with clients from a culture in which one can move toward something like recovery from shameful neglect of a dying parent by carrying out a ritual in which one asks for forgiveness from the spirit of the deceased parent. A counselor may learn about such rituals, may attend them, may learn how to carry some of them out, and may come to feel personally open to the healing from such rituals in her or his personal life.

REFERENCES

Abou-Zeid, A. (1966). Honour and shame among the Bedouins of Egypt. In J. G. Peristiany (Ed.), *Honour and shame: The values of Mediterranean society* (pp. 243–259). Chicago: University of Chicago Press.

Armstrong, M. K. (2006). The connection between shame and war. *Journal of Psychohistory, 34,* 35–42.

Berndt, R. M. (1962). *Excess and restraint: Social control among a New Guinea mountain people.* Chicago: University of Chicago Press.

Brandt, R. B. (1954). *Hopi ethics: A theoretical analysis.* Chicago: University of Chicago Press.

Counts, D. A. (1980). Fighting back is not the way: Suicide and the women of Kaliai. *American Ethnologist, 7,* 332–351.

Dalziell, R. (1999). *Shameful autobiographies: Shame in contemporary Australian autobiographies and culture.* Melbourne, Australia: Melbourne University Press.

De Zulueta, F. (2006). Terror breeds terrorists. *Medicine, Conflict and Survival, 22,* 13–25.

Dumencic, B., Matuzalem, E., Marjanovic, K., Pozgain, I., & Ugljarevic, J. (2006). Infanticide in eastern Croatia. *Collegium Antropologicum, 30,* 437–442.

Hahn, W. K. (2009). Shame. In W. O'Donohue & S. R. Graybar (Eds.), *Handbook of contemporary psychotherapy* (pp. 303–320). Thousand Oaks, CA: Sage.

Hecker, M. (1993). Family reconstruction in Germany: An attempt to confront the past. In B. Heimannsberg & C. J. Schmidt (Eds.), *Collective silence: German identity and the legacy of shame* (pp. 73–93). San Francisco: Jossey-Bass.

Hezel, F. X. (1984). Cultural patterns in Trukese suicide. *Ethnology, 23,* 193–206.

Hezel, F. X. (1987). Truk suicide epidemic and social change. *Human Organization, 46,* 283–291.

Heimannsberg, B., & Schmidt, C. J. (1993). *The collective silence: German identity and the legacy of shame.* San Francisco: Jossey-Bass.

Hsu, H. T., Kahn, D. L., & Hsu, M. (2002). A single leaf orchid: Meaning of a husband's death for Taiwanese widows. *Ethos, 30,* 306–326.

Iyer, A., Schmader, T., & Lickel, B. (2007). Why individuals protest the perceived transgressions of their country: The role of anger, shame, and guilt. *Personality and Social Psychology Bulletin, 33,* 572–587.

Kilborne, B. (1992). Field of shame: Anthropologists abroad. *Ethos, 20,* 230–253.

Kittikorn, N., Street, A. F., & Blackford, J. (2006). Managing shame and stigma: Case studies of female carers of people with AIDS in southern Thailand. *Qualitative Health Research*, *16*, 1286–1301.

Leys, R. (2007). *From guilt to shame: Auschwitz and after*. Princeton, NJ: Princeton University Press.

Li, L., Lin, C., Wu, Z., Wu, S., Rotheram-Borus, M. J., Detels, R., & Jia, M. (2007). Stigmatization and shame: Consequences of caring for HIV/AIDS patients in China. *AIDS Care*, *19*, 258–263.

Lindisfarne, N. (1998). Gender, shame, and culture: An anthropological perspective. In P. Gilbert & B. Andrews (Eds.), *Shame: Interpersonal behavior, psychopathology, and culture* (pp. 246–260). New York: Oxford University Press.

Macdonald, C. J.-H. (2007). *Uncultural behavior: An anthropological investigation of suicide in the southern Philippines*. Honolulu: University of Hawaii Press.

Marshall, M. (1979). *Weekend warriors: Alcohol in a Micronesian culture*. Palo Alto, CA: Mayfield.

Maschio, T. (1992). To remember the faces of the dead: Mourning and the full sadness of memory in Southwestern New Britain. *Ethos*, *20*, 387–420.

Meng, L. (2002). Rebellion and revenge: The meaning of suicide of women in rural China. *International Journal of Social Welfare*, *11*, 300–309.

Palmer, G. B., Bennett, H., & Stacey, L. (1999). Bursting with grief, erupting with shame: A conceptual and grammatical analysis of emotion-tropes in Tagalog. In G. B. Palmer & D. J. Occhi (Eds.), *Languages of sentiment: Cultural constructions of emotional substrates* (pp. 171–200). Amsterdam, The Netherlands: John Benjamins.

Pentikainen, J. (1983). Voluntary death and single battle: Suicidal behavior and Arctic world views. *Psychiatria Fennica*, (Suppl. 1983), 123–136.

Rasmussen, S. J. (2007). Revitalizing shame: Some reflections on "Changing idioms of shame: Expressions of disgrace and dishonour in the narratives of Turkish women living in Denmark." *Culture and Psychology*, *13*, 231–242.

Rosaldo, M. Z. (1983). The shame of headhunters and the autonomy of self. *Ethos*, *11*, 135–151.

Rosenblatt, P. C. (2008). Grief across cultures: A review and research agenda. In M. Stroebe, R. O. Hansson, H. Schut, & W. Stroebe (Eds.), *Handbook of bereavement research and practice: Advances in theory and intervention* (pp. 207–222). Washington, DC: American Psychological Association.

Rosenblatt, P. C. (2009). *Shared obliviousness in family systems*. Albany, NY: State University of New York Press.

Rosenblatt, P. C. (2010). *Racism comes home: The impact of racism on African American families in novels by African American authors*. Unpublished manuscript, University of Minnesota.

Rosenblatt, P. C. (in press). Providing therapy can be therapeutic for the therapist. *American Journal of Psychotheraphy*.

Rosenblatt, P. C., & Nkosi, B. C. (2007). South African Zulu widows in a time of poverty and social change. *Death Studies, 31*, 67–85.

Rosenblatt, P. C., Walsh, R. P., & Jackson, D. A. (1976). *Grief and mourning in cross-cultural perspective*. New Haven, CT: Human Relations Area Files Press.

Sargent, C. (1984). Between death and shame: Dimensions of pain in Bariba culture. *Social Science and Medicine, 19*, 1299–1304.

Scheff, T. J. (2003). Shame in self and society. *Symbolic Interaction, 26*, 239–262.

Shalhoub-Kevorkian, N. (1997). Tolerating battering: Invisible methods of social control. *International Review of Victimology, 5*, 1–21.

Sharpe, J. (1987). "Shame" in Papua, New Guinea. *Group Analysis, 20*, 43–48.

Shiang, J., Barron, S., Xiao, S. Y., Blinn, R., & Tam, W.-C. C. (1998). Suicide and gender in the People's Republic of China, Taiwan, Hong Kong, and Chinese in the U.S. *Transcultural Psychiatry, 35*, 235–251.

Shweder, R. A. (2003). Toward a deep cultural psychology of shame. *Social Research, 70*, 1109–1130.

Smith, J. (1981). Self and experience in Maori culture. In P. Heelas & A. Lock (Eds.), *Indigenous psychologies: The anthropology of self* (pp. 145–159). New York: Academic Press.

Stadler, J. J. (2003). The young, the rich, and the beautiful: Secrecy, suspicion and discourses of AIDS in the South African lowveld. *African Journal of AIDS Research, 2*, 127–139.

Strathern, M. (1968). Popokl: The question of morality. *Mankind, 6*, 553–562.

Strathern, M. (1972). *Women in between: Female roles in a male world, Mount Hagen, New Guinea*. London: Seminar.

Street, A. F., & Kissane, D. W. (2001). Discourses of the body in euthanasia: Symptomatic, dependent, shameful and temporal. *Nursing Inquiry, 8*(3), 162–172.

Turner, W. L., Wallace, B. R., Anderson, J. R., & Bird, C. (2004). The last mile of the way: Understanding caregiving in African American families at the end-of-life. *Journal of Marital and Family Therapy, 30*, 427–438.

Wikan, U. (1990). *Managing turbulent hearts: A Balinese formula for living*. Chicago: University of Chicago Press.

Yang, S., & Rosenblatt, P. C. (2001). Shame in Korean families. *Journal of Comparative Family Studies, 32*, 361–375.

Languages of Art

CHAPTER 8

Mask of Shame, Mask of Death

Some Speculations on the Shame of Death

Hilary Clark

In the scandal over the American military's abuse of prisoners at Abu Ghraib, photographs were the primary evidence: indeed, it seems that these abuses were performed for the eye of the camera. Images of naked Iraqis in humiliating positions or dead circulated the Internet, and a handful of these became icons: Private Lynndie England with a naked prisoner on a dog leash; snarling dogs threatening a naked, cowering prisoner; a pair of jokers, grinning broadly, giving the thumbs-up next to a human pyramid of naked buttocks and plastic-hooded heads ("The Abu Ghraib Pictures," 2004). "Shame and torture have a secret intimacy," John Limon suggests, and we saw their "coalescence at Abu Ghraib" (2007, p. 556). The cruelty or torture particularly involved nakedness and exposure, particularly exposure of genitals, to a camera—the archetypal shame situation in a culture where nakedness is deemed to be shameful.

In perhaps the most notorious image, however, the prisoner is not naked: standing on a rickety box with his arms extended and attached to electrical wires—he has been told that if he falls off the box, he will be electrocuted—the man is dressed in a blanket and masked with a black hood (Figure 8.1). His face and most of his body are covered, but this image of the hooded man records a shame just as terrible, if not more so, than that of the naked, sexually humiliated prisoners in the other images. Why is this so? Is it because we are looking at someone who

FIGURE 8.1 Abu Ghraib prisoner.

FIGURE   8.2 London Underground   bombing victim.   Photo   credit: Gareth Cattermole/Getty Images News. Copyright Getty Images. Reprinted with permission.

must be experiencing the terror of death? Is it because his arms are outstretched as if nailed to a cross? Is it because the man's face is masked, his head covered with what looks like the hood of a hanging man?

A figure of shame, the hooded man in the Abu Ghraib image is also a figure of death. In this chapter I will explore some relations between masks and shame, and masks and death, in order to think about the intimate relation of shame and death: shame's deathliness and death's shamefulness, a relation captured in the word *mortification*. That childhood abuse has been termed *soul murder* (Shengold, 1999) also suggests the proximity of toxic shame and death. And it is in the mask that we find this proximity most potently figured.

Another famous news image, another iconic mask: A female victim of the July 7, 2005, London Underground bombings is being helped to walk by a young medic wearing a white jacket and blue surgical gloves (Figure 8.2). With both hands, she is pressing to her face a white burn mask. In the days following the bombings, this image appeared in many newspapers under headlines like "Al-Qa'eda Brings Terror to the Heart of London" (*Daily Telegraph*, 2005; also see "Burn Mask Photo," 2005). The mask has a hole cut for the mouth, a slit for the nose; the eyes should have holes, but they have not yet been punched out, so the mask has blank or unused eyes. The face in the photo looks like the white-painted face of a mime, or the wrapped face of a mummy, registering the skull beneath. Like the Iraqi prisoner under the black hood, the woman under the mask is both present and absent; the mask has been substituted for the face. We can only imagine the damaged face beneath.

It is telling, I think, that both mask images I have mentioned set off a search for the identity of the real person beneath the mask. In the case of the woman in the burn mask, within a few days of the bombings newspapers were carrying stories identifying the woman's name and her profession (barrister). A story in the *Daily Mail* emphasized her pluckiness and good cheer despite her burns and her mother's death the month before

("Tragedy of the Woman," 2005). The search for the Iraqi prisoner under the black hood involved a bizarre twist: a man came forward claiming to be that prisoner; he had even had his business card stamped with the famous image. But he was eventually found to be an imposter—wearing another mask, as it were. However, the imposter had been a prisoner at Abu Ghraib and had endured similar abuse ("Cited as Symbol," 2006). In both cases, the need to ascertain the correct identity of the person behind the mask—to the exclusion of all the other nameless wounded and traumatized—is symptomatic of the fear that masks inspire: we cannot see what is behind them, but sense it may be something terrible, or worse, death itself. In both images, death is very near: dead Iraqi prisoners, bruised and bound, packed in ice; dead London commuters retrieved from the depths of the Underground. In both, shame is implicit in the exposure of these terrible images, via the Internet and newspapers, to the probing eyes of millions.

In *The Mask of Shame*, Léon Wurmser asks, "What is the real meaning of masking?" (1994, p. 302). Noting the traditional use of masks both to represent the dead and, in carnivals and similar contexts, to ridicule or shame, he asks: "How can we account for this close connection between death and shame? Can it be that the shaming by masks is, paradoxically, the mask for shaming death itself?" (p. 302). The latter question could be suggesting that shaming by masks hides (is a mask for) "shaming death itself," that is, a (shameless) shaming or rejection of death. At the same time, the question could be suggesting that shaming by masks hides (is a mask for) our shaming *by* death—a mask to hide our inescapable mortality. Masks are objects of deep anxiety and fascination—ritualistic objects across many cultures and over human history—that both manifest death and disguise it through laughter or contempt: "In short, the anxiety about the uncanniness of the dead and of death ... is defended against by ridicule and returns as punishment in the form of degradation" (Wurmser, 1994, p. 305). We could not find a better analysis of the shaming and degradation of the Iraqi prisoners at Abu Ghraib: a grotesque pantomime of omnipotence, a shaming (through feminizing or bestializing) of the Other that would be masking an "unmanly" fear of death, inadmissible in the military culture. To pursue Wurmser's insight further, recalling the media image of the white burn mask, one might argue that the public anxiety about bomb attacks and shame at the inability to foresee or forestall violent death found its focus in this white mummy mask—which was not, however, the target for ridicule or abuse. Arguably, the identification of the (white) face beneath the white mask—and the healing properties of the burn mask itself—deflected the fear of death, as it so often *is* deflected, into maudlin sentiment.

Death wears a mask, or at least a hood, in conventional images of the Grim Reaper. I remember as a child shrinking back in terror with Scrooge when, in the old Alastair Sim movie, he cowered before the Ghost of Christmas Future—black-hooded, with no face—pointing to Scrooge's grave. Violent death often arrives as a masked figure: a robber, a high school gunman, a sniper, an executioner. Personal identity is not an issue, or is so only after the impersonal exchange of the killing. And Wurmser reminds us that masks cover not only murder but also ritualized humiliation such as rape and plunder in wartime: "Endless indeed are the forms of humiliation the masked troop engages in with impunity" (1994, p. 302). Even in the benign, commercialized territory of North American Halloween, where masks cover children's candy-sticky faces, death appears at the door in the form of skeletons, ghosts, and ghouls—the more horrible and decaying, the more fun.

The mask of death speaks to the need both to show death and to hide (from) it—to hide from the eyes of our victims, to cover over our animal vulnerability to wounding and extinction. The impulse to cover the dead crosses cultures, even as the impulse is countered by traditions such as (ritually circumscribed) "viewings." Martha Nussbaum (2004) suggests that the earliest shame arises out of the inevitable frustration of the infant's boundless narcissism, and this "primitive shame" can persist, a "painful emotion grounded in the recognition of our own non-omnipotence and lack of control" (p. 182). The shame of death persists—it is, perhaps, especially acute—in Western medical–technological culture where life has been extended (indefinitely, with the prospect of cloning), a culture in which death and disease are enemies against which we fight valiant metaphorical battles (Sontag, 1990, pp. 63–67).

A mask that is explicitly both the manifestation of a dead face and its replacement or "cover" is the death mask: a representation of the face of a person who has died made by molding onto it a material such as plaster or wax. Although death masks were made in the West prior to the 19th century, the interest in phrenology at this time drove the making and collecting of a great number of masks of both celebrated personages and criminals (Gibson, 1985). Literary scholars, for example, can gaze upon the death mask of John Keats, Samuel Taylor Coleridge, Henry James, or James Joyce, seeing imprinted on it the features of the dead face, its final expression down to the last eyelash and wrinkle. Due to its intimate contact with the dead face, the mask, as one looks at it, could be the dead man himself; after all, both are dead material. The effect is unpleasantly intimate; the viewer feels like a voyeur, ashamed yet fascinated at looking.

FIGURE 8.3 James Joyce mask, three-quarters profile. Image courtesy of the James Joyce Museum, Dublin, Ireland.

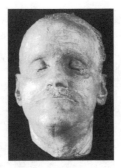

FIGURE 8.4 James Joyce mask, full face. Image courtesy of the James Joyce Museum, Dublin, Ireland.

James Joyce's death mask can be found at the James Joyce Museum in Sandymount, Dublin. The images available online include one of the mask full face and one of the mask in three-quarters profile (Figure 8.3 and Figure 8.4). Simply by looking at the mask from these different angles, I find an uncanny shift from life to death. The latter image could be taken for a photograph of a living man: the hair of the mask is a little stiff, certainly, and the eyes closed in sleep—but pensively, a slight smile playing on the lips. Any blemishes are those of age, those of the care-worn genius. The full-face image is another matter. Here, the mask looks like a dead face: rigid, rough, granular. The eyelids are sealed shut. The half-smile from this angle looks defiant, like a grimace. This mask could *not* be mistaken for the dapper Joyce of the famous photographs. One wonders which face is the uncanniest: the one that looks like it could be alive, just sleeping, or the one that has crossed over and become inert material?

An image of Henry James's life mask, held at the Houghton Library at Harvard University, brings together both this lifelikeness and this inert otherness (Figure 8.5).* The photo is a close-up, so we can see every pore and freckle of the skin; the lips are slightly parted, as though the face is about to speak. However, the image is quite shocking insofar as it appears as if brittle paper patches have been pasted over what seem to be unnaturally protruding eyes. Indeed, as Andrew Cutting points out, we *are* looking at patches, which were placed over James's eyes before the plaster was applied: "These are very unusual in a death mask, as the plaster is usually applied directly over the closed eyelids so as to reveal, in the finished sculpture, their every expressive wrinkle and contour" (2005, p. 71). The latter method was used in the case of Joyce's mask, with the result that the eyes, even closed, have

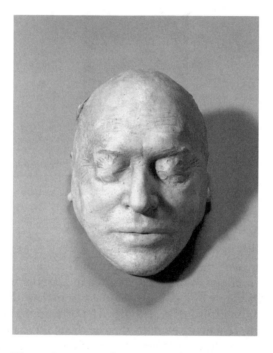

FIGURE 8.5 Henry James mask. Reprinted with the permission of the Houghton Library, Harvard University (library call number *45Z-1a).

---

* The Houghton Library refers to James's mask as a life mask. Indeed, it was sometimes the custom to make a mask of a living person's face. Andrew Cutting, however, refers to James's mask as a death mask. Whether James was living or dead when the mask was made, it is a deathly object.

expression. In contrast, the eyes of the James mask look wounded, like the blinded eyes of Oedipus; masking the eyes—creating two layers of mask—the patches prevent us "from seeing the most intimate signs of James's personality" (Cutting, 2005, p. 72). As shame is associated with covered or downcast the eyes, the shame response "stand[ing] in the same relation to looking and smiling as silence stands to speech" (Tomkins, 1995, p. 134), James's mask signifies shame in death, the shame *of* death.

In a short essay on James's death mask, biographer Lyndall Gordon (2004) describes her own first encounter with the mask at the Houghton Library, and she meditates on the meaning of the experience. Suggesting at the outset that biography is a shameful enterprise—that what "we [biographers] do is morally indefensible" in its "prying and determined curiosity"(p. 1)—Gordon acknowledges that she never felt this way while reading private writings unintended for her eyes, even knowing James's own phrase for the biographer, "the posthumous exploiter" (as quoted in Gordon, 2004, p. 5). It took her encounter with James's death mask to bring her to this conclusion. Acknowledging that she had some qualms about viewing the mask, Gordon describes the effect of lifting the lid of the box containing it, and looking in; oddly, she does not mention the patched eyes:

> It was like looking down into a grave. I saw a white face, thinner than in life but shockingly lifelike, as though the eyes might open at any moment and look at you.... As, transfixed, I stared into that bared face, I felt horribly intrusive. ... I thought uneasily of his late tale "The Real Right Thing" where the ghost of a writer appears to a biographer ... and bars his way. (pp. 2–4)

More acutely than other masks, the molded death mask in its nakedness—simultaneously both the man and something other—forces the viewer to experience the proximity of life and death, of the drive to know and shameless voyeurism.

The vogue for the making of plaster death masks was only one manifestation of an association of masks with death and death rites that goes back to the beginnings of human culture. For instance, masks have been buried with the dead, identifying that person; in Ancient Egyptian rites, where corpses were mummified, death masks covered the wrapped face in the tomb, "ensuring [the] spirit an everlasting life" in the underworld (Nunley & McCarthy, 1999, pp. 77–78). Sometimes masks were representations of gods like Osiris, the god of the underworld. Sometimes burial masks seem to have been portraits of the dead, however stylized, as in the golden death masks of the Qidan in China (Nunley & McCarthy,

1999, p. 306).* The most basic death mask was the human skull itself—
for example, the skull of an ancestor or an enemy. A striking example is
a Mixtec funerary mask made of a skull with a mosaic inlay of turquoise
and mother-of-pearl.† The decoration is on the face; the back of the skull
is bare. The eye sockets are filled in but the nose hole is not, and the jaw
gapes open. A few discolored teeth remain.

Wurmser remarks that "there is an archetypal relation between …
shame and mask. The mystery deepens when we read that masks originally represented the dead who come back asking for justice and putting
the living on trial" (1994, p. 302). The mask figures the revenant; it
covers the unthinkable face of one who cannot bear the light of day, one
who, like the ghost of Hamlet's father, is "[d]oom'd for a certain term
to walk the night" (act 1, scene 5, line 10), seeking justice and recognition from the living. Masks and masquerade have been used in funerary
rites and in initiatory rites involving ancestors. If the spirits of the dead
live on, they need to be remembered and if necessary appeased. They
may also need to be helped to reach their new state, out of respect but
also to ensure the boundaries between living and dead are maintained.
Melanesian masked dancers, for instance, would wear masks represent-
ing the deceased (Figure 8.6), and a type of pantomime would be played
out, in which the spirits would leave the living: funerary rituals would
"ensure that these spiritual elements no longer wander in the world of
the living but arrive at the place … that must be theirs" (Pernet, 1992,
p. 99). Those spirits of the deceased who are not given these rites might
become resentful and unstable, presenting a risk to the social order
(Pernet, 1992, p. 99). In these rites, reverence for the dead coexists with
fear.

To shame the dead is thus to invite disaster. The desecration of the
dead as a form of revenge is usually thought to be a deeply shameful
act. Nonetheless, even while masks are used to ensure that boundaries
are established and that the dead (and the living) receive due respect,
we know that masks are also used to hide behind when violating these
limits; they can be a symbol of shameless evil. (One thinks of the white
hoods of the Ku Klux Klan, for example.) The need to shame death and
the need to revere the dead are both motives for masking. As Wurmser
writes in concluding *The Mask of Shame*, "Masking, understood as a
defense against the fear of death, shames death by ridicule, but it also
impersonates the uncanny force of the dead ancestors—the heroes—and
vanquishes the fear by identification" (1994, p. 307). Impersonating

---

* Liao dynasty, 907–1125 (Nunley & McCarthy, 1999, p. 306).
† Late Post-Classic period, 15th to early 16th century (Nunley & McCarthy, 1999, p. 306).

FIGURE 8.6 Melanesian mask. Copyright Otago Museum, Dunedin, New Zealand. Reprinted with permission.

or imitating the terrifying dead through masking is a form of "identification" that nonetheless creates the crucial (aesthetic) distance of representation—"it's just a mask"—and hence a sense of mastery.

Mastery is also at issue in thinking about the relation between masks and trauma. As imitations or repetitions, masks both represent the scene of trauma and, through their multiplication, act as a means of mastering it. As Freud points out in *Beyond the Pleasure Principle* (1920/1966–1974), in recounting his grandson's repeated reenactment of his mother's departure and return, the rehearsal of traumatic loss—however painful—is a way of gaining some control over it. Voluntary rehearsal of traumatic loss—in masking, as well as in literature and art—can be a defense against the uncanny, attempting to forestall or at

least defuse an involuntary return of the repressed in the form of flashbacks and hauntings. Funerary or mourning rituals in many cultures
seem to involve this carefully circumscribed and controlled reenactment
or representation as a gesture of mastery (in the current term, "closure").
In one culture, dancers and elaborately decorated masks of the ancestors; in another, plaster death masks, black mourning garb and prayers;
in another, teddy bears, votive candles and mountains of cellophane-
wrapped flowers—all of these symbols and rituals respond to a need
to limit the loss, cauterize the wound by (one might say) shamelessly
revisiting it instead of leaving it alone. All of these mourning "masks"
"chang[e] the shamefully exposed into the shameless exhibitor": all
defend against fear and the shrinking invisibility of shame through
"powerfully fascinating images, gestures, and music" (Wurmser, 1994,
p. 306), through representations and fictions—thus, in the very gesture
of reverence, "ironizing" our ghosts and "exposing [them] to ridicule"
(Freud, 1919/2003, p. 158). Yet despite such defenses, the ghosts return.
As Jeffrey Kauffman suggests, mourning in its ambivalence involves the
"conjunction of integration and dissociation"; the integration of death
into our lives can only be "gradual" and remains "incomplete" (1993,
p. 33). We integrate death by abjecting the dead, ensuring that they
"respect borders" (Kristeva, 1982, p. 4) and stay in their night world.

Earlier in this chapter, I suggested that the word *mortification*
indicates the intimate relation between shame and death: this word for
shame or humiliation can also denote the death of tissue (necrosis) or the
death of an extremity (gangrene).* Piece by piece, one "dies" of shame
as an emotional necrosis. Or one turns to stone: the mask represents the
petrification involved in both death (the corpse is a "stiff") and extreme
shame. The mask—"rigid, immobile, frozen"—imitates[†] the "rigidity
of shame" and the "rigor ... of death," rigor mortis (Wurmser, 1994,
p. 305). This kinship of death and shame in the mask "reflect[s the]
horrifying power that turns a living being into a spellbound, fascinated,
charmed puppet," a power "typically vested in the eye"—the evil or
shaming eye (Wurmser, 1994, p. 306).

This process of petrification or freezing also characterizes certain
symptoms of the severely traumatized, such as the shell-shocked WWI
soldiers whose symptoms—loss of speech and paralysis, limbs frozen
into particular positions, behaviors locked into repetitive patterns—
were studied by the psychoanalysts Sandor Ferenczi and Abram Kardiner

---

* *Oxford English Dictionary Online.* Retrieved December 3, 2009, from http://www.
  oed.com.
† Wurmser uses the word "counterfeit(s)," which has more negative connotations. The
  mask's frozen face is false currency; it is neither the red, downcast face of the shamed
  nor the disintegrating or absent face of the dead. Or is it both of these?

(Leys, 1996, p. 48). A traumatic event such as the nearby explosion of a shell, in breaking through the victim's psychic shield, acts like the evil eye; this horrific invasion of boundaries is as shaming as a rape. The detachment and emotional petrification that defend against further wounding are a kind of masking, a "death mask": "[T]he mask is thus ... the image of the traumatic *failure* of defense" (Leys, 1996, p. 63). If traumatic symptoms such as tics and numbness are, as Leys argues, mimetic in that they are "unconscious imitation[s] of, or emotional identification[s] with, the traumatic event" (1996, p. 59), they are nonetheless also antimimetic in that they are defenses *against* the (shaming) event: the symptom as a mask both reveals and conceals, split as it is "between the double connotation of mimesis and antimimesis that exemplifies the traumatic situation" (Leys, 1996, p. 63). The mask is thus "[s]imultaneously a representation of defense and of the failure of defense" (Leys, 1996, p. 63). Inadequate as it is, we wear it because we have always been, and always will be, shamed by our vulnerability to wounding and death.

Masks in popular culture are no less marked by these contradictions and paradoxes arising from the mask's association with shame and death. From the Lone Ranger to Spider-Man to rock bands like Kiss and Slipknot, the popular media are full of masked figures (usually young men) who are antihero outsiders, avengers, or in-your-face "shit disturbers."* Masked superheroes and masked supervillains are cult favorites in comic books, graphic novels, and Hollywood movies such as the *X-Men* and *Batman* series. Both heroes and villains are often survivors of a horrible accident or trauma, the heroes overcoming the past in fighting evil, the villains perpetuating it in their evil deeds. A particularly interesting example of a masked antihero is V in *V for Vendetta*, originally a comic-book series and graphic novel, made into a movie in 2005 (McTeigue, 2005). The story is set in a *1984*-type dystopian Britain. V is a vigilante character who, to do his work of resisting the totalitarian government and plotting to blow up the parliament buildings, wears a stylized smiling Guy Fawkes mask, greenish white, that makes him look rather like a male geisha. In his troubled past, V was tortured in a government detention center, and this trauma fuels his "personal vendetta" against the government and the evil doctors who tortured him.[†] With all the clichés, V's mask has the function Wurmser (1994, p.306)

---

* Kiss is a rock band whose members mask their faces with heavy face paint. See http://www.kissonline.com. Slipknot is a metal band whose members wear grotesque masks (like those in horror movies) while performing. See http://www.slipknot1.com.

† Details and phrase taken from http://www.imdb.com/title/tt0434409/. An image of V fighting off villains can be found at http://www.imdb.com/media/rm243964160/tt0434409.

points out: "The mask changes the shamefully exposed into the shame-less exhibitor"—V taking over the TV station to rally the citizens against the government—and defeats shame. As in the Abu Ghraib images, the shame of torture, the traumatic violation of privacy and dignity, is insep-arable from the shame of mortality itself. V's frozen smiling mask, like the plaster death mask, the white burn mask, and the black hood of Abu Ghraib—indeed, all masks, whether of shamer or of shamed—speak to our terrible vulnerability, "feel[ing ourselves] naked, defeated, alienated, lacking in dignity or worth" (Tomkins, 1995, p. 133).

Our most intimate sense of our selves is as bodies—desiring, hungry, diseased, in pain: "The obtrusive and insistent life of the body ... [is] par-ticularly associated with complex feelings of shame" (Adamson & Clark, 1999, p. 15). In the splitting of soul from body that has characterized Western religious and philosophical thinking for millennia, the body is "meat,"* just this side of death and decay. In both life and death, the body's shame is its naked vulnerability, its materiality. Like the grass, we wither and die; but the soul lives on, we say, defying death. The shame of death is in the gap between our immortal aspirations and our mortal imperfec-tions. Masks hide this shame—and, shameless, show it to the world.

REFERENCES

The Abu Ghraib pictures. (2004, May 3). *The New Yorker*. Retrieved January 26, 2008, from http://www.newyorker.com/archive/2004/05/03/slideshow_040503?viewall=true#showHeader

Adamson, J., & Clark, H. (Eds.). (1999). *Scenes of shame: Psychoanalysis, shame, and writing*. New York: SUNY Press.

Al-Qa'eda brings terror to the heart of London. (2005, July 12). *Daily Telegraph*. Retrieved March 2, 2008, from http://www.telegraph.co.uk/news/main.jhtml?xml=/news/2005/07/08/nbomb08.xml

Burn mask photo woman stable. (2005, July 9). *BBC News Online*. Retrieved March 2, 2008, from http://news.bbc.co.uk/2/hi/uk_news/4667825.stm

Cited as symbol of Abu Ghraib, man admits he is not in photo. (2006, March 18). *New York Times*. Retrieved March 2, 2008, from http://www.nytimes.com/2006/03/18/international/middleeast/18ghraib.html

---

* The body is referred to as "meat" throughout William Gibson's *Neuromancer* (1984), the novel that inspired the cyberpunk science fiction genre.

Cutting, A. (2005). *Death in Henry James*. New York: Palgrave Macmillan.

Freud, S. (1966–1974). Beyond the pleasure principle. In J. Strachey (Ed. & Trans.), *The Standard edition of the complete psychological works of Sigmund Freud*, Vol. XVIII (pp. 1–64). London: Hogarth Press. (Original work published 1920)

Freud, S. (2003). The uncanny. In D. McClintock (Trans.), *The uncanny* (pp. 121–162). London: Penguin Books. (Original work published 1919)

Gibson, I. I. J. M. (1985). Death masks unlimited. *British Medical Journal, 291*, 1785–1787.

Gordon, L. (2004). The death mask. In M. Bostridge (Ed.), *Lives for sale: Biographers' tales* (pp. 1–6). London: Continuum.

Kauffman, J. (1993). Dissociative functions in the normal mourning process. *Omega: Journal of Death and Dying 28*(1), 31–38.

Kristeva, J. (1982). *Powers of horror: An essay on abjection* (L. S. Roudiez, Trans.). New York: Columbia University Press.

Leys, R. (1996). Death masks: Kardiner and Ferenczi on psychic trauma. *Representations, 53*, 44–73.

Limon, J. (2007). "The shame of Abu Ghraib." *Critical Inquiry, 33*(3), 543–572.

McTeigue, J. (2005). *V for vendetta* [Motion picture]. United States: Warner Brothers.

Nunley, J., & McCarty, C. (1999). *Masks: Faces of culture*. New York: Harry N. Abrams.

Nussbaum, M. (2004). *Hiding from humanity: Disgust, shame, and the law*. Princeton, NJ: Princeton University Press.

Pernet, H. (1992). *Ritual masks: Deceptions and revelations* (L. Grillo, Trans.). Columbia: University of South Carolina Press.

Shengold, L. (1999). *Soul murder revisited: Thoughts about therapy, hate, love, and memory*. New Haven, CT: Yale University Press.

Sontag, S. (2001). *Illness as metaphor and AIDS and its metaphors*. New York: Picador. (Original works published 1978 and 1989).

Tomkins, S. (1995). Shame–humiliation and contempt–disgust. In E. K. Sedgwick & A. Frank (Eds.), *Shame and its sisters: A Silvan Tomkins reader* (pp. 133–178). Durham, NC: Duke University Press.

Tragedy of the woman behind the mask. (2005, July 11). *Daily Mail*. Retrieved February 3, 2008, from http://www.dailymail.co.uk/pages/live/articles/news/news.html?in_article_id=355379&in_page_id=1770

Wurmser, L. (1994). *The mask of shame*. Northvale, NJ: Jason Aronson. (Original work published 1981)

CHAPTER 9

Using the Representation of Grief and Shame in Contemporary Literature and Film to Train Mental Health Professionals

Maureen M. Underwood and Laura Winters

> There is a pain—so utter—
> It swallows substance up—
> Then covers the Abyss with Trance—
> So Memory can step
> Around—across—upon it—
> As one within a Swoon—
> Goes safely—where an open eye—
> Would drop Him—Bone by Bone.

—Emily Dickinson (1960)

There has been increasing awareness since September 11, 2001, of the necessity for mental health practitioners to understand the dynamics of grief and loss and to be able to translate that understanding into therapeutic interventions. Professional publications in the area of bereavement have increased and national continuing education seminars are available that address the rudiments of bereavement and its application to counseling.

Most mental health bereavement training incorporates both didactic content with some form of experiential exercises to reflect what is generally acknowledged to be the most effective and best-practice model for death education courses (Durlack & Reisenberg, 1991). While theoretical content addresses cognitive learning goals and cognitive attitudes on death-related issues, the experiential aspects of these programs generally focus on personal fears of death (Durlack, 1994). These experiential approaches may also be effective in preparing practitioners for what Neimeyer (1998) has described as the role of the grief counselor: "to act as a fellow traveler rather than consultant ... and walking alongside rather than leading the grieving individual along the unpredictable road to a new adaptation" (p. 881).

Helping the bereaved attain this "new adaptation" requires practitioners to empathically engage with the mourner's loss experience in both its practical and subtle dimensions. The practical aspects of adjustment to the changed environment occasioned by the loss can often be facilitated by referral to self-help support groups, where mourners exchange strategic advice and coping techniques. While some of the emotional processing of grieving may take place in these settings as well, mourners facing more complicated deaths like suicide or homicide often need skilled professional intervention.

Understanding the affective experience of the griever is obviously essential to acting in Neimeyer's (1998) "fellow traveler" role. Much has been written for practitioners about the broader emotional elements of the grieving process, starting with the early work of Kübler-Ross in the 1970s, and there is an increasing body of literature detailing the dimensions of more complicated mourning (Doka, 2002; Rando, 1993). Yet one of the more nuanced, significant, and underrepresented aspects of complicated grief resolution is the role of personal shame.

As Lester (1997) has noted, shame is sometimes viewed as a more developmentally primitive emotion than guilt. Whereas guilt includes a determination that personal behavior was wrong, shame contains the element of personal inadequacy or unworthiness (Lewis, 1992). As Kurtz (2007) notes, shame is a more subjective experience than guilt. Whereas the reference point of guilt is the line crossed, the rule that is broken, shame reflects the self-reproach of "the goal fallen short of, the limited self-ideal" (Kurtz, 2007, p. 7).

Experiences of shame expose the self to its most sensitive and intimate vulnerabilities. It can incorporate the perception of failure in a major social role and the anticipation of negative reactions from others (Breed, 1972). Ultimately, however, the significant exposure of shame is to one's own eyes (Kurtz, 2007). Its ultimate power is encapsulated in its need for emotional secrecy, to hide from not only the judgment of others but the judgment of the self as well. When attendant to grief, shame subverts bereavement by preoccupation with the failure of the self and distraction from the loss of the essential relationship between the deceased and the bereaved.

Another aspect of shame that is significant in understanding its relationship to grief is the fact that its genesis is in the death of the other, which is an involuntary, nonmoral lapse. This involuntary quality is concomitant with shame's focus on the deficiencies of the self (Breed, 1972, p. 24). At its base, death bears no relationship to personal power or moral transgression; it is the ultimate reflection of the limitation of the human condition. While the circumstances of an individual death may engender feelings of guilt—that there was something that should have been done to prevent the death—an aspect of shame resides at a more existential level, the effort to will what cannot be willed. Death is the ultimate reminder of one's personal helplessness, and shame-related grief subverts the opportunity to accept and embrace this essential reality.

OVERVIEW OF THE TRAINING PROGRAM

The events of September 11, 2001, created unprecedented needs in New York metropolitan communities for trained mental health professionals to address the bereavement and trauma recovery needs of survivors (Galea et al., 2002). The authors, who are professional colleagues, had collaborated with other local mental health providers to design a community-based intervention to provide needed bereavement support services. The Families' Going On After Loss program (Underwood, Milani, & Spinazzola, 2004), the result of that collaboration, was a series of psychoeducational support groups that was eventually expanded to include community members bereaved under other traumatic circumstances. Group content was carefully structured to address not only the challenges of complicated mourning but also to highlight both personal and family resiliency.

The initial training program in 2002 was designed to prepare mental health practitioners to facilitate those groups. It included didactic content related to disaster mental health, complicated bereavement, group process, resiliency, and family systems theory (Underwood, Kalafat, & Spinazzola, 2006). The overall goal of the training was to prepare practitioners, all of whom had previous experience in grief counseling, to provide both individual and group therapy for people who had been bereaved on September 11. Since that initial program, the training design expanded to include content related to deaths under other traumatic circumstances, like suicide and homicide. While the training obviously included a variety of specific content areas designed to increase both the knowledge level and skills of providers (Underwood, 2004), this particular chapter will focus on the ways in which the training used poetry and film to explore the dimension of grief-related shame. These materials were subsequently used in 9/11 bereavement support groups for widows and parents of New York City firefighters (Underwood, 2004). They have also been incorporated into more generic bereavement support programs.

The authors had previously developed a number of training protocols for mental health professionals that used poetry, novels, and films to explore complicated bereavement. They used these techniques for several reasons. At its most basic level, this training design reflects the symbolic nature of human beings, who perceive and experience their social world largely through figurative and symbolic metaphors (Esslin, 1987). Metaphors are ways of filtering and shaping apprehensions of social reality and facilitating the understanding of things that are unfamiliar, like death (Esslin, 1987).

Their choice of film and poetry as teaching tools also reflects the authors' agreement with Appelfeld's (1994) proposition that "art constantly challenges the process by which the individual person is reduced to anonymity." Especially when addressing the dimension of shame that begs secrecy from the eyes of all observers (Kalafat & Lester, 2000), the authors believe that exploration and interrogation of film and literature directly engage the viewer/reader in the helplessness, loss of control, and attributions of personal unworthiness and failure in which shame is rooted.

Because most of their training content focused on losses related to traumatic and violent circumstances like suicide and homicide, the authors thought it was important to include not just experiential activities that touched this difficult content directly, but to provide participants with some degree of emotional distance from the subject matter by incorporating material that was couched in metaphor. The language of metaphor, which is exquisitely expressed in the voice of poetry, speaks to the unconscious and stretches abstract reasoning skills. In this training, it provided a respite from complex didactic concepts and invited training participants to decide on a personal meaning for some of the more transcendent and existential aspects of mortality (Barker, 1985; Underwood & Clark, 2005).

Particularly after September 11, poetry seemed like an appropriate choice as a training tool. As Billy Collins, the former United States poet laureate, has commented, poems are what people turn to in crisis. "Poetry also can assure us that we are not alone; others, some of them long dead, have felt what we are feeling. They have heard the same sea, watched the same sky, looked up to see the same moon" (Collins, 2008, p.xvi). The authors, aware of the dangers of compassion fatigue inherent in providing services to traumatized populations (Figley, 1995), felt that this sense of connection to the larger universe offered by poetry might provide a respite from the chaos of that day's events and perhaps ameliorate some of the isolation and uncertainty practitioners felt in responding to the needs of those bereaved on that day. Their inclusion of poems as part of the training curriculum supported Collins's (2008, p. xvi) observation: "Poetry is thus seen as a kind of flotation device for those who find themselves at sea on troubled waters."

Literature, poetry, and films were selected for the training with the intention of not only assisting participants in recognizing their feelings about death but also enhancing their therapeutic capacity for empathic engagement. In particular, the multisensorial experience of viewing a movie has been demonstrated to facilitate increased empathy with the characters involved and to enhance the empathic skills of viewers (Gladstein & Feldstein, 1983). Because shame as an emotion is difficult to define in the abstract, the authors felt that the opportunity to review carefully selected scenes multiple times for both verbal and nonverbal levels of communication would increase the possibility that the training participants would begin to understand and empathize with some of shame's unspoken dimensions.

Movies have also been used to assist in the identification of countertransference responses (Hills, 1987). Because a component of shame is related to the expectation of a negative reaction from others, it creates a desire to hide from public responses (Kalafat & Lester, 2000). Awareness and management of countertransference related to shame are essential because it could so easily support the bereaved's anticipation of negative moral judgment, shut down the therapeutic process, and increase rather than help ameliorate the shameful feelings. Training participants were encouraged to make connections between their own experiences and the experiences of the characters in the movies and to explore the ways in which these reactions might support or subvert the therapeutic process.

USE OF LITERATURE AND FILM

In *The Redress of Poetry* Seamus Heaney defines the role of the artist: "If our given experience is a labyrinth, then its impassibility is countered by the poet's imagining some equivalent of the labyrinth and bringing himself and the reader through it" (1995, p. 191). Heaney's definition has guided the authors' work with both therapists and bereavement groups. The maze of grief and shame can feel impassable, but the poet's and filmmaker's work can encourage the audience to reflect on ways to manage the feelings of helplessness, loss of control, and powerlessness. Because the viewer has the remove of being participant/observer, he or she is offered the emotional control to empathize and then strategically disengage from the content and, ultimately, construct new meaning about the loss. In sum, art effectively allows its audience knowledge of loss and understanding of shame, yet provides the observer with the power to distance from the suffering and therefore reconstruct a new narrative that includes personal reconciliation and resiliency.

Trainings begin with "The Voice You Hear When You Read Silently," by Thomas Lux (1997). Here the speaker of the poem explores "your voice / caught in the dark cathedral / of your skull"; that is, the poem explores the way we construct meaning about loss. The following passage is read aloud by the trainer and then the listeners are asked to mentally substitute a word about grief and shame for the word *barn*:

> It is your voice
> saying, for example, the word barn
> that the writer wrote
> but the barn you say
> is a barn you know or knew. The voice
> in your head, speaking as you read,
> never says anything neutrally—some people
> hated the barn they knew,
> some people love the barn they know
> so you hear the word loaded
> and a sensory constellation
> is lit: horse-gnawed stalls,
> hayloft, black heat tape wrapping
> a water pipe, a slippery
> spilled chirr of oats from a split sack,
> the bony, filthy haunches of cows ...

The group is asked to reread the passage aloud and pause in silence every time the word *barn* appears, substituting their own word choice. The trainer then asks what words the members of the group would select for the "horse-gnawed stalls" and "bony, filthy haunches of cows." This initial exercise encourages participants to recognize how much they create meaning around words and the nature of the words that speak to them about grief and shame. This exercise is designed to encourage participants to decide on a personal meaning for some of the more elusive and wordless aspects of bereavement. Both the content of the poem itself and the personal sharing of reactions in a group format demonstrate for participants the range of interpretations made to the same words and validate the importance in clinical situations to explore beyond the surface meaning of a word choice, especially when it is related to grief. This exercise in metaphor is an activity that allows participants to take as much emotional distance as they need from the topic through their choice of response. It is interesting to note, however, that as discussion progresses, participants who initially chose less evocative words often amend their selections to more significant and personal choices. Self-disclosure that touches profoundly private aspects of grief and shame generally emerges when sections of the poem are reread aloud.

This transformational power of poetry—to take ordinary experiences, thoughts, and emotions and change them into something that becomes personal and memorable for the reader—was also used to reinforce the importance of clinical listening skills, especially as they relate to the anomalies of individual grief. The variety and depth of participants' reactions to the single word *barn*, for example, concretely demonstrated the importance of exploring the evocative meaning of everyday words, especially in the context of loss.

The technique the training used to maximize the effectiveness of the selected poems was to have participants read them aloud, which was based on the teaching experience of one of the authors. As a professor of English her teaching is infused with classroom exercises and assignments designed to engage the reader's voice and imagination through multiple out-loud readings of the same poem. Her technique for helping readers intuit the poet's purpose and meaning mirrors Pinsky's (Moyers, 1999, p.xxi) reflection that "poetry is a vocal art that requires a physical response." As Hirsch (1999, p. xxi) has written: "Poems communicate before they are understood ... Let the poem work in you as a human experience. Listen to the words, and pay attention to the feelings they evoke." As part of the training protocol, this paying attention to the feelings evoked by words of the poem is an ideal method for helping participants recognize the ways in which they infuse a situation with personal meaning and how this might affect their countertransference.

The following is an example of another poem read aloud that the authors have incorporated into both the practitioner trainings and the support groups.

Although the wind
blows terribly here,
the moonlight also leaks
between the roof planks
of this ruined house.

—Izumi Shikibu (Hirshfield & Aratani, 1990)

When used in the training program, this poem usually generated inter-pretation of its images as a juxtaposition of the disastrous impact of sudden death with inklings of recovery. There was, in truth, only superficial explo-ration of application of the "wind" to the experience of grief or the ways in which the house or self was "ruined" by a sudden, violent death. Nothing in the poem was ever connected to the concept of shame. Instead, it seemed to provide what one participant referred to as "a ray of transcendent hope" that lightened both the emotional heaviness and the concrete losses of com-plicated grief. Indeed, without even addressing the Buddhist symbolism of moonlight as enlightenment, the mental health practitioners moved to the core challenge of trauma work: to find meaning that transcends the death.

With women who were widowed on September 11, discussion pro-ceeded in a somewhat different direction. Although they initially focused on the concrete image of the ruined house and the comparison it sug-gested to the Twin Towers and the Pentagon, their discussion quickly moved to a more personal identification with the ways in which their lives had been changed and damaged by the events of that day. Although the authors anticipated that these changes would include a myriad of feelings related to absence of a partner and coparent, they were sur-prised when the women included the "shame of notoriety" as one of the ways in which their lives had been ruined. Their explanations included the ways in which their grief had been made public by the continuing media coverage of the events and the instant celebrity they experienced in their small-town communities. "Wherever we go," one group mem-ber explained, "people point and stare. When we get together with each other and go out to dinner as a group, the restaurant is generally full of whispers. 'It's those 9/11 widows,' we can hear them say." "And what they're talking about," another member continued, "is what we're going to do with all the settlement money." Their individual and collective shame related to the government's financial compensation, which was initiated after discussion of this short poem, became a frequent topic in subsequent group sessions. Members recounted ways in which they were spending money: buying cars, sending children to private schools, adding onto houses, which were changes they had anticipated making when their spouses were still alive. What they had not expected was to be ashamed of spending this money and feeling embarrassed that friends and neighbors would see their expenditures as a sign of their benefiting from the deaths of their spouses. This feeling was unfortunately rein-forced by national press that hinted at similar, greedy motives. For all of them, this was an unexpected and unwelcome source of shame.

One group member expressed a different reaction to the poem. She sheepishly admitted to one of the group leaders that she actually did not like poetry and had simply feigned interest when the poem was initially read in the group. "I didn't relate to it," she stated, "and thought I had forgotten it. A couple of weeks later," she went on, "I was alone in my car running errands, when the thought came to me out of the blue 'you know, I *have* seen some of the moonlight.'" Such is the power of poetry, writes Raccah (2001), to speak to us at another level, below consciousness.

Certainly the exploration and interrogation of film and literature can help the participant understand that he is not alone as he experiences the helplessness, the loss of control, and fear that often leads to the shame that can surround grief and mourning. Because film is such an effective medium for allowing viewers to become voyeurs to the private experiences of others, three films were selected for the training that provide an intimate vantage point for observing some of humanity's deepest, silent, and most collective fears. There is an unfortunate universality in the experience of shame and the selected films can open our eyes to the ways in which we, the viewers, are not unlike the characters on the screen. The authors also felt the selected film clips could stand as Rorschach tests for the viewer to project his or her own experiences of grief and shame onto the images on the screen and through that process, and develop a more nuanced understanding of the experiences of the bereaved.

The first clip used is a powerful sequence from *In the Bedroom* (Field, 2001), about the shame of parents whose son is a victim of homicide. In the film, a jealous ex-husband kills a young man who has become involved with his former wife. Because of claims of self-defense, the killer is out on bail and will likely receive a minimal sentence. The paralyzing grief of the mother of the slain young man and the helplessness of his doctor father lead the couple inevitably to blame each other. Each suggests that the other was responsible for the son was death. The father calls the mother cold and unloving; he blames her for the son's decision to go out with an attractive, loving townie. The mother excoriates the father for encouraging the son in the affair because the son was able to have his father's "fantasy piece of ass." Underscoring all of this is their unspoken shame at their personal and collective failure as parents in not having been able to protect their son from his premature death. While parents who have lost children can easily identify with the projection, blame, and shame in this clip, even viewers unacquainted with personal loss can feel the unspoken weight of the moral judgments of inadequacy that fill the scenes. As the tension between the parents escalates, the tension shifts from marital discord to reconciliation as the parents wordlessly develop a plot to kill the murderer.

In the Bedroom is about the trap of revenge, about how feelings of powerlessness and the silent burden of shame drive these model citizens to do the unthinkable. Both parents agree that murder is the only option; they are both complicit. This sequence explores their perceptions of having failed in their major social role of parenting and the unstated assumption that others hold them accountable for their parental inadequacy. The depth and intensity of these unspoken feelings hint at their sense of moral failure as well. Their inability to articulate this failing, their need to keep their shame secret from perhaps even themselves, leads to their conclusion that their only absolution is in homicide. These parents are paradoxically isolated and desperate due to their shared shame and grief.

Reactions to this film clip are initially wordless, stunned silence. The embarrassment of helplessly witnessing the parents' pain and grief-induced rage is only eclipsed by the shock of their plan for revenge. Because didactic training content has focused on the variety of ways in which uncomfortable and perhaps personally unacceptable grief reactions like shame can be projected and displaced, participants have no difficulty connecting those theoretical constructs to the emotions portrayed on the screen. While the intensity of the scene facilitates empathic engagement, viewers are also aware of the need to strategically detach as the direction of the dramatic resolution—murder—begins to unfold. Discussion centers on strategies for therapeutically holding the pain of the parents while naming and addressing the underlying shame that isolates them from each other.

The training also uses two scenes that involve family dinner scenes. The first is from *Brokeback Mountain* (Lee, 2005) where Ennis del Mar, after the death of his beloved friend Jack Twist, visits the impoverished farm of Jack's parents. Almost nowhere is the relationship between form and content, style and meaning, clearer than in this clip. What it looks like *is* what it means. Ennis feels shame for his attraction to and love for Jack. He feels shame about his unwillingness to make a life with Jack. He feels shame for Jack's premature death. The story and particularly the film suggest that Jack was killed by bigots wielding tire irons to Jack's body.

The Twist home is entirely bare—like the Wyoming landscape surrounding it. Ennis is invited to sit at the kitchen table and the quiet discomfort in the scene becomes palpable. The viewer is again the uninvited witness to the unspoken pain and shame that sits just below the surface. Jack's father's strategy for dealing with his grief and shame is cruelty and control. In a flat tone of repressed rage, he refuses to let Ennis bury his son's ashes on Brokeback, which was Jack's wish. He handles his shame at his son's homosexuality by cruelly telling Ennis that Jack spoke of another man in his life. On the other hand, Jack's mother, in a quiet, understated way, provides a degree of counterpoint in her remarkable generosity of spirit toward Ennis. She suggests he might want to look at Jack's boyhood bedroom; she gives Ennis the shirt Jack kept from their time on Brokeback, and she invites Ennis to come back.

When Ennis climbs the stairs to Jack's bedroom, the filmmakers convey the starkness of grief and shame by their shots of the staircase, the balustrade, and the almost empty room. Nowhere in film is there a more powerful depiction of the paradox of grief and loss and the importance of tangible, material objects. The sequence shows simultaneously that after loss things do not matter and that things matter deeply. Ennis slowly circles the room, almost reverently touching the artifacts of Jack's boyhood that still occupy the room. Moving through Jack's closet, he buries his face in the remaining clothes, trying, as those who have experienced death can imagine, to recapture the scent of his dead lover. As he opens the window to look at the desolate view of the landscape, the visual metaphor of emptiness captures the starkness of death. Though he leaves quietly, carrying Jack's shirt in a brown paper grocery bag, the feeling of shame still hangs uncomfortably in the air.

Although the feelings in *In the Bedroom* were screamed and shouted, the understated affect in *Brokeback Mountain* is, for some viewers, even more powerful. Discussion usually addresses the therapeutic challenge of helping the bereaved who were generally inexpressive prior to the death find words for that which is hard to articulate under the best of circumstances, the moral inadequacy of shame. The ability to view this scene multiple times and pause at individual frames to observe both the verbal and nonverbal communication helps viewers identify and understand some of shame's unspoken dimensions. With the more empathic engagement facilitated by this multiple viewing, training participants become more facile intuiting the unspoken messages decipherable in facial expressions, which they then use to develop intervention strategies.

When the *Brokeback Mountain* clip has been used in bereavement support groups, the literal details of the film—Wyoming, ranch hands, closeted gay men—seem insignificant to the participants. The mothers of firefighters from downtown Manhattan, for example, used this clip as a prompt for discussion about the death of a child and the helplessness and sorrow they experienced in coming to terms with their loss.

A different kind of dinner table scene occurs in *Little Miss Sunshine* (Dayton & Faris, 2006), a movie about a dysfunctional family's car trip to a junior beauty pageant in which the young daughter is a contestant. At the table is an uncle who has recently tried to take his own life; a grandfather who hides his heroin addiction from some members of the family; a brother who has taken a nine-month vow of silence; and a father whose nine-step, self-help manual *Refuse to Lose* is an utter failure. Olive, the 9-year-old child, is the healthy questioner who breaks the family's silence. She asks the question that is silently hovering above the table—unspoken but powerful. Looking at the wrist bandages that announce her uncle's suicide attempt, Olive asks, "What happened to your arms?" In its shame, the family tries to silence her, but Olive persists. "How did it happen?" she asks. When her mother tells her that her uncle tried to kill himself, Olive pauses, and again asks sincerely, "Why did you want to kill yourself?" and "Why were you unhappy?" Olive is the model for the therapist, the fellow traveler, who may ask the difficult questions and break the silence that begins the healing of shame. In fact, Olive's questions liberate her uncle to explore his own desperation honestly. In her mature innocence, Olive has the courage to ask the tough questions about the shameful suicide attempt without the expectation of a negative reaction from others.

To end a training session, participants usually sit or stand in a circle to recite a poem that both encompasses loss and promotes resiliency. One of the poems that is always well received and poignantly summarizes the task of the therapist as the fellow traveler on the journey of grief is Mary Oliver's (1992) "In Blackwater Woods." With an economy of words, the final lines of the poem capture the essence of grief:

> To live in this world
> you must be able
> to do three things:
> to love what is mortal;
> to hold it
> against your bones knowing
> your own life depends on it;
> and, when the time comes to let it go,
> to let it go.*

SUMMARY

The challenge for mental health professionals exploring the feelings of shame attached to a death is that these feelings generally remain unspoken and often even outside the consciousness of the bereaved. Because they incorporate the expectation of negative reaction from others, these feelings can be displaced or projected, making therapeutic intervention even more difficult. Film and literature, with examples that range from the individualized private space of poetry to the social, collaborative landscape of movies, offer compelling teaching tools for helping mental health practitioners access some of these more private aspects of grieving. Although the training described in this chapter was conducted in a group setting, individual mental health practitioners might consider incorporating exploration of the arts into their professional development regimes. Poets and filmmakers often speak the words and create the images that touch on

---

* From *American Primitive* by Mary Oliver. Copyright© 1978, 1979, 1980, 1981, 1983 by Mary Oliver. Reprinted with permission of Little, Brown and Company.

the nature of mortal existence. Elusive emotions like shame come alive in film and poetry. The thoughtful viewer or reader can glimpse not just the visceral manifestation of this complicated emotion but also a way to make the human, therapeutic connection that is the foundation of healing.

REFERENCES

Appelfeld, A. (1994). *Beyond despair: Three lectures and a conversation with Philip Roth* (p. 23) (J. M. Green, Trans). New York: Fromm International.

Barker, P. (1985). *Using metaphors in psychotherapy.* New York: Brunner-Mazel.

Breed, W. (1972). Five components of a basic suicide syndrome. *Life-Threatening Behavior, 2,* 4–18.

Collins, B. (2008). Preface. In J. Shinder (Ed.), *The poem I turn to* (p. xv). Naperville, IL: Source Books.

Dayton, J., & Faris, V. (Directors). (2006). *Little Miss Sunshine* [Motion picture]. United States: Fox Searchlight Pictures.

Dickenson, E. (1960). *The complete poems of Emily Dickinson.* Boston: Little, Brown & Company.

Doka, K. (Ed.). (2002). *Disenfranchised grief: New directions, challenges and strategies for practice.* Champaign, IL: Research Press.

Durlack, J. A. (1994). Changing death attitudes through death education. In R. A. Neimeyer (Ed.), *Death anxiety handbook: Research, instrumentation, and application.* Washington, DC: Taylor & Francis.

Durlack, J. A., & Reisenberg, L. (1991). The impact of death education. *Death Education, 1,* 41–56.

Esslin, M. (1987). *The field of drama: How the signs of drama create meaning on stage and screen.* London: Methuen.

Field, T. (Producer/Director/Writer). (2001). *In the bedroom* [Motion picture]. United States: Miramax Films.

Figley, C. R. (1995). *Compassion fatigue: Secondary traumatic stress disorder in those who treat the traumatized.* London: Brunner/Routledge.

Galea, S., Ahern, J., Resnick, H., Kilpatrick, D., Bucuvalas, M., Gold, J., et al. (2002). Psychological sequelae of the September 11 terrorist attacks in New York City. *New England Journal of Medicine, 346,* 982–987.

Gladstein, G., & Feldstein, J. (1983). Using film to increase counselor empathic experiences. *Counselor Education and Supervision, 23,* 125–131.

Heaney, S. (1995). *The redress of poetry.* London: Farber & Farber.

Hills, M. (1987). The discovery of personal meaning: A goal for counselor training. *Counselor Education and Supervision, 27,* 37–43.

Hirsh, E. (1999). *How to read a poem and fall in love with poetry*. New York: Harcourt.

Hirshfield, J., & Aratani, M. (1990). *The ink dark moon*. New York: Vintage Books.

Kalafat, J., & Lester, D. (2000). Shame and suicide: A case study. *Death Studies, 24*, 157–162.

Kurtz, E. (2007). *Shame & guilt*. New York: iUniverse.

Lee, A. (Director). (2005). *Brokeback Mountain* [Motion picture]. United States: Focus Features.

Lester, D. (1997). The role of shame in suicide. *Suicide and Life-Threatening Behavior, 27*, 352–361.

Lewis, M. (1992). *Shame: The exposed self*. New York: Free Press.

Lux, T. (1997). *New and selected poems*. Boston: Houghton-Mifflin.

Oliver, M. (1992). *New and selected poems*. Boston: Beacon Press.

Moyers, B. (1999). Robert Pinsky. In *Fooling with words: A celebration of poets and their craft*. New York: William Morrow & Co.

Neimeyer, R. (1998). *Lessons of loss: A guide to coping*. New York: McGraw Hill.

Raccah, D. (2001). Notes from publisher. In E. Paschen & R. Mosby (Eds.), *Poetry speaks* (pp. xi–xx). Naperville, IL: Source Books.

Rando, T. (1993). *Treatment of complicated mourning*. Champaign, IL: Research Press.

Underwood, M. (2004). Group interventions for bereavement following traumatic events. In B. Buchele & H. Spitz (Eds.), Group *interventions for the treatment of psychological trauma* (pp. 1–23). New York: American Group Psychotherapy Association.

Underwood, M., & Clark, C. (2005). Using metaphor to help children cope with trauma: An example from September 11th. In J. Webber, D. Bass, & R. Yep (Eds.), *Terrorism, trauma, and tragedies: A counselor's guide to preparing and responding*. Alexandria, VA: American Counseling Association Foundation.

Underwood, M., Kalafat, J., & Spinazzola, N. (2006). Children and terrorism: A psychoeducational approach. In B. Bongar, L. M. Brown, L. E. Beutler, J. N. Breckenridge, & P. G. Zimbardo (Eds.), *The psychology of terrorism* (pp. 311–337). New York: Oxford University Press.

Underwood, M., Milani, J., & Spinazzola, N. (2004). *Families' GOALs: A training manual*. Verona, NJ: Mental Health Association of New Jersey.

Social Conscience and the Psychology of Shame

CHAPTER 10

The Long Road to Relevance
Disability, Chronic Sorrow, and Shame

Susan Roos

I saw one morning
a swan that had broken out of its cage,
webbed feet clumsy on the cobblestones,
white feathers dragging in the uneven ruts,
and obstinately pecking at the drains,
drenching its enormous wings in filth
as if in its own lovely lake, crying
"Where is the thunder, when will it rain?"

—Charles Baudelaire, "Le Cygne" (p. 81)

HISTORICAL CONTEXT AND OVERVIEW

Human impairment and its associated grief have significantly impacted people's lives from time immemorial. Although often rationalized in some positive way, attitudes and practices in response to these realities do not always reflect humane and compassionate group values. In competitive societies, attributes such as competence, physical attractiveness, intelligence, charm, and personal autonomy are esteemed as group ideals. Whether overtly articulated or developed as a shadow characteristic of the society, marginalization, rejection, and abhorrence of those who fall too far from acceptable standards may occur as a result of perceived threats to the integrity and viability of large group identity. Hence, people with chronic illness, deformities, and permanent disabling and debilitating conditions are devalued and often considered deviant, sometimes to such an extent as to be rendered socially invisible. Correspondingly, as Cheyfitz (2000) has noted, intermittently throughout recorded history a series of ideas not initially seen as related to each other have consistently converged. These ideas include: suicide, euthanasia, infanticide, maternal or paternal filicide, eugenics, genocide, and, more recently, physician-assisted suicide.

Trace archeological evidence, as far back as hunter and gatherer groups, indicates that some babies with birth defects were killed (Gerdtz, 1993; Scheerenberger, 1983). Both the impaired child and the mother were killed in the New Hebrides (Sumnar, 1906). In Greece, Sparta, many Asian cultures, and during the Roman Empire, abandonment and exposure to the elements and mercy killings were often accepted "solutions." In all versions of the drama of the legend of Philoctetes (e.g., those of Aeschylus, Euripides, Sophocles, and even the contemporary version by Seamus Heaney [1991]), the Greeks abandon Philoctetes as damaged goods on the island of Lemnos because of his incurable, odiferous, excruciatingly painful, and oozing foot wound. He was deserted on the island for 10 long years and would have remained there forever had the Greeks not been told by an oracle that they would win against Troy only if they used a bow in Philoctetes's possession. Through subterfuge and, eventually, honest negotiation, Philoctetes and the bow were retrieved from the island, leading ultimately to a satisfactory outcome for all parties—except, of course, the Trojans. An implication of this story is the veiled suggestion that the larger group may, like it or not, *need* its marginalized, shunned, and disowned members who are physically or mentally disabled, a need worthy of its own analysis and articulation.

During the Inquisition, demon and satanic possession and witchcraft were associated with conditions such as psychotic states, mental retardation, and epilepsy. Persons with these conditions were ridiculed at best and at worst persecuted, tortured, and burned at the stake (Gerdtz, 1993). Some royal and upper-class families kept persons with mental deficiencies and certain physical anomalies for their entertainment value, as their "pets" or buffoons. Until a few decades ago, circus and carnival sideshows regularly featured people with "exotic," "believe it or not" deformities. However, there have been leaders throughout history (e.g., physician and philosopher Avicenna; physician and chief rabbi of Cairo Maimonides; religious leader Vincent de Paul; and philosophers Francis Bacon, René Descartes, and John Locke) who have advocated for a just society and for respect and better conditions for persons with disabilities (Gerdtz, 1993; Marmura, 1963; Roos, 2002, 2007a).

Following European incursions into the New World, most individuals with disabilities continued to be cared for by their own families or foster families who were paid by state governments. Ordinances and laws were enacted for the protection of those with "naturall or personall impediment ... defect of minde, fayling sences, or impotence of Lymbes ... Children, Idiots, Distracted persons ..." (Eliot, 1938, pp. 67–68). In actual practice, however, people with disabilities were often treated no better than criminals, and government-sponsored "solutions" were generally of poor quality by design due to fear of attracting those with disabilities to lives of indolence at public expense (Gerdtz, 1993; Roos, 2002, 2007a). An increase in concern and the emergence of hope for neglected and disfranchised people occurred in the late 18th and early 19th centuries in Western Europe and America (Ingalls, 1978; Trent, 1994). In the United States an institutional movement gathered momentum. By 1898, there were 24 publicly funded institutions in 19 states (Trent, 1994). Reflective of societal values, early admissions to institutional care and habilitation were restricted to those deemed capable of training for job placement in the community. A more covert goal for women was to prevent pregnancy, a foreshadowing of the eugenics movement in America (Roos, 2002, 2007a; Trent, 1994).

As the early promise of institutions soon faltered, the backlog of residents continued to increase as superintendents requested their retention due to fears of what would become of them if they were discharged (Scheerenberger, 1982; Trent, 1994). A severe lack of options for families led to expanding admission criteria to include "custodial" cases, such as adults and children with severe and profound defects and impairments: the so-called vegetables and subtrainables (those thought to be incapable of any education whatever), and those with cerebral palsy, seizure disorders, craniofacial anomalies, physical deformities, and other complications. Meanwhile, special education programs and other community-based services were very slow to develop. The concept of permanent institutionalization became accepted. A policy of "out of sight, out of mind" was America's answer, especially to the problem of mental disabilities.

When an infant was born with obvious defects, it was quite common for physicians to recommend that the child be placed immediately, a practice still occurring in many parts of the world (e.g., Serbia). Some mothers did not even see or hold their babies. Out of concern for the family, this practice was well intentioned and based on the erroneous assumption that it was best for both mother and child that they be separated before they became attached. Another, often unvoiced intent was to protect the family from social ostracism and shame. Some mothers were advised to forget the child and to have another one, that is, a replacement child. When children and adults with significant impairments were kept at home, they were sometimes hidden from society, their very existence a family and community secret (Roos, 2002). In instances such as these, consequences frequently were inevitably tragic. Today, for the betterment of all, we know far more about the nature of attachment, loss, continuing bonds, and unseverable relationships.

During the first half of the 20th century, stigma and ostracism continued to flourish. As described by Scheerenberger (1982) in specific reference to developmental disabilities, "science and prejudice walked hand in hand" (p. 57). Based on flawed and highly biased research, a eugenics movement began to emerge. The goal was to eliminate all inherited disorders (including character defects) in as many places as possible (Davies, 1959; Goddard, 1912). Despite protests from some professionals and families, increased retention of women of child-bearing age in institutions and compulsory sterilization became widely accepted in the United States, Canada, Europe, and Japan. In the United States, from 1907 until 1958, 30 states had laws permitting involuntary sterilization of persons deemed unfit (Davies, 1959).

In 1927, deciding for the constitutionality of involuntary sterilization of those with "mental defects," U.S. Supreme Court Justice Oliver Wendell Holmes wrote in *Buck v. Bell* (1927, pp. 207–208): "It is better for all the world that the manifestly unfit be stopped from reproducing. Three generations of imbeciles are enough." It is hard to imagine policies and practices any more flagrantly shame-based than a eugenics program, for society in general, families with disabilities in particular, and for individuals with disabilities specifically. Unfortunately, a link exists between the eugenics program in the United States and acts committed in Germany's eugenics campaign, where compulsory sterilization preceded systematic killing of adults and children who were disabled, frail, sick, and weak. Among other things, the link is evidenced by the University of Heidelberg's 1936 award of an honorary degree to Harry Laughlin, one of several leaders and activists for eugenics in the United States (Kevles, 1985).

In 1929, 2 years following the *Buck v. Bell* decision by the U.S. Supreme Court, and presaging the most distorted and unforgivable use of "mercy killing" ever documented, Adolf Hitler advocated the removal of weak and disabled persons (i.e., "superfluous beings" and "freakish people") from German society. The numbers of infants, children, and adults with disabilities of all kinds who were killed between 1930 and 1945 are staggering and incomprehensible. For example, physician-implemented "euthanasia" took the lives of more than 70,000 persons whose existence was deemed unworthy (Goldhagen, 1996). By 1941, 200,000 persons with disabilities had been exterminated in six killing centers, including the well-known Hadamar Clinic (Burleigh, 1990, 1991). Disabled individuals were the training ground on which methods were perfected to carry out the Holocaust that ensued. Interestingly at the least, it does not appear that the atrocities committed against defenseless individuals with mental and physical disabilities have been nearly so well recognized as those that occurred during the Holocaust, nor do I know of any public symbols of remembrance or monuments that have been constructed for them.

In a rather compelling thought process, from a sociocultural and psychoanalytic framework, Koenigsberg (2007) has focused on Nazism and has attempted to explain how Hitler, Himmler, Goebbels, and millions of other Germans invested themselves in the cleansing of the social body (i.e., restoring and maintaining large group identity) through segregating the sick, being alert to contagions, exclusion of so-called deviants, eugenics, and quarantine of "degenerates." Those with disabilities and Jews were characterized as diseases that should be removed from the body politic. The goal was to forge a social body that would be immune from "infection" attributed to these targeted populations. Therefore, Nazi discourse was a fantasy about the body politic. The discourse was embraced because it allowed Nazi leaders and followers to escape their mortal and flawed bodies and to imagine fusion with an omnipotent body that is not prone to death and decay. Koenigsberg points out that each of us contains weakness and illness, that is, a death principle, in our own bodies. Those we deem to be social deviants (e.g., criminals, the sick, the mentally ill or deficient, those with physical anomalies and disabilities, those we view as our national enemies, etc.) are the people onto which principles of weakness, frailty, and death can be projected. In Nazi Germany, to kill off Jews and those with disabilities was to kill off the death principle by eradicating a disease imagined to be residing within the body politic.

Following World War II, family members, concerned citizens, and some professionals became more vocal about poor and inhumane conditions, widespread neglect, and scarcity of treatment and care options for individuals with disabilities. Parents—especially those of children with mental disabilities—began to insist that inalienable rights granted by the Constitution belonged equally to their children as human beings and citizens. Demands were made for improved services. Grassroots coalitions were formed. Exposés of atrocious conditions in overcrowded and understaffed institutions were aired on television by Geraldo Rivera (1972) and appeared in Blatt and Kaplan's (1966) landmark publication of their photographic essay, *Christmas in Purgatory,* a book that was also reproduced in a popular magazine (Blatt & Mangel, 1967). These exposés of unconscionable treatment of defenseless children and adults shattered the shell of public complacency. "Out of sight, out of mind" could no longer prevail.

Voluntary advocacy, service, and research organizations grew in strength and numbers (Roos, 2002). The Kennedy administration supported and promulgated improvements in many areas, including public opinion. If the president of the United States could openly speak of his sister who had mental deficiencies, ordinary citizens could, too. A few celebrities came forward with a kind of confessional, admitting to having sons and daughters who were impaired and who had theretofore been hidden away as shameful secrets. Federal funding became available for research and demonstration projects aimed at improving care and increasing functionality. Funds were allocated for staff training and overall improvement of institutional settings and programs.

Paving the way for the eventual passage of the Americans with Disabilities Act (ADA), class-action litigation, a desperate but effective recourse, was instigated as a means to secure previously denied constitutional rights, such as: the right to treatment and habilitation, individualized programs, freedom from harm and abuse, due process, and freedom from servitude or peonage (Roos, 2002). Involuntary sterilization was ruled to be an unconstitutional infringement of a fundamental freedom. Other reforms included mandates on facility standards and quality of care, including adequate nutrition and staffing, the right to choice, and rights to the least restrictive environment, as well as to an array of services and environments similar to those afforded nondisabled persons. Some professional groups urged their members to develop a social conscience that would translate into advocacy and legal actions to right the wrongs that had been perpetrated against those of us who are the most vulnerable (Roos, 2002).

Conditions have improved considerably since the 1970s and 1980s. Great strides have been made in surgery, rehabilitation, orthotics, prosthetics, and other technologies that promote more freedom and normative living for persons with chronic illness and disabilities. However, the deinstitutionalization movement in conjunction with the failure to develop adequate community services, especially for those who are mentally ill, has consequently resulted in many persons who are only marginally able to care for themselves being among the homeless on the streets of all major urban areas (Alexander-Eitzman, 2006; Forchuk, Russell, Kingston-Macclure, Turner, & Dill, 2006). As mentally ill and drug-addicted people are relegated to the streets (sadly and ironically, the "least restrictive environment"), in times of sickness and failing health, emergency rooms have become dumping grounds for people who are incompetent to negotiate the system for much-needed services. With no other recourse available, some people literally wait days in hospital emergency rooms.

Generations bequeath to one another timeless histories of conscious and unconscious attitudes related to ways of living with one another and ways of rejecting one another. One form of rejection is expressed by redirecting (projecting) negative, even hate-filled self-appraisals and self-doubts onto those who are without equal power. As enacted, these internal working models are cryptic, elusive, and so familiar and engrained that they are deeply embedded in the fabric of society, the ground from which we extract our support and resources. We become so accustomed to ever-present, seemingly eternal attributes of society and our large group identity that we often fail to apprehend what is obvious, reflective of the principle: We see where we put our focus. Seen or unseen, prejudicial attitudes and ignorance are alive and well in America and, no doubt, elsewhere. Further, all people with disabilities, families, caregivers, advocates, and professionals do not embrace the same opinions, needs, goals, and desires (Roos, 2002, 2007a). Moreover, governmental allocations for services are perpetually under threat of reductions or discontinuation. Unfortunately, abuse and neglect can occur in community settings just as easily as in institutions. Community-based services are often fragmented, with inconsistent oversight. Cost containment mandated by managed care organizations, medical facilities, and federal and state government is also a frequent dominant factor in the quality of support.

CONTEMPORARY MODELS

From the vast history of disability, four essential models have emerged (Kaplan, 1999). The *moral model,* by far the oldest of the four, regards disability as resulting from sin or as divine retribution for wrongs committed by the affected individual or by previous generations. Vestiges of the model can be found in cases where there is an assumption that the person has contracted the disabling condition or cannot recover from it due to lack of faith. Even today, many thousands of people, desperate for a cure, throng to revival tents for faith healing or go on pilgrimages to Lourdes and other places where it is believed that miracles have occurred, signifying these special sites as loci of healing, if only one has sufficient faith. Although associating disability with sin and faulty faith is not so exacting and prevalent today in most Western societies, guilt (even if not based on religious beliefs) remains a prominent complication of conditions that diminish autonomy and deviate from prevailing social values and expectations. The moral model is associated with shame and guilt, often on an entire family. In reality, there are some situations in which shame and guilt are rational and appropriate, for example, sustaining a spinal cord injury in a car crash occasioned by driving while intoxicated, or leaving one's child with a person known to be violent who then batters the child, causing permanent and severe head injuries and broken bones.

The *medical model* views disability as an internal defect or illness that requires medical intervention. Individuals with disabilities are cast in the sick role. Until recently, according to Kaplan (1999), most disability policy issues have been seen as health issues, and physicians have been considered the primary authorities in this area, including public policy. The influence of this model can be seen in the Social Security system in which disability is defined as the inability to work. This definition is the source of insurmountable distress for people who want to work but would risk losing all benefits, such as health care coverage or access to personal assistance services, as disability status would be lost by going to work. In addition, practices of confinement that are associated with the sick role are no longer viewed as acceptable. Likewise, bearing the "sick" label has many negative implications for self-image and identity development.

Similar to the medical model, the *rehabilitation model* views the person with a disability as in need of rehabilitation delivered by professionals who can provide physical therapy, vocational training, counseling, transport, and other services and interventions to increase functioning and decrease obstacles caused by or associated with the disability. People with disabilities have leveled much criticism against both the medical and rehabilitation models. There are some similarities in these two models and, in broader contexts, the beliefs that underlie patterns of reflexively blaming the victim (e.g., finding fault with a person who is seen to have exhibited poor judgment and, hence, "asked to be raped" and "should be ashamed").

The *disability model* emphasizes social context, viewing prejudice and discrimination as the most significant problems faced by persons with disabilities and as causing many of the difficulties often regarded as intrinsic to the disability as it is depicted by other models. In this model, disability is regarded as a *normal fact of life*, not as a deviance. Most people will experience disability, either permanent or transient, over the course of their lives; hence, it should be expected. If disability were more commonly recognized and accepted, we would design our environments and our systems differently, in a manner more accommodating and considered more normal than abnormal. However, the larger society continues to focus predominantly on the *condition of the person* as the source of problems, rather than on handicapping aspects of social attitudes, ostracism, and the harsh physical environment. Hence, to a very large extent, disability is a social construct.

Political Doctrine and Exclusion

Embedded in both our political culture and the history of disability is the traditional model of society that is based on a contract entered into by free, equal, and independent people for mutual advantage (Nussbaum, 2006). The contract is based on the premise that people get something by living together that they would not have as individuals on their own. Nussbaum (2006) contends that, despite the traditional model's value and important contributions, it falls short in addressing "three frontiers of justice," namely, disability, nationality, and species membership (p. 14). To some extent, contemporary contract doctrines have rectified traditional exclusions of previously marginalized persons, such as women, children, and elderly people, from the bargaining table. Despite the existence of the ADA, Nussbaum explains that even today no social contract doctrines include people with severe physical and mental impairments as among the parties who choose basic political principles or who participate in the creation of political institutions—even after these institutions are created by an initial contract. She points out that until recently, exclusion and stigmatization were the norm, and people with disabilities simply were not included in society.

The 19th century philosopher Friedrich Nietzsche (1990) went so far as to describe the invalid as a parasite on society, indicating that "in a certain state it is indecent to go on living. To vegetate on in cowardly dependence on physicians and medications after the meaning of life, the right to life, has been lost ought to entail the profound contempt of society" (p. 99). As recently as the 19th and early to mid-20th centuries, exclusion has been so deliberate as to be specifically mandated by "unsightly" ordinances. An example of such an ordinance from the Chicago Municipal Code states:

> No person who is diseased, maimed, mutilated or in any way deformed so as to be an unsightly or disgusting object or improper person to be allowed in or on the public ways or other public places in this city, or shall therein or thereon expose himself to public view, under a penalty of not less than one dollar nor more than fifty dollars for each offense. (Cited by Boles, 2007, p. 1)

The intent of unsightly or ugly laws was to preserve the aesthetically pleasing façade of the community from being blighted by the sight of people who were poor or disabled, especially those with cerebral palsy and other disfiguring conditions. Although much of Western society promulgates the myth of equal opportunity, the best interests of people with disabilities have usually not been considered germane to political process and power. In general, as nonparties to the decision-making process, they have been relegated to charity, being dependent on the good will of power structures and transitory political conceptions of compassion. Clearly, contemporary political theorists have been slow to construct models that reflect important advances made by the disability rights movement (e.g., reforms in the language of disability, principles of inclusion, rights to education and access, normalization, and so on).

CHRONIC SORROW

Chronic sorrow refers to frequently unrecognized and misunderstood, pervasive, continuing, and resurgent grief responses that result from coping with loss due to significant and permanent injury, illness, disability, or progressive deterioration of oneself (self-loss) or another living person (other-loss) to whom there is a deep attachment (Roos, 2002, 2007a, 2009). As the source of the loss is ongoing and involves frequent (and often creative) adaptations, grief responses are usually lifelong. The experiential core of this type of grieving is a painful disparity between perceptual reality and thoughts of what might have been, should have been, and still may be hoped for. Introduced in the 1960s, the concept of chronic sorrow was based on observations by rehabilitation professional and researcher Simon Olshansky (1962, 1966) of parents of children with significant developmental impairments. The concept heralded a paradigm shift by challenging professional perceptions prevalent at that time and which, to some extent, linger today. These perceptions included stereotyping, negative labeling, and pathologizing of parents who were commonly seen as neurotic, autistogenic, schizophrenogenic, overprotective, depressed, and never satisfied. Instead, Olshansky observed that, while functioning devotedly and with a paucity of resources to help their children, these parents were coping with a grief process, that is, chronic sorrow, a normal response to the tragedy of having a child with severe and permanent disabilities.

As a result of research, the concept has undergone an expansion to include other ongoing loss situations (Roos, 2002, 2007a). It is now considered useful to the understanding of the effects of a wide range of chronic diseases, disabilities, and progressive physical and mental deterioration (e.g., spina bifida, ALS [amyotrophic lateral sclerosis], multiple sclerosis, Parkinson's, chronic mental illness, AIDS, Alzheimer's and dementias, spinal cord injury, hydrocephalus, and protracted coma). The concept has been empirically validated in many of these conditions. Since it pertains to losses that are ongoing, chronic sorrow may also apply to a limited number of other situations as well (Roos, 2007b, 2009). Many mothers who have relinquished babies for adoption and are unable to determine what happened to them report pervasive and resurgent grief responses, some more than 20 or 30 years following relinquishment (Millen & Roll, 1985). The concept is also suggested as a useful perspective for understanding and ameliorating experiences of refugees and immigrants who have lost their culture, their country, the language of their birth, and intimacies of friends and family members left behind. It may also be applicable to some cases of infertility, as well as to loved ones of people who have vanished (e.g., MIAs, kidnap victims, and those who have inexplicably disappeared, their fates unknown).

Losses central to chronic sorrow are characterized by great complexity, whether derived from the self or from another person who is deeply loved and cherished. Usually inaugurated by trauma, the onset of chronic sorrow can be considered a severe life narrative interruption, that is, a shattering of the assumptive world and the self, whether it is momentous (e.g., sudden paralysis due to spinal cord injury, birth of a child with previously undetected anomalies) or consists of gradual, incremental concerns that culminate in a realization of the loss or its true severity (e.g., symptoms being confirmed as multiple sclerosis, worsening misperceptions being diagnosed as schizophrenia). Reconstructing and relearning the world and self to make the new reality believable as well as bearable may require a full lifetime as a work in progress. Referred to as "spread" in disability literature (Wright, 1983), the risk of taking on a "defective" identity that is dominant and tends to override other options is immense and is often reinforced by reductionist social stereotypes. Mental and physical disabilities carry the mantle of unwantedness everywhere. For those affected, breathing in this unwantedness is toxic, whether it exists in the media; incidental social contacts; the self, parents, or family; or in the professional tasked with helping the situation.

Interpretation of the loss, at the time of onset and throughout one's lifetime, determines the existence of chronic sorrow, as well as its intensity and frequency of resurgence. Cultural context, group affiliations, primary relationships, and other spheres of influence affect the perception and meaning of loss. Fantasies, although idiosyncratic, are the product of our culture and even of our collective unconscious. Fantasies of the life that was meant to be produce both positive and negative responses. While keeping dreams alive can forestall depression or incapacitating grief responses and can be a primary motivating force for bringing us through very difficult times, activation of the dream that is lost can also trigger intensification of grief responses. Reminders are inevitable. It often requires years to know what parts of the dream are forfeited and how the unchosen and initially terrifying new reality will unfold. It is often impossible to know which of many potential outcomes one is grieving. Hence, interpretations may vary over the course of a lifetime for the same individual. Given the undying nature of dreams, even when one is functioning adaptively and optimistically, the world and the self are seen through the lens of loss and chronic sorrow. During the course of chronic sorrow, the intensity of grief is commensurate with the potency and magnitude of the discrepancy between reality and the dreams we cling to.

Despite its challenges, in almost all cases, chronic sorrow is *not* a state of permanent despair. It can be the basis of a life that has increased meaning and richness and is more deeply appreciated. The beauty of a life itself can be aesthetically cherished. We can, of course, learn far more from an unconventional life that tests our mettle than we ever can from a more conventional one, and we are usually stronger and "better people" as a result. We can, for instance, learn to make sacrifices with grace and to love without expectation. We can develop a keener wit and humor that includes a broader sense of proportion in appraising and dealing with all facets of living in the world.

Complications in Chronic Sorrow

Although chronic sorrow per se is normal, it can increase susceptibility to complications over the life span. These include (a) clinical depression, (b) problems with identity development and poor self-esteem, (c) guilt, (d) anger, (e) stress (chronic and episodic) and stress-related ailments, (f) anxiety and clinical or subclinical trauma symptoms, (g) a deep sense of loneliness and alienation, (h) disordered intimacy and attachment (e.g., enmeshment, prohibitive fears of closeness, or of having wants and desires), (i) existential angst (e.g., disillusionment and spiritual conflicts), (j) addictions relapse, and (k) periodic affective flooding or loss spirals that may be so overwhelming as to be temporarily disabling (Roos, 2002, 2009). Shame can be implicated in all these complications. In addition, chronic sorrow is frequently characterized by disenfranchisement (Doka, 2002). Often there is little or no social recognition that a loss has occurred, and there may be only scant social recognition of the person who is the source of the loss. There are no socially sanctioned ways in which to grieve the loss and no customary rituals or other systemic resources that provide support for grieving. Understandably, there are qualitative experiential differences in how chronic sorrow is manifested by people who are the locus of the loss as compared to those who are emotionally close to them (e.g., parents, siblings, partners, devoted friends). In some situations, self- and other-loss, accompanied by resurgences in the impact of chronic sorrow, are reciprocal and interactive, for example, in some caregiver–care receiver relationships.

Stress and Suicide

Chronic sorrow situations represent lifetimes of chronic and episodic stress. Stressful events are not only those involving crisis and emergency; they are also part of the grind of day-to-day hassles of living. In developing her recurrent stress model, Hewson (1997) has observed a similar range of responses in both those who sustain a loss of ability and in their close family members. These responses include (a) emotional states (e.g., shock, sadness, anger, guilt), (b) physical responses (e.g., feeling hollow, headaches, fatigue), (c) cognitive responses (e.g., denial, questioning, confusion, rumination, a sense of going crazy), and (d) behavioral responses (e.g., social withdrawal, sleep disturbances, restless overactivity, crying). Social isolation and alienation are common in self-loss as well as in other-loss, and they are associated with stress and with diseases traceable to immune dysfunction. Since grief responses are at the heart of chronic sorrow, it is reasonable to assume that added significant stressors—especially those related to other-losses—can result in decreased immune efficiency. Mitigating factors that may reduce depression and other severe complications of chronic sorrow include protective relationships, social support, and close or affectionate caregiver–care receiver relationships (Horowitz & Shindelman, 1983; Roos, 2002; Williamson & Schulz, 1990).

Professionals should be especially aware of the high incidence of suicidality in people with chronic illness and disabilities. Based on my observations, reasoning, and clinical intuition, my opinion is that people with self-loss are much more likely to commit suicide than those coping with other-loss (Roos, 2002). Those with self-loss are better able to justify the decision to end their lives (e.g., on the basis they can no longer be a burden to others). Nietzsche (1990) and those involved in the eugenics movement would have agreed with this justification. For those with other-loss, justifications are more complicated and difficult. In reciprocal and interactive chronic sorrow situations, suicidal thoughts can be accompanied by fantasies of ending the lives of both caregiver and care receiver. In fact, these fantasies are sometimes brought to fruition. However, there is usually an internalized injunction against such a drastic and tragic action. Causing the death of the loved one in order to be free to take one's own life is seen as the ultimate betrayal of the other and the antithesis of what has given central meaning to the life of the caregiver (Roos, 2002).

Disaboom (2008), an online community for people affected by disability, recently conducted a study via survey to determine American citizens' perception of disability. When asked, "Which would you choose:
Living with a severe disability that forever alters your ability to live an
independent life, or death?" responses indicated that more than half of
all Americans would rather be dead than disabled. Attitudes varied by
age, income, geographic location, and level of education. The founder
of Disaboom, Glen House, a physician who has been quadriplegic since
his early 20s, feels that these disturbing responses are based on serious
misperceptions.

Based on a review of 73 studies of neurologic disease, Arciniegas
and Anderson (2002) found the risk of attempted or completed suicide is
increased in patients with migraine with aura, epilepsy, stroke, multiple
sclerosis, traumatic brain injury, and Huntington's disease. People who
are at risk for certain neurological disorders are also at increased risk for
suicide. Risk is especially high among people who have a genetic propensity for developing Huntington's disease, independent of the known presence or absence of the Huntington's gene mutation. The risk of attempted
or completed suicide in neurologic illness is strongly associated with
depression and social isolation, as well as cognitive impairment, recent
onset or change in illness status, prior psychiatric illness or suicidal
behaviors, and a lack of future plans or perceived meaning in life.

From a historical, societal, and ethical perspective, I suspect that
disability is a factor in a disproportionate number of cases of mercy
killing and assisted suicide. My suspicion is supported by a few arti-
cles and books. In *Right to Die versus Sacredness of Life,* an in-depth
empirical and theoretical analysis of mercy killing, Kaplan (2000) sum-
marily states: "The preponderance of disability as opposed to terminal-
ity in the Kevorkian–Reding cases raises a red flag" (p. 287). The risk
of faulty assessments about quality of life may be higher for people with
disabilities than for those facing certain and imminent death. After all,
it was only decades—not centuries—ago that nutrients were withheld
from some infants born with Down syndrome, a regrettable practice
that is now rightfully abandoned. It is quite apparent that children with
Down syndrome and other genetic disorders, given love and adequate
support, are capable of living good and rewarding lives. I do wonder, as
perhaps more of us should, about the true prevalence of mercy killing
and assisted suicide in disability. In many cases it is relatively easy to kill
someone who is fragile, helpless, and defenseless, and to do so without
leaving traces. In equivocal death, I also wonder if medical examiners
and investigators do as thorough a job in determining cause in cases of
severe disability, coma, and other severely compromising conditions, as
compared with others.

Caregiver Depletion

When caregivers age, become incapacitated, or wear out, family dynamics change significantly. Caregivers often provide a layer of protection for other family members and close friends. When this protection crumbles, those who have managed to avoid their own issues with regard to the person with impairments may confront not only the stress of reassigning responsibilities but their old and previously dormant issues as well. As distressing intrapsychic and interpersonal conflicts break the surface of denial, old injuries, deprivations, misunderstandings, longings, and resentments are afforded one more (sometimes final) arena for reenactment. Caregivers who are no longer resilient and who must contend with complaints, accusations, and conflict may experience a loss of the last vestiges of certain hopes and fantasies that have bolstered and sustained them during times of exacerbated grief and discouragement. Family members who have been ashamed or begrudging of the one with impairments and have warded off closeness may face difficult soul-searching.

The subject of dying or becoming infirm, often a charged and over-determined source of shame and inadequacy, can be so daunting for some caregivers that they postpone unduly or totally fail to prepare for these overwhelming events. Some may delegate the care and future of their loved one to God or to fate. Some are so terrified of what could happen to the loved one that they make great and inordinate sacrifices in their late years to prevent actualization of their worst fears, only to find that they themselves may need increased resources to manage their own frailty and waning capabilities. The person who takes on the fallout may assume large financial as well as emotional burdens for her lifetime. Even high socioeconomic status does not necessarily protect family caregivers from burnout and depletion, as skilled home care and respite services are not guaranteed commodities. Caregivers who are disqualified from receiving some services and wanting to maintain the same level of care following their own infirmity or death may encounter obstacles they could not anticipate.

Family ideology and how members feel about one another greatly influence decision-making processes. Families who function according to the belief that "we take care of our own" and who function cooperatively, avail themselves of services, empower themselves with knowledge, maintain a sense of humor and perspective, and whose members have a healthy internal locus of control will negotiate depletion and burnout of caregivers much better than families who are fractured by lengthy intergenerational histories of disconnection and unresolved conflicts. Positive changes during the past few decades (e.g., mainstreaming, early intervention, family support groups, lawyers with specialized training in trusts and guardianships) have made it easier for families to be more open with themselves and others outside the family. No matter how they are negotiated, family developmental transitions are marked by increased stress. In this particular transition, aging and weakened caregivers may be engaging in life reviews and revisions in order to strengthen meaning, value, and coherence in their lives that have been so different from most of their cohorts. Hence, this is a time when chronic sorrow may deepen and feelings of loss and grief may escalate.

Minilosses

Critical stress points are a fact of life in other-loss and most self-loss. Resurgence of grief can be triggered internally by thoughts and imagery, and externally by special occasions (e.g., anniversaries, birthdays, special holidays), crisis events, idiosyncratic reminders (anticipated and unanticipated), and—perhaps most predictably—by those times when developmental milestones should occur but cannot. Dreams of what should, might, and could have been are reactivated by a series of experiential and symbolic "minideaths" that occur during the course of a lifetime, lending validity to the expression "We die in inches." The same can be said for the dream or enduring fantasies about our lives. During the course of chronic sorrow, these fantasies are usually given up in fragments, as we acknowledge over an extensive time span that they (or parts thereof) are like Don Quixote's "Impossible Dream." We mourn the loss of these fragments. In addition, we may mourn the progressive loss of function in such conditions as ALS, Alzheimer's, multiple sclerosis, cerebral palsy, Huntington's, Parkinson's, and so on. The meaning that is attributed to these microlosses and how or whether they are integrated into the person's life story will affect comprehension, decision making, and subsequent adjustment.

It is important that helping professionals be aware that emotional support and therapy are often sought when a crucial dream or expectation can no longer survive in the face of mounting and distressing evidence of its unreality. For example, a mother who has been driven by the family motto that "desire and hard work can accomplish anything" is in a sudden collapse. She breaks down one day when she sees her friends' daughters and sons graduating from high school and going on to college. She takes a new look at her own daughter who is developmentally disabled, and instead of seeing the "funny looking, adorable kid," she sees the daughter almost as others see her: as a young woman who walks clumsily; speaks haltingly; converses sparingly on a concrete, simplistic level; and who has recently begun to strike out in anger and frustration, actually hitting the mother who loves her so much. This mother sees clearly in that instant that she has lost the code she has lived by, that her extended family have made themselves scarce in her life, and that while her very hard work has reaped important benefits, her daughter is likely not to have the life she expected her to have. She feels shame and failure. It is in this context that she reaches for help from a psychotherapist, pastoral counselor, or other similarly trained professional.

What seems unbearable and so broken now is not entirely irretrievable and unmendable, but she will need help in identifying what parts of her dream are no longer working for her, what remains as helpful and potentially valid, and what she can, with integrity, hope for and see as her own enlightened truth. If relief is to be found, it is usually in a gradually achieved embrace of what actually is, accompanied by releasing those parts of dreams and fantasies that are clearly a detriment to living fully in the moment and to being open to the gifts that are found in the life that was actually meted out to us. Choosing hope that is based on the real situation and is different from wishful thinking and forced optimism is instrumental in support of grieving and the prevention or alleviation of despair.

DISABILITY AND SHAME

Frederick Turner (1991) has stated: "Shame, fundamentally, does not come from a lack of ability to *have,* or *possess*; it comes from the consciousness of a lack of ability to *give*" (p. 26). Further elaborating, he indicates that the feeling of shame at being excluded from the communion of the "right" people and not getting a share of the hunter's prey derives from a suspicion that one's own gifts to society are unacceptable and that being barred from the human exchange system may be justified. "It is the shame of Cain" (p. 26). While guilt and shame are sometimes experienced as one and the same thing, guilt refers to acts of omission or commission that are believed to be wrong, hurtful to others, or to have injurious consequences of some nature. Guilt can be assuaged by atoning or making amends; it also implies more possibility of control over one's life. Shame, on the other hand, is self-referential and inescapable. Some theorists believe that shame propensity is virtually universal. In childhood, shame can be induced through awareness of one's powerlessness, dependency, and "puny" self-image. Shame may be induced in adolescence when the maturing body triggers embarrassment, awkwardness, and feelings of exposure. It is at this time too when one might work very hard not to appear different. In adulthood the realization of how far the distance is between one's self-ideal and what one may actually be able to accomplish in one's life may deepen shameful affect and experiences. Aging has its own perils and associated shame. In its most extreme consequences, shame is the basis for being unable to feel either belongingness with the community of humankind or that one is an individual with wholeness, a person who is a force in the world.

Speaking with the voice of Shame (as an ego state), Laura Minges (2004) contends that some common ideas about disability make Shame's job easy. It takes very little for Minges to be reminded that she is contributing much less than what is needed to come out ahead on the resources poured into her. Situations of debilitating chronic disease and disability are open invitations for shame, as they involve the realization of weakness, need, inadequacy, and mortality itself. As is posttraumatic stress disorder (PTSD) subsequent to the trauma that often initiates chronic sorrow, somatic disturbance is also at the core of shame (McNish, 2004; Roos & Neimeyer, 2007; Rothschild, 2000). Shame evokes some of the same physical manifestations, such as freezing, numbing, feeling one's very life is threatened, hypervigilance, and the flight-or-fight stress response. There is a cogent argument that shame goes deeper than guilt (Lynd, 1999). Moreover, there is risk that it may permeate and dominate self-image and personality.

As emphasized by Triano (2003), speaking for people with disabilities, "the single greatest obstacle we face as a community is our own sense of inferiority, internalized oppression and shame" (p. 1). She contends that the sense of shame associated with disability has reached epidemic proportions, and she makes an important point, consonant with this chapter, when she acknowledges that one's history and culture are essential components in development of a positive appraisal of self and community. The history and culture of disability, described previously, provide many reasons—some quite chilling—for why people with disabilities do not benefit from generational transfer. Also, a person may be the first or only known disabled family member so that intergenerational transfer relevant to disability is nonexistent.

In varying degrees, oppression and trauma may be part of ordinary life. Yet, when a person with a disability (mental, emotional, physical, educational, etc.) meets the external environment, there are factors that mediate the consequences of disability. Mental disorders and deficiencies (e.g., schizophrenia, mental retardation) are especially evocative of primitive negative societal responses and constructions. Even in infancy, babies must struggle with the impact of disability internally and in interactions with parents and other caregivers who are coping with their own fears and grief. The critical process of parent–infant bonding, attunement, and the infant's growing sense of self are affected. The biologically-based bond between child and caregiver is the ground upon which the security, survival, and well-being of the child is ensured. Insecure patterns or failures of attachment are seen as the basis for later pathological development of relational or attachment style(s). A worried and fearful mother's mirroring of a severely disabled child and whether she can reliably contain her own distress as well as her child's has powerful implications for the child's development and future sense of trust and self-esteem. (For more information specific to attachment theory, please see Chapter 3 of this volume.)

As the child is the major focus of concern, effects on the mother are often inadequately recognized. She is usually deprived of time, space, and support for her grief, as she is caring for a child who has more (and more constant) needs than a normal child. If the child has autism or profound brain anomalies, she is deprived of the pleasure of attuning with her child through a special and powerful synchrony of responses. If her child cannot attune with her she misses out on important pleasures and satisfactions of parenting. Autistic infants and children often turn away from, reject, or physically attack mothers who are simply trying to connect with them and express their love. These mothers are trapped in and by their bonds with a child who is emotionally hurtful to them. This kind of role-entrapment can be fraught with a deep sense of inadequacy and is a fertile ground for development of guilt and shame.

In regard to subjectivity and disability, in his classic work *Stigma*, Goffman (1963) refers to a "spoiled identity." How can one redeem such an identity? Can it be through promotion of disability pride? Does disability pride resonate internally as truth, or is it a defense, a reaction formation that disallows self-awareness and introspection? From earliest childhood, our culture exerts subtle and usually unquestioned power over definitions of good and bad, desirable and undesirable, people of value and those to shun. Children's stories have long equated beauty with goodness. Snow White is beautiful and good; the wicked Queen is ugly and evil. The Ugly Duckling cannot possibly be all right until transformed into a graceful swan. With this kind of early influence, can movements such as neurodiversity rights, autism rights, civil disobedience protests, and redefinitions such as "Disability is beautiful!" offset messages promulgated in an age of cosmetic surgery, obsession with thinness, genetic engineering, in vitro fertilization, artificial insemination, "designer babies," abortion of fetuses with impairments, wrongful life and wrongful birth litigation, assisted suicide, and other practices associated with the "new eugenics"?

Buchanan, Brock, Daniels, and Wikler (2000) have predicted that by 2020 many parents will consider unborn babies who may have an increased risk of certain cancers or Alzheimer's as "undesirable," resulting in abortion of otherwise healthy fetuses. I value as a precious right a woman's freedom to choose termination of a pregnancy. I have also extrapolated from scenarios developed by Buchanan et al. (2000) to predict that conditions related to chronic sorrow will be increasingly unacceptable and socially ostracized. Parents of children with serious anomalies may be blamed more frequently for their misfortunes. The gap between those who have been "custom designed" and those with impairments will widen, resulting in increased alienation and more intense chronic sorrow (Roos, 2002, 2007a). Extrapolating even further, shame may become more entrenched.

CLOSING THOUGHTS

In concentrating my thoughts on individual and social meanings of disability and chronic illness, the process of writing this chapter has been both beneficial and unsettling, as I have turned inward on memories of personally humiliating experiences related to the severe and profound congenital impairments that have bombarded my two children. Reliving these experiences has strengthened my resolve to forge a meaningful, if largely invisible, legacy for the three of us. Writing is an integral part of that legacy. A helpful realization emergent in the replay of scenes of humiliation is a clearer understanding of a turning point that occurred more than a decade ago in relation to the way I cope with chronic sorrow and its periodic resurgence, especially in response to snubs or snide and derogatory remarks—in any milieu—about people who are disabled in some serious way. I am tuned in. The ominous implications of such expressions are not lost on me, and they occur more often than one might ordinarily imagine.

The shift occurred when I stopped "taking cover" and began to confront these events and my anger, pain, sorrow, and shame. I realized I had made an unconscious and subtle error. My goal had been to defeat my sense of inadequacy and the stinging consequences of others' humiliating judgments and belligerent ignorance. Rather than overcoming, choosing instead to *manage* these circumstances has its advantages. Concluding that *all* of us mortal human beings contend with feelings of lack (if not shame), I believe that staring them squarely in the face and getting to know them leads to less fear and alienation, more self-acceptance, and to being better equipped to respond in an authentic, constructive way, should I choose to respond at all.

Writing about chronic sorrow as a professional and parent does occasionally trigger familiar and extremely uncomfortable feelings of exposure, aloneness, and alienation, as well as very complicated shame, part of the underlying structure of these feelings. However, within certain boundaries, I do not fear writing close to the heart, and I no longer shade my perceptions when something is acutely illuminated by mind sight. It is from this perspective that I think of others with far more access to public and professional dissemination of life experience than I will ever have, those whose works have unquestionable, worldwide importance and impact. Two of these individuals are: Erik Erikson (1902–1994), the famous child psychoanalyst known as "identity's architect" (Friedman, 2000) because of his innovative contributions to human development theory; and Arthur Miller (1915–2005), the internationally acclaimed playwright who was extolled as the moralist of the past American century (Andrews, 2007). Rather than expose themselves as parents of children with disabilities, these men hid these personal facts from friends and the world and, much worse, rejected and unrelentingly deleted these children from their lives as if they were nonexistent.

The acknowledged children of Arthur Miller are: producer Robert Miller; Rebecca Miller, writer, film director, and wife of Daniel Day-Lewis; and Jane Doyle. Never acknowledged was a fourth child, Daniel. He was not included in Miller's 1987 memoir, *Timebends,* and he was omitted as a survivor from the 2002 obituary for Inge Morath, Daniel's mother and Miller's wife (Andrews, 2007). When Miller died in Connecticut, only one major newspaper, the *Los Angeles Times,* mentioned Daniel, referring to him as another son, born in 1962 with Down syndrome and placed in an institution where Miller apparently never visited him. Daniel was not mentioned in his father's will, but from information that has been gleaned following Miller's death it is known that he is named in separate trust documents that were signed the same day Miller's will was executed, making his portion of the inheritance no different from that of his siblings. Ironically, in this dramatic gesture, among other serious complications, by not establishing a "special-needs" trust, Miller made Daniel too wealthy to receive government assistance.

Daniel left the institution in early adulthood and has been able to live in group-home settings in the community. He had a very hard life in the institution but apparently shows no bitterness. Miller was adamantly against Inge's periodic attempts to bring him home. Daniel currently lives with an elderly couple who have loved him and taken care of him for a long time, and he continues to be visited by a social worker. He has a job, is active, and apparently is happy. Helping people is reported to be his greatest joy. Andrews (2007) writes that some who knew Miller judge him harshly, as a weak, narcissistic hypocrite who perpetuated a cruel lie. She appropriately raises questions about the relationship between Miller's behavior and his art. Miller excised a central character whose presence was unacceptable to the desired plot of his life, creating a palpable absence at the heart of his story. Andrews states that Miller's choices regarding Daniel may have cost him as a writer, contending that he never wrote anything approaching greatness after Daniel's birth. She speculates that Miller may have been sitting on his greatest unwritten play. Someone who knows Daniel well is reported by Andrews as saying that Danny transcended his father's failures; the loss is Miller's in never seeing how extraordinary his son is. In his memoir, Miller wrote that a character is defined by challenges he cannot walk away from and also by those challenges he *has* walked away from that cause remorse.

Erik Erikson never knew who his biological father was (Friedman, 2000). He postponed and ultimately failed to follow up on two potential leads. In reinventing himself, he changed his last name from Homburger to Erikson after he and wife Joan brought their two young sons, Kai and Jon, from Europe to live in America. The sons' names were also changed. Their daughter Sue (now Bloland) was born in the United States and is a psychotherapist in New York. Kai is a well-published social psychologist; Jon became somewhat peripheral to the family and has worked in a number of occupations. There was a fourth child, Neil, who had Down syndrome. Immediately after his birth, Erikson consulted physicians and his friend, the cultural anthropologist Margaret Mead. Consistent with norms of that time, they recommended immediate removal of Neil to a home for children with similar disabilities. Joan did not see Neil after his birth. When she returned home without the baby, the children were told that Neil had died. Despite Erikson's objections, Joan went to see him when she was well enough, and she later wanted to take care of him, but Erikson was unalterably opposed and she didn't insist. Silence, shame, and sorrow won out. Neil and the lie were divisive forces in the family. Neil's existence was eventually revealed to one of his siblings who then was responsible for keeping the secret, even from his siblings. The other two siblings later discovered that Neil was alive. No pictures of Neil exist. When he died, Erikson and Joan were vacationing in Italy. In an ironic twist of fate, Kai, Jon, and Sue—by then adults—were responsible for arranging a burial for the brother they never knew, while Erikson and Joan continued their vacation.

It is impossible to know what influence these and other admired world figures could have had if they had not chosen secrecy about an impaired family member. Their work shaped thought, attitudes, perception, and emotions of a wide range of intellectuals and lovers of the arts.

Hence, there is no reason *not* to assume that, given their discernment and fame, they could have made powerful inroads in changing many people's views of disabilities and chronic illness. Some of their contemporaries chose to use their public access to foster a more enlightened, compassionate understanding of disabilities. A sterling example is Peter Nichols's play, *Joe Egg* (1967), with successful runs in Glasgow, New York, and throughout the world. It has endured and recently had performances in Dallas. In a somewhat more current generation, the now-deceased, fine actor Christopher Reeve, who became paralyzed from the neck down due to sustaining a spinal cord injury, unquestionably captured public esteem and accomplished a great deal by establishing the Christopher Reeve Paralysis Foundation whose mission is to promote awareness and research on spinal cord injury and the development of innovative treatment interventions. He managed to live a very full, refocused life in the wake of his devastating losses, a life cut tragically short in 2004 at the age of 52. He experienced profound meaning and purpose, reflected in his two books (Reeve, 1998, 2002). Still, he was known to humorously quip that he had liked it better when he was "shallow."

My thoughts have also been on unmarked graves. Perhaps it would be fitting to add "unmarked graves" to Cheyfitz's (2000) list of convergent ideas (euthanasia, suicide, eugenics, etc.) not readily seen as related, although they reflect societal attitudes toward unwanted people. Large, monolithic institutions of the recent past often buried "inmates" on the outer edges of the institutional grounds or in areas given over to that purpose by state or local government. These areas are sometimes referred to as potter's fields. Unmarked in untended ground, these souls were "throwaways" who lived and died unknown and unnoted. These graves are sad indictments of our society's disdain and neglect of those who cannot meet definitions of acceptability. As such, they are repositories of shame that more reasonably belongs to society and its extensive history of rejection and hostility toward those in many chronic sorrow situations.

On some recent occasions, I have strolled through a patch of ground located in the far reaches of the sprawling campus of a state school for mental retardation an hour away from my home. (The school is now an array of group homes that have been reconstructed from the original dormitories.) The patch is a cemetery. The ground there is sunbaked and hard. There is no grass, but the weeds are cut short. Someone has cared enough to put a wood, mostly open, white-painted fence about 4 feet high around it, and there is a gate. Ten years ago most of the graves were unmarked. Everyone has a marker and a name now. While some markers are granite or bronze, obviously provided by families, the majority of markers consist of an ordinary, red, house brick, with a name and year of birth and death almost illegibly etched into it. Someone has cared enough to do this. Some children died early, before the age of 5, and some people buried there had almost normal life spans. A mother's son died on his birthday, 40 years later. The place is peaceful. Branches of nearby trees rustle in the breeze. Even now, those buried there can teach the rest of the world so much. They create longing for a more evolved society whose worth can be measured not so much by its superior aggression, laissez-faire materialism, competition, and unreasoned reliance on technology and power, but by "immeasurables," such as how the society values and treats its weakest members and their families.

REFERENCES

Alexander-Eitzman, B. E. (2006). Examining the course of homelessness: Right direction, wrong approach. *American Journal of Public Health, 96*(5), 764–765.

Andrews, S. (2007). Arthur Miller's missing act: Fame & scandal. *Vanity Fair*. Retrieved July 2, 2008, from, http://www.vanityfair.com/fame/features/2007/09

Arciniegas, D. B., & Anderson, C. A. (2002). Suicide in neurologic illness. *Current Treatment Options in Neurology, 4*, 457–468.

Baudelaire, C. (1961). Poeme XXXIX, Le cygne, Les fleurs du mal. In C. Baudelaire, *Oeuvres completes* (Pleiade edition, p. 81) Paris: Gallimard.

Blatt, B., & Kaplan, F. (1966). *Christmas in purgatory*. Needham Heights, MA: Allyn & Bacon.

Blatt, B., & Mangel, C. (1967, October 31). Tragedy and hope of retarded children. *Look, 41*, 96–99.

Boles, D. W. (2007). Enforcing the ugly laws. Retrieved July 5, 2008, from http//urbansimiotic.com/2007/05/01/enforcing-the-ugly-laws/

Buchanan, A., Brock, D., Daniels, N., & Wikler, D. (2000). *From chance to choice: Genetics and justice*. New York: Cambridge University Press.

Burleigh, M. (1990). Euthanasia and the Third Reich. *History Today, 40*, 11–16.

Burleigh, M. (1991). "Euthanasia" in the Third Reich: Some recent literature. *Social History of Medicine, 4*, 317–328.

Carrie Buck v. James Hendren Bell, Superintendent of State Colony for Epileptics and Feeble Minded, 274 U.S. 200, 207–208 (May 2, 1927).

Cheyfitz, K. (2000). Who decides? The connecting thread of euthanasia, eugenics, and doctor-assisted suicide. In K. J. Kaplan (Ed.), *Right to die versus sacredness of life* (pp. 5–16). Amityville, NY: Baywood.

Davies, S. (1959). *The mentally retarded in society.* New York: Columbia University Press.

Disaboom. (2008). *52% of Americans would rather die than have a disability.* Retrieved on July 22, 2008, from http://www.disaboom. com/forums/p/28045/80894

Doka, K. (Ed.). (2002). *Disenfranchised grief* (2nd ed.). Champaign, IL: Research Press.

Eliot, C. (Ed.). (1938). *American historical documents.* New York: Collier.

Forchuk, C., Russell, G., Kingston-Macclure, S., Turner, K., & Dill, S. (2006). From psychiatric ward to the streets and shelters. *Journal of Psychiatric Mental Health Nursing, 13*(3), 301–308.

Friedman, L. J. (2000). *Identity's architect: A biography of Erik H. Erikson.* Cambridge, MA: Harvard University Press.

Gerdtz, J. (1993). Introduction: Historical summary. In M. McGarrity, *A guide to mental retardation* (pp. 1–33). New York: Crossroad.

Goddard, H. (1912). *The Kallikak family: A study in the heredity of feeblemindedness.* New York: Macmillan.

Goffman, E. (1963). *Stigma: Notes on the management of a spoiled identity.* Englewood Cliffs, NJ: Prentice Hall.

Goldhagen, D. (1996). *Hitler's willing executioners: Ordinary Germans and the holocaust.* New York: Alfred A. Knopf.

Heaney, S. (1991). *The cure at Troy: A version of Sophocles' Philoctetes.* New York: Noonday Press, Farrar, Straus and Giroux.

Hewson, D. (1997). Coping with loss of ability: "Good grief" or episodic stress responses? *Social Science Medicine, 44*(8), 1129–1139.

Horowitz, A., & Shindelman, L. (1983). Reciprocity and affection: Past influences on current caregiving. *Journal of Gerontological Social Work, 5,* 5–20.

Ingalls, R. (1978). *Mental retardation: The changing outlook.* New York: John Wiley & Sons.

Kaplan, D. (1999). Definition of disability: Perspective of the disability community. *Journal of Health Care Law and Policy, 3*(2), 352–364.

Kaplan, K. J. (2000). *Right to die versus sacredness* of life. Amityville, NY: Baywood Publishing Company.

Kevles, D. J. (1985). *In the name of eugenics: Genetics and the uses of human heredity.* New York: Alfred A. Knopf.

Koenigsberg, R. (2007). *Hitler's ideology: Embodied metaphor, fantasy and history.* Charlotte, NC: Information Age Publishing.

Lynd, H. (1999). *On shame and the search for identity.* London: Routledge.

Marmura, M. E. (1963). Avicenna, healing: Metaphysics X. In R. Lerner & M. Mahdi, *Medieval political philosophy* (pp. 98–112). Ithaca, NY: Cornell University Press.

McNish, J. (2004). *Transforming shame: A pastoral response.* Binghamton, NY: The Haworth Pastoral Press.

Millen, L., & Roll, S. (1985). Solomon's mothers: A special case of pathological bereavement. *American Journal of Orthopsychiatry, 55*(3), 411–418.

Minges, L. (2004). *Disability shame speaks: I am alive and doing very well.* Retrieved June 4, 2008, from http://www.raggededgemagazine.com/life/shamespeaks1.html

Nichols, P. (1967). *Joe Egg.* New York: Grove Press.

Nietzsche, F. (1990). *Twilight of the idols and the anti-christ: Or how to philosophize with a hammer.* New York: Penguin Classics.

Nussbaum, M. C. (2006). *Frontiers of justice: Disability, nationality, species membership.* Cambridge, MA: Belknap Press of Harvard University Press.

Olshansky, S. (1962). Chronic sorrow: A response to having a mentally defective child. *Social Casework, 43*(4), 190–193.

Olshansky, S. (1966). Parent responses to having a mentally defective child. *Mental Retardation, 4*(4), 21–23.

Reeve, C. (1998). *Still me.* New York: Random House.

Reeve, C. (2002). *Nothing is impossible: Reflections on a new life.* New York: Random House.

Rivera, G. (1972). Willowbrook: A report on how it is and why it doesn't have to be that way. New York: Random House.

Roos, S. (2002). *Chronic sorrow: A living loss.* New York: Brunner-Routledge.

Roos, S. (2007a). Disability, chronic sorrow, and end-of-life decisions In T. H. Lillie & J. L. Werth (Eds.), *End-of-life issues and persons with disabilities* (pp. 100–112). Austin, TX: PRO-ED.

Roos, S. (2007b). Relinquishing mothers: Silent and invisible. *The Forum, 33*(4), 1–5.

Roos, S. (2009). Chronic sorrow. In C. D. Bryant, & D. L. Peck (Eds.), *Encyclopedia of death and the human experience* (pp. 196–199). Thousand Oaks, CA: Sage Publications.

Roos, S., & Neimeyer, R. A. (2007). Reauthoring the self: Chronic sorrow and posttraumatic stress disorder following the onset of CID. In E. Martz & H. Livneh (Eds.), *Coping with chronic illness and disability: Theoretical, empirical, and clinical aspects* (pp. 89–106). New York: Springer.

Rothschild, B. (2000). *The body remembers: The psychophysiology of trauma and trauma treatment.* New York: Norton.

Scheerenberger, R. (1982). Treatment from ancient times to the present. In P. Cegelka & H. Prehm (Eds.), *Mental retardation: From categories to people* (pp. 44–75). Columbus, OH: Charles E. Merrill.

Scheerenberger, R. (1983). *A history of mental retardation.* Baltimore: Paul H. Brookes.

Sumnar, W. (1906). *Folkways.* New York: Ginn.

Trent, J. W. (1994). *Inventing the feeble mind.* Berkeley and Los Angeles: University of California Press.

Triano, S. (2003). *Disabled and proud.* Retrieved June 4, 2008, from http://www.disabledandproud.com/power.htm

Turner, F. (1991). *Beauty: The value of values* (p. 26). Charlottesville and London: University Press of Virginia.

Williamson, G., & Schulz, R. (1990). Relationship orientation, quality of prior relationship, and distress among caregivers of Alzheimer's patients. *Psychology and Aging, 5,* 502–509.

Wright, B. A. (1983). *Physical disability: A psychosocial approach* (2nd ed.). New York: HarperCollins.

Author Index

Subject Index

A

Abu Ghraib, 141, 142
ADA, *see* Americans with
    Disabilities Act
Advanced health care directives, 94
AIDS, 42, 117, 120
American jeremiad, 19
Americans with Disabilities Act
    (ADA), 176, 179
"The Appointment in Samarra," 93
Association for Death Education
    and Counseling, 94
Assumptive world, 41
Attachment, 33–57
    AIDS, 42
    alcoholism treatment, 51
    anlage, 40
    assumptive world, 41
    attachment disorders, 37
    brain cells, 39
    clinical practice and
        examples, 42–52
      counseling, 42–44
      mourning in shame-based
        client, 44–46
      psychotherapy, 42–44
      self-destructive
        behavior, 50–52
      shame–grief nexus, 46–50
      supermother, 48
    counselor–client relationship, 43
    death as great equalizer, 35
    death instinct, 36
    depersonalization, 52
    disconnect, 36
    disorders, 37
    disrupted attachments, 37, 41
    early nonverbal attachments, 38
    exclusion, 35, 42
    false self, 50
    family image, 49
    fragmentation, 50
    guilt, 34
    here-and-now interaction, 41
    hierarchical primacy of
      relationships, 39
    holding environment, 41
    holding provided by
      counseling, 43
    homosexuality, 43
    hospice care, 43
    infant–caregiver interactions, 53
    infant experiences with
      caregivers, 36
    infantile derailments, 52
    infantile disconnect, 44
    infant's pleasurable feeling, 39
    infant's procedural memories, 36
    insecurity, 47
    life force, 47
    London Blitz, 53
    maternal attachment,
      disruption in, 46
    mirror neurons, 39
    model of maternal care, 43
    mother–infant relationship,
      disruptions of, 33, 40
    mourning process, 37
    narcissistic behavior disorder, 46
    nonverbal attachments, 38
    numinous, 38
    object constancy, 48